THE *NATIONAL POLICE GAZETTE* AND THE MAKING OF THE MODERN AMERICAN MAN, 1879–1906

List of Previous Publications

Unequal Justice: Wayne Dumond, Bill Clinton and the Politics of Rape in Arkansas (Prometheus, 1993)

Co-author: *The Blood of Innocents* (Kensington, 1995)

THE *NATIONAL POLICE GAZETTE* AND THE MAKING OF THE MODERN AMERICAN MAN, 1879–1906

Guy Reel

palgrave
macmillan

THE *NATIONAL POLICE GAZETTE* AND THE MAKING OF THE MODERN AMERICAN MAN, 1879–1906

First published in 2006 by
PALGRAVE MACMILLAN™
175 Fifth Avenue, New York, N.Y. 10010 and
Houndmills, Basingstoke, Hampshire, England RG21 6XS
Companies and representatives throughout the world.

PALGRAVE MACMILLAN is the global academic imprint of the Palgrave Macmillan division of St. Martin's Press, LLC and of Palgrave Macmillan Ltd. Macmillan® is a registered trademark in the United States, United Kingdom and other countries. Palgrave is a registered trademark in the European Union and other countries.

ISBN 1–4039–7165–X

Library of Congress Cataloging-in-Publication Data

Reel, Guy.
     The *National Police Gazette* and the making of the modern American man, 1879–1906 / by Guy Reel.
        p. cm.
     Revision of thesis (doctoral), Ohio University.
     Includes bibliographical references and index.
     ISBN 1–4039–7165–X
        1. Masculinity—United States—History. 2. Sex role—United States—History. 3. National Police Gazette (New York, N.Y.). 4. Sensationalism in journalism—United States—History. 5. Crime and the press—United States—History. 6. Sports—United States—History. 7. Sex—Press coverage—United States—History. 8. Sports in journalism—United States—History. I. Title.

HQ1090.3.R44 2006
305.31097309′034—dc22   2005053525

A catalogue record for this book is available from the British Library.

Design by Newgen Imaging Systems (P) Ltd., Chennai, India.

First edition: April 2006

10 9 8 7 6 5 4 3 2 1

Printed in the United States of America.

To my father, who provided support and encouragement throughout the production of this book

CONTENTS

LIST OF TABLES

ACKNOWLEDGMENTS

This work began as a dissertation for my doctorate at the E.W. Scripps School of Journalism at Ohio University. The members of my dissertation committee—Drs. Patrick Washburn, Joseph Bernt, Martin Schwartz, and David Mould—deserve special thanks. Also offering invaluable help were Dr. Daniel Riffe and two of my College of Communication colleagues, Lee Anne Peck and Abhinav Aima.

INTRODUCTION

Yes, I used to stare at those pictures, and so did all the boys that I knew.
—Franklin P. Adams, 1930

One afternoon in the sweltering New York City summer of 1881, three beautiful young ladies—pupils of a female seminary—decided to quench their thirst by bumming drinks from a beer garden next door. It was a risky and risque act, but far from being outraged by the apparent breach of morality, the editor and publisher of one of New York's up-and-coming publications took delight in their initiative. He ran a huge front-page woodcut illustration of the young women drinking and holding their beer bottles aloft, having just obtained them from the other side of a high fence. Pink-tinted newsprint showed their ample figures clad in frilly dresses boldly displaying calves and ankles. An accompanying editorial comment congratulated the women for showing more ingenuity than the famous Greek lovers Pyramus and Thisbe, who had merely made love through a crack in a wall "and knew nothing about beer." The New York girls were simply "Tippling Under Difficulties," the caption read, finding "stimulus for their exhausted mental faculties"[1] (figure I.1).

Did this rather racy picture shock the readers of 1881 New York? Perhaps it did some of them. But many of those who picked up that July 2, 1881, issue of the *National Police Gazette*—most of them men and boys—had come to expect exactly this sort of tantalizing whimsy. For they were readers of one of the most lurid and sensational journals of the era, and it was for precisely this kind of picture that they eagerly beheld the *Gazette* each week.

Over the years, the weekly *Gazette* has delighted historians as a chronicler of debauchery: "Victorian didacticism and moral certitude were absent from these pages," historian Elliot J. Gorn noted drily.[2] But it also lived on the memories of its readers, who recalled it fondly for its prurient content. Franklin P. Adams wrote in 1930 that the *Gazette* was quite familiar to him when he was growing up in Chicago in the 1880s and 1890s. The many pictures of women in the *Gazette*

TIPPLING UNDER DIFFICULTIES.

HOW THE PUPILS OF A FEMALE SEMINARY ADJOINING A BEER-GARDEN OBTAIN STIMULUS FOR THEIR EXHAUSTED MENTAL FACULTIES; NEW YORK CITY.

Figure I.1

beckoned him to sneak peaks of it at Frank's barbershop on the south side of Thirty-fifth Street:

> [I]t was ankles and legs that really got me. Those were the days when a woman's shoe-top was considered, as you might say, uptown. And these pictures showed some women's skirts—thousands of skirts—in abandoned disarray. Women were running, and were ostentatiously careless whether they displayed their legs almost to the knee. Yes, I used to stare at those pictures, and so did all the boys that I knew.[3]

Partly through these large illustrations, the *Gazette*, in its New York City heyday in the late 1800s and early 1900s, became a sort of go-between in Victorian America's transition from rigidly suppressed sexual desires to the rapid onset of modernity and consumerism that turned sex into a commodity. Sniggering schoolboys and men in barbershops and saloons flipped through it as a guilty pleasure made all the more exciting because it *was* frowned upon, by "respectable" people, rival editors, and moral absolutist crusaders such as Anthony Comstock, who decried the "vile illustrated weekly papers" that, with their lurid tales and sensationalist pictures, acted on children "to defile their pure minds by flaunting these atrocities before their eyes."[4]

Of course, one of the purposes of the *Gazette*-style sensations was to increase hand-to-hand readership by quickening the circulation of eager-eyed readers. James Joyce wrote in *Ulysses*:

> —And here she is, says Alf, that was giggling over the *Police Gazette* with Terry on the counter, in all her warpaint.
> —Give us a squint at her, says I.
> And what was it only one of the smutty yankee pictures . . . Misconduct of society belle. Norman W. Tupper, wealthy Chicago contractor, finds pretty but faithless wife in lap of officer Taylor. Belle in her bloomers misconducting herself, and her fancyman feeling for her tickles and Norman W. Tupper bouncing in with his peashooter just in time to be late after she doing the trick of the loop with officer Taylor.[5]

Like many readers, Joyce considered the *Gazette* to be a type of soft-core pornography, and clearly, sex was what made the *Gazette* into the legend it would become. This book, however, looks not just at the *Gazette*'s use of sexual suggestion, for the magazine satisfied other (frequently male) appetites; it was the leading sporting journal of its kind, taking the lead in boxing as well as other sports promotion, and it served as a chronicler of sensational crimes and disasters that exposed the duplicity, vulnerability, folly, and hypocrisy of the human race. In the process it became filled with seeming contradictions—it championed the underclass but was an outlet for bigotry; it cheered strong, independent women but illustrated them as sex objects; it decried crime but celebrated vice, winking at famous outlaws such as Jesse James. Thus, it highlighted various aspects of masculine culture in an era when the American manhood was developing into its modern form. And it accomplished this largely through its splashy drawings that depicted aspects of sex, crime, and sports. In the process, it helped create a culture of news coverage that frustrates, enrages, and captivates readers and journalists even today—the sensational, celebrity-baiting, gossip-hounding, "reality-based" reporting and programming that is now known as tabloid journalism.

How did the *National Police Gazette*, founded in New York City in 1845 ostensibly as an organ to help police capture criminals, become a national and international publication and leave a legacy that helped change the way we look at the world? Much of the answer comes in an editorial published thirty-one years after the *Gazette*'s founding. An ambitious new publisher had taken control of the magazine, and, he announced in 1876, it was his intent to make it the greatest journal of sport, sensation, the stage, and romance in existence. This brash new magazine "proprietor," as he liked to call himself, was an Irish immigrant, Richard Kyle Fox.

Fox's early stewardship of the *Gazette*, and the way the magazine reflected New York and the journalism of its day, serves as the defining time frame for this work. For Fox, more than any other person, was the creator of the *Gazette* that is well known even today. In addition to publishing pictures of pretty girls, Fox also made the *Gazette* into what it said it was on its flag, "The Leading Illustrated Sporting Journal in America," and a promoter of prizefights, rowing events, aerial jumping, shin-kicking duels, oyster-eating contests, and all manner of other competitions that emerged in the late-nineteenth century's brand of masculine competitiveness. The *Gazette* served as the perfect answer to the questions that men faced arising from rapidly changing workplaces and sex roles, and its blend of crime stories, sporting promotions, and woodcut illustrations (and later, photographs) of scantily clad, often athletic, or talented young women helped create a national culture of male fans.

Gazette illustrations reflected different emphases at different times during this era of New York history, with depictions of dastardly crimes common in the early years (from about 1845 to the early 1870s), followed by increasing numbers of illustrations featuring sports or games, and sexual content, including the confusion of sex roles, consistently prominent from the 1880s until the twentieth century's flapper era. As part of this work, *Gazette* illustrations were examined in a content analysis because of the way they illustrated Fox's priorities as a journalist; in a real sense, the *Gazette*'s woodcuts *were* the *Gazette*, and they were the New York that the *Gazette* wished to portray. Perhaps without realizing it, Fox was reflecting and helping shape the emerging modern American culture by showing different types of men, women, masculinities, and reactions to numerous threats to masculinities.

Thus, a variety of factors were at play during this era as the *Gazette* relentlessly hawked its portrayals of crime, sex, and sports. These include the emergence of tabloid media; the links between masculinity, crime, sports, and mass media; and the evolution of publishing and image-making technology and its relation to depictions of crime, sexuality, and sports. Of course, pictures don't tell the whole story. News and sports stories that appeared throughout Fox's editorship offer additional insight into the *Gazette*'s style of journalism.

What was this style? To be sure, it was more than just mere idle amusement to New York's unwashed. The pictures and the copy in Fox's *Gazette* represented responses to challenges to masculinities that had appeared at least a decade before Frederick Jackson Turner noted the 1890 census' declaration of the closing of the Western frontier.[6] By the end of the century the typical American male was no longer a tough frontiersman or even a hardworking farmer; many were immigrants and lived in cities while working factory jobs. In addition, tradesmen were threatened by a rapidly changing economy, including the creation of national markets and the development of mass production and distribution. Although democratic ideals had helped many men assert a sense of personal autonomy, they were not independent when it came to their jobs.[7] Without the challenges of nature facing the city dwellers, the taming of the male wildness was in full force. Certainly, women were part of this taming, as disparate forces changed their paths in different ways—for example, toward domesticity, the working world, suffrage, or temperance. Responses to the challenges to masculinity included the creation of the Boy Scouts, the development of taverns as male-only domains, a frenetic health, sports and youth craze, and the socializing at the barbershop.[8] By 1890, Fox was running an average of full page and a half of boxing illustrations in every issue, was regularly profiling barbers, and was printing jokes about drinking. In 1901, the sportsman, hunter, and rancher Theodore Roosevelt became the nation's twenty-sixth president, and he used the bully pulpit to promote fitness, health, and recreation. The *Gazette* reflected and encouraged these trends while leading the way in a new kind of promotional journalism that built circulation while it advocated an agenda that was pro-sports, anticrime, and for entertainment of a romantic and sexual sort. During this period men and women were attempting to define themselves according to new roles and expectations, and in its framing role the *Gazette* was portraying both sides of the coin—the changing sex roles as well as the traditional notions of hegemonic masculinity that served many of its male readers in barbershops and saloons.

A large body of scholarly study concerns itself with the development and perception of masculinities, with the years covering the late nineteenth and early twentieth centuries seen by many historians as a watershed era, particularly in United States men's history. In an influential essay, John Higham in 1970 identified a cult of masculinity at the end of the nineteenth century and argued that beginning in the 1890s, America had an "urge to be young, masculine, and adventurous," because of a reaction against "the sheer dullness of an urban industrial culture."[9] Later, social historians Elizabeth Pleck and Joseph Pleck named the years 1861–1919—including the most successful years of the *National Police Gazette*—as the period of the "strenuous life" in America, one of four major periods of men's history in the United States. The others, according to Pleck and Pleck, were the years of "agrarian patriarchy" (1630–1820), the "commercial age" (1820–1860), and an era of "companionate providing" (1920–1965).[10] The definition of periods of history is always somewhat arbitrary, but these authors argued that certain economic and political forces set apart the late nineteenth and early twentieth centuries as especially important in the development of perceptions of masculinities. Many of these forces have been cited repeatedly by scholars and historians as key factors that contributed to beliefs, portrayals, actions, and reactions that shaped what it meant to be a man in America.[11] Fox's *Gazette*, and other publications like it, reflected these forces and in so doing helped shaped what the twentieth-century American male would look and act like.

Of course, it seems unlikely that threats to masculinities had the direct effect of causing great numbers of individual men to quake at the notion of their lost manhood. Men were and are of types, not of a stereotype. Some men sought "masculine domesticity" and the companionship of wives and security of homes, according to Margaret Marsh; this type helped define the masculinities sought by others who found satisfaction in bodybuilding or bachelorhood.[12] But there was a cumulative effect to portrayals, forces, and reactions to those forces that was by definition part of the culture of the age, when men were admonished to adopt "manly" postures to respond to the events around them. Each week the *Police Gazette* and other publications presented weekly illustrations similar to that on the cover of the February 18, 1882, issue, showing a "discarded Romeo" publicly protesting the "derelictions" of his faithless actress girlfriend, only to be turned away by a male defender carrying a revolver. In addition to the illustration, the *Gazette* carried a small story sympathetic to the "eminent sport" who had lost his "manly" honor. It added that his gentlemanly bearing had disappeared because drink caused him "in a great measure [to be] incapacitated from acting with coolness and judgment."[13] So for the (mostly male) readers of the *Gazette* there it was: a gentleman's manhood was threatened by a woman; he understandably reacted against the threat, was thwarted by another man, and then was shamed because he had lost his composure. It was just a single illustration in the thousands in the *Gazette*, as well as in other publications, that showed aspects of threatened masculinities and the proper way to deal with them.

In his study of the sexual revolution of the Victorian era, Kevin White contended that the masculine crisis of late-nineteenth-century America was partly the result of the erosion of moral constraints that had given men concrete purpose in an agrarian society. Before industrialization and modernization, hard, physical labor, self-control, discipline, delayed gratification, and self-sacrifice had contributed to a man's sense of self. But the "Self-Made Man with his firm sense of personal autonomy and independence gave way increasingly to the bureaucrat and salesman, who felt all the more enclosed and confined and limited in the corporations" that were growing larger as the century turned, White wrote. In addition, the closing of the frontier, "with the concomitant crisis in America's sense of manifest destiny, only served to aggravate the middle class's sense of being hemmed in and trapped." Crises of faith brought about by Darwinism and the "watering down" of Protestantism, which became more vague as it played down hell and the punishments of sin, were also significant. White wrote that for many men, the question became, "Without religious structures, why not then behave badly?"[14]

Women, too, behaved badly; one needs to up virtually any copy of the *Police Gazette* during this period to find examples. For instance, the June 25, 1881 issue carried a front-page illustration of a posted sign at Long Beach warning women bathers against "loud" bathing suits; the sign, of course, was being read cheerfully by two belles in revealing swimwear.[15]

Women, wrote White, began to imitate men by smoking, drinking, swearing, petting, and dating freely. But that was merely one side of it. On the other, men were told by many females that their drinking was destructive and should be outlawed, that they should eschew lewd magazines, and that they should support more equality for the sexes and give women the right to vote.

It was not until 1920 that women finally achieved suffrage, but that milestone was preceded by a fifty-two-year effort that had influenced generations of men. The result of the campaign was an erosion of will. Pleck and Pleck wrote:

> The final stronghold of male public privilege was the voting booth. . . . Because men held political power, the campaign for suffrage involved persuading a male electorate to enfranchise women . . . [and] male supporters of suffrage often had to brave the view that they were betraying their sex.[16]

In many ways, the *Gazette* was able to attract readers on a large scale because of technological advances earlier in the nineteenth century. In 1814 a steam engine was first used to run presses for the *Times* of London, and the application gave newspapers the ability to produce large numbers of copies to distribute to thousands of readers. But as historian Mitchell Stephens noted, it took America's particular form of sprawling society to give the masses a true feeling of involvement in the mass media by making journalists "public ministers" of information.[17] The mass audience may have been born from the mother of technology, but information was the ever-willing father. According to James Madison, "A popular government without popular information, or the means of acquiring it, is but a prologue to a farce or a tragedy."[18] By 1825 the voracious American public was consuming more newspapers than any other nation, with content that, according to one editor from New London, Connecticut, was "neither wholly false, nor wholly true." Less than half a century after that, Fox would take full advantage of this willing, wide-eyed mass readership, to the benefit of his pocketbook as well as to *Gazette* readers.[19]

The growth of the consumer society and the mass media may not have caused the changes in attitudes about masculinities, but they certainly helped place them at the center of the popular imagination. As Fox's fortunes improved, so did those of many other publishing barons. Not only did circulation of newspapers and magazines increase, but also the demand for photographic materials (including postcards and cigarette cards). Boxing and wrestling grew in popularity and "strongman acts," long a feature of the circus, transferred to the music hall. Wrote historian John Beynon, "This coincided with a renewed nostalgia for the Olympian movement and presentations (using the new media of photography, slide shows and, later, silent film) of the ideal male body modeled on the warrior of antiquity displaying Herculean power."[20] In addition, women were presented in more sexual, independent, and gender-defying roles. In publications such as the *Gazette*, men were warned against deviance of women as well as the deviance of criminal activity while that very behavior was sensationalized.

The masculine ideal was revered; it amounted to a sort of "quiet grandeur," wrote historian George L. Mosse, that was of a physically strong, tenacious male "whose external appearance reflected the moral universe, a normalcy that set the standard for an acceptable way of life." Yet this stereotype needed "enemies" through which it was contrasted, and thus America saw conflicting images pour forth in the race to promote the ideal.

Who were the outsiders who reflected poorly on modern masculinity? Mosse answered, "Those who were said to be unsettled, without roots, were usually considered outsiders: Gypsies, vagrants, and Jews. . . . Habitual criminals, the insane, and so-called sexual deviants must be added to the list."[21] For *Gazette* readers, one may also add to these outcasts Chinese immigrants, African Americans, drunks, and dangerous, sexy, strong, or masculine women.[22] By sensationalizing these types while promoting the ideal, Fox was able to serve his readers a double helping—the model man and the perilous, exciting, and enticing threats to the model.

After about 1876, the issues associated with masculinities, and the forces that influenced them, became an integral part of *Gazette* portrayals; this coincided with the the most successful years of the Fox era. A glance at most any issue during this period shows evidence of the period's physical culture, criminal misbehavior, sexual excitation, and deviance—and the parallel masculine reactions and defenses. For more than a quarter of a century, these portrayals became important reflections and constructions of masculinities and their oppositional forms.

The depictions took on a peculiar variety. Fox loved to show women as criminals, aggressors, and victors over men. In 1882 a woman was shown rebuking a black male admirer by hitting him over the head with a banjo; in 1894, a scantily clad young woman, in the Mardis Gras parade at New Orleans, was depicted nearly killing a man by beating him with a stone (figure I.2); in 1900, an "angry burlesquer" was featured getting the better of a "Milwaukee masher" (a man who preyed on women) with a broom[23] (figure I.3).

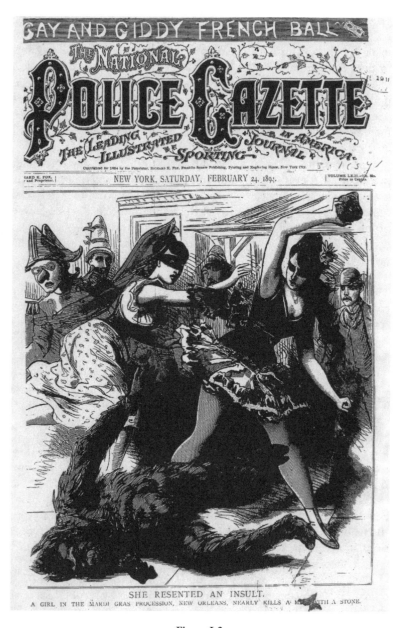

Figure I.2

SHE GAVE IT TO HIM GOOD.
ANGRY BURLESQUER MADE A MILWAUKEE MASHER THINK THE ROOF HAD FALLEN.

Figure I.3

At first glance these depictions might appear to be *anti*masculine, but juxtaposed with cheesecake and beefcake (innumerable pictures of beautiful women, boxers, and bodybuilders), the pictures have a cumulative effect of challenging, embracing, and reinforcing masculinities all at once. For example, on covers in 1879, a daring, well-dressed beauty had herself lowered from a cliff to seek thrills, and in 1902, actress Hope Booth showed off a strapless dress and pearls, a "charming young woman who will shortly appear in a sensational dancing act."[24] But both issues, more than twenty years apart, also had several pictures of males bodybuilders or other athletes displaying their hairless chests.

Fox could not have known that a few decades after the *Gazette* flourished and then faded, historians would cite the era's preoccupation with manliness, physical fitness, sexual politics, and criminal heroes as evidence of a cult of masculinity. All he knew was that boxing matches, showgirls, and crime stories sold magazines. Simply put, the interplay of men, women, and their bodies made for good pictures.

For many years, the *Gazette* was the most important of the tabloid publications and it was thus in a position to most obviously personalize, dramatize, and sensationalize issues of the greatest importance to its readers—primarily men. Thus, to better understand the issues of masculinities that have been discussed by many historians, and to glimpse the treatment of these issues by the most popular men's magazine of the day, the subject matter of *Gazette* illustrations was quantified over the twenty-seven-year period of 1879–1906, the prime years of Fox's heyday (and the beginning of the *Gazette* decline). In addition, issues beyond those years were examined qualitatively to supplement the study. The quantitative examination covered 278 issues, with a sampling procedure used in which an issue was chosen randomly for content analysis in each month of each year.[25] In the study, cover and inside illustrations were coded according to three basic categories—(1) crime; (2) sports/physical recreation; and (3) sex-related or provocative activities of actresses, showgirls, or other women. In addition, two other categories, disasters and an "other" designation, also were included, and each category included subheadings.[26] Cover illustrations were also coded to determine the sex and race of those depicted.

The results are discussed in more detail later, but they show that for more than two decades, the *Gazette* displayed a relative consistency in sports and sexual/theatrical portrayals, with depictions of crime dropping dramatically after the beginning of the twentieth century. One reason for the decline in crime portrayals was the improvement in picture production. With halftone technology the use of photographs became more common, and Fox did not choose to continue to use woodcuts to depict criminal acts that his illustrators had often imagined in the past. But he was consistent in his promotion of masculinities, for decades showing acts of physical prowess as well as showgirls and boxers in provocative portraits and poses. These quantitative findings help shape the material that follows—an analysis of the way Fox's *Gazette* covered the world through the lens (or pens) of sensationalism. Simply put, the *Gazette*'s illustrated portrayals of sport, crime, and sex defined and described emerging trends and conflicts of masculinities in Victorian and post-Victorian America.

Printed on pink paper to attract attention in much the same way as today's flashy graphics or "O.J.'s Murder Weapon Found in Oprah's Closet" headlines are used, the weekly *Gazette* (the "Barbershop Bible," as it was called) was part of the flourishing of New York's daily penny press. This remains true even though the *Gazette* is often considered a magazine. For example, one of the *Gazette*'s rivals, Joseph Pulitzer's *World*, had its similarities to the *Gazette*, with a mix of part sensationalism ("A Quintuple Tragedy. An Entire Family Annihilated By Its Murderous Head," read a *World* headline on March 5, 1884) part Progressivism (often backing laborers in disputes with capitalists), and part event promotion (it took the lead in 1885 to erect the Statue of Liberty). William Randolph Hearst purchased of the New York *Morning Journal* in 1895, and his decisions to cut the price to a penny and embrace sensationalism had forced Pulitzer to adopt similar tactics.[27] While for most of Fox's reign the *Gazette* was relatively expensive at a dime, it practiced, to an even more extreme degree, the same kinds of journalistic traditions that were so popular during this era. However, its relentless sponsorship of prize belts and awards, particularly in the manly art of boxing, set the *Gazette* apart from its competitors. In this context Fox can be seen as a sort of P.T. Barnum of journalism—a man who knew how to create a spectacle and make money off it at the same time.

This type of promotional activity was common among contemporary publishers. Races and contests abounded, and publishers offered prizes—sometimes cash or trips—to winners. In 1890 reporter Nellie Bly became famous when Pulitzer sent her on an around-the-world trip that beat the fictional Phileas Fogg's eighty-day journey; in 1895 the Chicago *Times Herald* staged a highly publicized race to promote the newly invented automobile. But Fox took the promotional activity a step further through his creation of contests and the backing of prizefights, and in the process he helped the great boxer John L. Sullivan become the nation's first sports superstar. Sports were ideal and idealized pastimes in an era in which masculinities were challenged by modern trends, and during this era newspapers and magazines seized upon the growth of sports as a way to boost circulation and promote themselves. In addition to promoting events that might boost the *Gazette*'s circulation, Fox was also a tireless self-promoter. In 1885, nine years after he took over the publication, he permitted the following to be printed in the *Gazette*:

> Richard K. Fox was born in Belfast in the year 1846, of that commingled Scotch and Irish parentage which has contributed so much to American enterprise and energy. The solid grit of the one and the mental acuteness of the other are both equally represented in him. His first employment was in the office of the *Banner of Ulster*, the celebrated organ of the Presbyterian Church in Ireland. After remaining with the *Banner* four years, Mr. Fox joined the staff of the *Belfast News Letter*, the richest and most powerful newspaper in Ireland. He remained with the *News Letter* for ten years, rising to the second place in its counting-room service. He arrived in New York in September, 1874. Although he had but a few shillings in his pocket, twenty-four hours after his landing he found profitable employment with the *Commercial Bulletin* of New York, a situation he left to connect himself with the *Police Gazette*— then at a very low ebb of prosperity, although the oldest weekly in America. Applying the most dauntless courage and industry to his work the new owner of the property which he had literally snatched from extinction, in less than ten years has made the *Police Gazette* building one of the sights of New York. It towers alongside the Brooklyn Bridge, and it occupies more space and machinery than any publishing house in America. To see the slender, almost boyish proprietor of this wonderful business moving modestly and good humoredly through its mazes . . . is to make one convinced that after all even Monte Cristo was a possible character, with the difference, however, that Monte Cristo had his fortune made for him, while Richard K. Fox forced fortune to smile on him by his own genius, good judgment and indomitable energy of will.[28]

Although a bit vainglorious, the portrait suited Fox, who would have been the first to say that no man ever made a dime from modesty. He came to America in 1874 virtually penniless. He died in 1922 as a millionaire. This is the story of how he did it, partly through grit and partly through the journalistic hat trick of sex, crime, and sports coverage. It was his wisdom to see, or at least exploit, the odd confluence of the cultural and historical influences that took hold during Gilded

Age America. During this time men were challenged by their wives, their jobs, the growth of immigration to cities in a newly industrialized, post–Civil War America, and astounding technological and engineering achievements, including railroads, the telegraph, and mass-produced publications. All of these forces were changing what it meant to be human, and with equal gusto, Fox seized on the wicked and the weird while often championing the weak. It was a formula that influenced modern journalism and helped foster and reflect the emerging notions of what it meant to be a modern man.

1

LIVES OF THE FELONS

We offer this week a most interesting record of horrid murders, outrageous robberies, bold forgeries, astounding burglaries, hideous rapes, vulgar seductions, and recent exploits of pickpockets and hotel thieves in various parts of the country.
—*National Police Gazette*, November 8, 1845

The New York City where Richard K. Fox disembarked from the *Tuscarora* in 1874 amounted to roiling contradictions of corruption and reform, of suffering and excess, of secret vices and high-handed morality. The king of Tammany Hall kickbacks, William "Boss" Tweed, the object of vitriolic Thomas Nast cartoons in *Harper's Weekly* that portrayed him as a corrupt, despicable oaf, was in jail.[1] Temperance leader Anthony Comstock was busy working up crusades against society's depravity. Workers had been petitioning for eight-hour workdays, and professional occupations were attempting to develop standards to winnow out amateurs. Apartment buildings were becoming a common habitat of the middle class, but tenements housed half of the city's residents, and beggars were an increasing nuisance. It was a city torn by conflicts of class and religion, of attitude and invective. Three years before Fox arrived, the "slaughter on Eighth Avenue" had been burned in memories when, on the 181st anniversary of Ireland's Battle of the Boyne, more than sixty people were killed and one hundred wounded when Irish Catholic and Protestant groups had clashed over the right of celebrants to hold a parade.[2] Fox would later tell a story about being drawn into the Protestant–Catholic conflict, only to emerge more wizened, ambitious, and focused on his task of media empire-building.[3]

Fox's personal industry represented what characterized many in the teeming city of immigrants: the notion that hard work and inventiveness could take one to the pinnacle of American society. That he symbolized many of the trends of the country in which he lived is not surprising; as an immigrant, he was, like many others, attempting to figure out what it meant to be an American as a new, modern century approached. Even more, he was driven to success and wealth from his memories of his hard work as a schoolboy in Ireland. When he arrived in New York he was a charter subscriber to the American dream.

This energy and drive—the *American* brand of energy and drive—was portrayed in the popular mythology of the day, as well as in the New York press that was the eager-eyed gazetteer of the daily spectacle of gotham. It is instructive that one of the city's press practitioners when Fox arrived was Horatio Alger.

Alger, born in 1832 in Revere, Massachusetts, was at first drawn to the ministry but was lured to writing after an 1866 scandal in his Unitarian church at Brewster, Massachusetts, when elders concluded that he had been engaging in "unnatural crimes" with young boys in the parish. Alger left for New York and began writing and helping out at the Newsboys' Lodging House, where newsboys and bootlicks stayed for a nickel a night. His adventures fed his fiction, and in 1867 Alger began publishing his serial, "Ragged Dick; or, Street Life in New York," in the children's magazine *Student and Schoolmate*. In the series Dick acts as a street guide for a well-to-do acquaintance, warning him, "A feller has to look sharp in this city, or he'll lose his eye-teeth before he knows it." The acquaintance returns the favor, teaching Dick about manners and dress, and he reforms from his ragged ways.[4]

The Alger stories were part of the lore of boyhood pluckiness that flourished in the press and in fiction at the turn of the century. It was a nation in need of heroes, since the changes of modernization, industrialization, and immigration had challenged people's perceptions of the proper conduct of their lives. The costs of modernity included alienation and ambiguity, and the press was a vehicle where people sought stories that simultaneously registered the appalling features of society while affirming the good. Wrote historian Susan Douglas,

> The adulation of heroes and the excoriation of villains became a dominant feature of American journalism during the late nineteenth century, when many aspects of American life were in flux. As the society navigated, and sometimes drifted, toward new horizons, heroes served as fixed points during an uncharted voyage.[5]

The notion of the hero as the "ideal man" (or boy) coping gracefully and inventively with life's new challenges was one image that affirmed masculinities which, as many historians have noted, came under increasing assault as the century drew to a close.[6] In Alger's stories there was often an element of luck in one's rise to success, as when one boy saved a young girl from peril and later learned her father was a millionaire. But in dime novels with characters such as Deadwood Dick, the heroes also asserted themselves through physical strength, sporting mastery, and the conquest of nature.[7] In the wildly popular Jack Harkaway stories, written by Bracebridge Hemyng, who later went to work for the *National Police Gazette*, Jack is a square-jawed hero with a sense of justice and adventure on a grand scale.[8] These very masculine pursuits fit in well with the overall portrait of the hero as resourceful, brave, and inventive.

The labeling of boys and men as heroes for their mastery of technology was no accident. The press seized on many inventions and their creators with wonder and enthusiasm; indeed, it was the advance of technology that had made the mass media a possibility. David E. Nye, in his 1994 book *American Technological Sublime*, contended that sublime faith in technological advances became an important part of the growth of America. The rapid development of railroads, bridges, skyscrapers, factories, and electricity led to the assumption that "sublime technological objects were . . . active forces working for democracy."[9] In America the sublime transcended traditional natural features, such as great rivers, canyons, or waterfalls, to include the amazing advances in science and development, so that the "American sublime transformed the individual's experience of immensity and awe into a belief in national greatness."[10] Caught up in this exalted faith in technology, an editor in 1874 breathlessly predicted the following:

By means of condensed air and cold vapor engines excursion parties may travel along the floor of the ocean, sailing past ancient wrecks and mountains of coral. On land the intelligent farmer may turn the soil of a thousand acres in a day, while his son cuts wood with a platinum wire and shells corn by electricity. The matter now contained in a New York daily may be produced ten thousand times a minute, on little scraps of pasteboard; and boys may well sell the news of the world printed on visiting cards, which their customers will read through artificial eyes. . . . The time is coming when the *Herald* will send a reporter to see a man reduce one of the Rocky Mountains to powder in half a day. Skillful miners will extract gold from quartz as easily as cider is squeezed from apples. A compound telescope will be invented on entirely new principles, so that one may see the planets as distinctly as we now see Staten Island. . . . And marvelous progress will be made in psychological and mental sciences. Two men will sit in baths filled with chemical liquids; one of them may be in Denver and the other in Montrial [*sic*], a pipe filled with the same liquid will connect the two vessels, and the fluid will be so sensitive that each man will know the other's thoughts. In these coming days our present mode of telegraphing will be classed with the wood ploughs of Egypt, and the people will look back to steamships and locomotives as we look back to sailboats and stage coaches.[11]

Some of that speculation was, of course, mere fancy, but in an accompanying comment, a writer could not resist the temptation to poke fun at a competitor, the New York *Herald*, and its lack of expertise on science matters. Under a headline, "The *New York Herald* as a Science Prophet," the item noted:

A recent number of *The New York Herald again* contains one of the would-be scientific articles as of little credit to its scientific editorial department as its criticisms on music and painting are to that department to which art has been assigned. The article commences thus:

"Wendell Phillips [a Boston lawyer and abolitionist who gained fame when he condemned the murder of anti-slavery editor Elijah P. Lovejoy] said in a recent speech that the time was coming when we might communicate instantly with San Francisco without either wire or operator. The audience laughed at him. Perhaps his statement is not so extravagant as it seemed. Had the ordinary work now done by the magnetic telegraph been predicted forty years ago, it would have been received with the same incredulity."

Now the fact is that not only did scientific men forty years ago believe the possibility of telegraphy by electricity, but it was successfully done in 1747 by Dr. Watron in England, in 1757 by Lomand in France, while in 1774 Lesage of Geneva made it a perfect success. See further our condensed history of the electric telegraph in our May number for 1873, from which those who attempt writing on this subject may obtain some preparatory information, or at least be placed on the right track as to learn where to obtain further light.[12]

Some of the wonder at new technology was well-directed, of course. James Gordon Bennett Sr. along with his son James Gordon Bennett Jr. had been the first to report on Samuel Morse's telegraph and Thomas Edison's lightbulb. They were prescient in their sense that the inventions would revolutionize communications and people's lifestyles. The elder Bennett also had dispatched boats to meet ships bringing news from Europe; the smaller boats would then hurry back to New York to get the news to the *Herald* well before the transatlantic ships arrived. In addition, Bennett's son founded the Commercial

Cable Company to help with transatlantic communication. The competition for speed and news, and the effort to reach wider audiences, helped establish modern journalism techniques.[13] This was a profession that was full of rambunctious rabble rousers and partisans, who took joy in the fierce competition and satisfaction in the humiliation of another editor. Fox would become heir to this tradition, which had lasted for many years, but its immediate ancestor in New York was the penny-paper-era rivalry between Benjamin Day of the *Sun*, James Gordon Bennett of the *Herald*, and Horace Greeley of the New York *Tribune*.

Day, the son of a hatter who was born in 1810 in West Springfield, Massachusetts, was, like many journalists before and after him, a printer and compositor who had broader ambitions. Against the warnings of his friends who had noted the death of penny papers such as the *Cent* in Philadelphia and the *Bostonian* in Boston, Day became determined to start a penny newspaper and finally did so, with the *Sun* beginning publication in September 1833. In a deliberate challenge to the six-penny papers aimed at mostly upper-class readers and businessmen, Day devoted less space to business and Congress and more to features and crime news. His first presses were powered by mechanical cranks, but a year into operation he was able to afford a steam-powered press that could produce 4,000 copies an hour. It took Day only a week of producing papers before he hired a reporter to attend police court and write up crime items of interest. Circulation grew to more than 8,000 as Day highlighted the racy, sensational, and the criminal.[14]

The *Sun* also published stories about sporting events, including one two-hour, fifty-two-round boxing match in which an Irish challenger was condemned for nearly biting off the finger of his American opponent.[15] Day's success led to both condemnation and imitation. One editor of a six-penny daily, James Watson Webb of the *Courier and Enquirer*, ridiculed the *Sun* as a proponent of trashy news. Meanwhile, imitators, such as *The Man* and the *New York Transcript*, flourished and then failed. *The Man* emphasized labor unions and women's rights but would survive only a year. The *Transcript*, however, more closely resembled a publication that would follow—the *National Police Gazette*. The *Transcript*, under Willoughby Lynde and William J. Stanley, emphasized sports, sexual gossip, and ribald humor, and it also published advertisements that touted quick cures for various ills. It rivaled the *Sun* in popularity, at one point achieving a circulation of more than 20,000 (the *Sun* grew to more than 35,000 before Day sold it in 1837). But the financial panic of 1837 doomed the journal and it folded in 1839. Six years later, the birth of the *Gazette* would follow.[16]

In the never-ending competition for readers, the newspapers of this day often carried items that were either untrue or unverifiable. In some cases, the gossip or intimations were reasonably accurate, but in others, rumors were presented as fact (often in the form of invective) that left their targets helpless. It was in 1835 that Day launched what would become the most famous of journalism's early winks at the truth, the great Moon Hoax. In August he began publishing a series of articles about the fantastic sightings made possible by a gigantic new telescope in Sir John Herschel's observatory at the Cape of Good Hope in Africa. The articles, supposedly containing descriptions already published in a Scottish science journal, were ostensibly written by Richard Adams Locke, a descendant of the English philosopher John Locke. They contained vivid accounts of blue goats with single horns; man-bats who collected fruit, flew around, and then idled about; biped beavers; and four-foot-tall moon people who looked like orangutans but whose lips were more human than those of the orangutans on Earth.[17]

The *Sun*'s circulation leapt to more than 20,000, and Day's competitors were forced to acknowledge the magnitude of the scoop. The more "respectable" six-penny newspapers, such as the *Daily Advertiser*, the *Commercial Advertiser*, the *Evening Post*, and the *Courier and Enquirer*, either reprinted the articles without comment or praised the *Sun* for publishing them. It was left to the *Journal of Commerce* to expose the hoax after Locke admitted authoring them, and James Gordon Bennett, publisher of a new penny paper, the New York *Herald*, said the *Sun* "can never thrive hereafter upon the moon or any other planet."[18]

Some historians have portrayed the early practice of deliberately printing falsehoods as a kind of experimental, whimsical journalism that was soon replaced by more objective, fact-filled reporting. However, a tabloid tradition relying on gossip, innuendo, and fabrication survived and flourished for many years and is still marketed today at supermarket checkout lines. The indifferent attitude toward the truth in the 1800s was not so much an attempt to fool readers but was rather a wink at the truth (and an attempt, at times, to tell "greater truths" through the use of fiction) and amounted to a reliance on the marketability of the entertainment of deception. One historian has suggested that style and tone were clues to the quality or veracity of the reporting, and that those who violated these conventions of tone—*not* necessarily those who violated the truth—were the ones who found themselves subject to criticism.[19] As editor of the *Gazette* five decades after the Moon Hoax, Fox would take advantage of these kinds of reader discernments. Although the *Gazette* often printed what was true, it also printed the kind of unverifiable suggestions that titillated readers who by the 1880s were used to the good, the bad, and the preposterous of nineteenth-century journalism.[20]

Historian Dan Schiller, in his 1981 study of how the forces and traditions of objectivity shaped the news, described the Moon Hoax as a clever attempt by the penny press to outwit the more prestigious six-penny rivals; the *Sun* charged that these rivals all too often lifted articles from the *Sun* without credit. For Schiller, this condemnation of the Moon Hoax amounted to a beginning of a more scientific journalism that contributed to enlightenment. The growth of positivism in the mid-nineteenth century, along with the idea of a uniform and objective world governed by immutable laws, gave a legitimacy to objective journalism whose role was to chronicle the facts of the world.[21]

Objectivty, Schiller argued, was a recurrent and conventionally generated strategy in the *Police Gazette*. Yet:

> Objectivity . . . was contradictory: the ideal of a universally recognizable, democratically accessible "web of facticity" was concretely verified and bulwarked by a specific social hierarchy. Belief that access to knowledge should be equal for all citizens was belied by the particular *form* through which knowledge was expressed. For in the *Police Gazette*, a specific social hierarchy authorized and defined a particular threshold of proof.[22]

Schiller argued that the Penny Press was a force for democracy. The *Sun*'s motto, "It Shines for All," is a case in point. Day was committed to making his newspaper a force for enlightenment, thus creating a central role for the press in public education. In the case of the *National Police Gazette*, Schiller argued, infringement of "natural rights" was tied up in a class context. For him, defense of natural rights and public good was the "enduring foundation upon which the structure of news objectivity was built."[23] These historical trends helped shape what the *National Police Gazette* became in its early years, because they helped focus journalism, at least in part, toward crime coverage.

A few months after the Moon Hoax[24] came another big story. On a spring day in 1836 James Gordon Bennett walked from his *Herald* office at Nassau and Beekman streets in Manhattan to a yellow house on Thomas Street. There, he viewed "a beautiful female corpse—that surpassed the finest statue of antiquity." The head of the woman, prostitute Helen Jewett, had been crushed by three ax blows, "either of which must have proved fatal, as the bone was cleft to the extent of three inches in each place."[25] In his account of the crime Bennett provided one of the most careful, elaborate, on-scene eyewitness accounts of early-nineteenth-century journalism. Commonly, crime reporters of the day relied on accounts of police and magistrates. Rarely did they quote eyewitnesses or conduct interviews. Bennett, however, in his reporting on the Jewett case, became the arbiter of "public duty" and privy to the crime scene himself.[26] He published conversations he had with the keeper of the house of prostitution where Jewett died, and Bennett biographers have credited him with inventing the art of the interview. But he also became something more: a detective and an investigator.[27] In addition, the Jewett case became a landmark because it marked the first long-term, ongoing exploitation of a crime story in major American newspapers.[28]

The suspect in the brutal hatchet murder was Jewett's paramour, Richard Robinson, making it perfect fodder for urban journalism. According to Schiller, crime news reached its early zenith with the case, and George Wilkes, the *National Police Gazette* editor, produced one of eleven "chapbooks" (small pamphlets usually sold by peddlers, or chapmen) on the case in 1849.[29] The case was highlighted as an indictment of society: all of civilization should be judged guilty because of the conditions that led to the crime, according to Bennett.

In this manner, crime news, Schiller contended, "led to another important development—the growth of a cheap urban culture," and "lavish description and detail were often used to flesh out cursory accounts from the police courts." Crimes also gave reporters a chance to develop *stories*—and to explore a narrative style. Schiller said, "Crime news intertwined with the lived experience of the new public and thus testified to the essential propriety of reporting the varied forms of urban social life."[30]

Bennett had founded the *Herald* the year before the Jewett murder, and it had grown quickly, like other penny papers. Many historians credit Bennett with fostering the growth of newsrooms and reporting staffs. He predicted that more common transatlantic shipping (the first steamship to cross the Atlantic was the British *Sirius* in 1838) would help smaller penny papers compete against their more wealthy rivals because the smaller papers could get news without having to pay for a shipping operation of their own. Bennett was aggressive in news gathering and other innovations, employing reporters to cover religious meetings and even overseas events.[31]

Like many of its competitors, the *Sun* was considered a way for the poor to keep up with the news, and the penny newspapers became symbols of Jacksonian democracy—outlets of politics and news for the common man. Politics was not much more than a hobby for Bennett, but another editor, Horace Greeley, who began the New York *Tribune* in 1841, was an active abolitionist and a socialist who was not afraid to voice his opinions in print.[32]

Greeley came from New Hampshire to New York City when he was twenty and at first found it difficult to find employment. He proved skillful as a printer, however, and eventually he saved about $1,500 and began a publication called the *New-Yorker*, which, in its first issue, published a story taken from *London Monthly* called "Delicate Attentions." The British author used the name of "Boz," which was the first time that Charles Dickens's work had been brought to the common men and women of New York City.[33]

The tall, stout, balding Greeley was prolific and sociable, and he contributed two columns a week to the *Tribune* and the equivalent of six other columns to other publications. In these letters to his readers, Greeley championed progressive causes and challenged Americans to build a utopia. He also published Margaret Fuller's *Woman in the Nineteenth Century*, the first feminist manifesto to be published in America, and he became an active supporter of "women's rights." In the 1850s, he was a frequent guest at the home of the "poet sisters" Alice and Phoebe Cary, who held dinner parties that included the likes of Phineas T. Barnum, Susan B. Anthony, Elizabeth Cady Stanton, publisher Robert Bonner, editor Samuel Bowles of the *Springfield Republican*, and the beautiful writer Kate Field, who wrote biographies of Dickens and the famed Italian actress Adelaide Ristori and became an expert on mysticism and the supernatural.[34]

At the urging of Susan B. Anthony and Elizabeth Cady Stanton, Phoebe Cary had served as an editor of *The Revolution*, a radical weekly that originated from a large, well-appointed house on East Twenty-third Street. Although they were both married and devoted to their families, Stanton and Anthony held radical ideas on feminism and the institution of marriage, with Stanton regarding it as legalized prostitution. It was during this period that the women who frequented the Carys on Sunday evenings were roused to action by the snubbing of a well-known female journalist by the New York Press Club. The reporter, Jennie June, had asked for a ticket to a banquet that the club was holding for Dickens. She was refused on the grounds that she was a woman. After she informed her friends of the slight, they decided to form a club of their own; they called it Sorosis, from the Greek meaning "aggregation," and they signed up fifty members.[35]

> Wrote historian Lloyd Morris in 1951,
>
> Perhaps the unchivalrous New York Press Club foresaw an ultimate collapse of masculine supremacy. After suitable preliminaries, it joined Sorosis in a public banquet—the first ever given in New York at which men and women sat down on equal terms, each paying their own way and sharing equally in the honors and responsibilities.[36]

At the banquet, one guest put Susan B. Anthony on the spot by asking her why it was that women did not propose marriage to men. She won admiration and laughter with the reply, "Under present conditions, it would require a good deal of assurance for a woman to say to a man, 'Please, sir, will you support me for the rest of my life?' "[37]

Greeley, Bennett, and Day were an unlikely trio to help set the agenda for Park Row. But their different approaches illustrated the riotous conflict that was at the heart of the newspaper wars in the sprawling, rapidly growing city. The emphasis on scandal and the salacious was nothing new. Two British journalists concluded in 1986 that audiences have always loved to watch scandals expose the depths of hypocrisy and deviance among the elite. An audience may gain satisfaction from the downfall of others and the knowledge that that the wealthy are just as subject to deviant temptations as "ordinary" people. The news coverage also provides diversion from the audience members' own, probably less-privileged, lives.[38] The sociologist Emile Durkheim maintained that the actions of the deviant test the limits of society and thus define acceptable behavior, while those less deviant use the deviants as "others" to prosecute.[39] In reading about scandal and reprehensible conduct, all readers, like the readers of the 1800s, are fascinated but often disgusted at their own fascination. The appetite for stories of murders, mutilations, disasters, and scandals may be explained by historian Mitchell Stephens's suggestion that human beings are motivated to read these items because they are preoccupied with all matters of life and death and are really on the lookout for possible threats as well as potential mates. In any case, the editors of the 1800s understood perfectly that crime news sold, and sold well.[40]

New York, like another great city of its day, London, had made possible the mass audience. By 1845 New York City had more than 300,000 people and it would grow to more than 500,000 in five years.[41] It was the perfect backdrop for an experiment in mass media content—an experiment in the reporting of gossip and scandal, of business and politics, of crime and punishment, and of reform and riots, which the people wanted and demanded. But it was also an experiment in the limits of what the public could tolerate. Many became appalled at what they considered the spread, and celebration, of immorality. But they had not read anything yet. For a new kind of publication was born in 1845 that would, by the end of the century, become notorious for its salacious, bawdy irreverence as it flourished on vice, self-promotion, and the celebration of manhood.

It is not an unreasonable speculation to consider the possibility that the idea for the *National Police Gazette* was at least partly born in a jail cell in New York City's Tombs. The Tombs Prison, which was officially known as the New York Halls of Justice, had housed a well-known repeat offender, George Wilkes. In 1844, he spent thirty days there after being convicted of libel.

Wilkes, who Schiller says was probably the son of an artisan, had worked as a law clerk, a journalist, a speech writer, a political boss, and a commentator on such diverse topics as Shakespeare, horse racing, boxing, and on the prospect of a national railroad.[42] Eventually he became editor of a four-page journal called *The Subterranean*, which sought to publicize the illegal sources of income for various political activities, and in so doing he had been shot at twice. After his imprisonment on libel charges, Wilkes, a handsome man with robust sideburns and a well-trimmed mustache, wrote a long account of his imprisonment in the Tombs, published in *The Subterranean*, and its details of corruption and wickedness were so vivid that, according to some, it led to the defeat of Mayor Robert H. Morris and the removal of the warden of the Tombs. *The Subterranean* soon went under, however, and Wilkes was looking for a new venture when he was approached by a capitalist lawyer, Enoch Camp. Their shared experiences with the law led them to the conclusion that what New York lacked, even with all of the dailies' devotion to crime and mayhem, was a reliable chronicler of vice and the police response to it.[43]

The *Gazette* was a product of a newly modern era, but historian Schiller noted that in the mid-1700s the seeds for crime reporting were sown in England after "the novelist Henry Fielding was determined to start a police force to suppress the thieves and robbers who too often enjoyed the freedom of the city." After his death, his half brother, John Fielding, took over and redoubled the effort. His 1761 proposal to Prime Minister Thomas Pelham Holles, the Duke of Newcastle,[44] said that as part of the crime-fighting effort, an official gazette, or chronicle, of police activities should be published so that information about wanted criminals could be distributed. Newcastle agreed; four years before the American Revolution, Fielding's police gazette (called the *Quarterly Pursuit* or, more frequently, the *Weekly or Extraordinary Pursuit*) began publishing.[45]

Eighty years later, the National *Police Gazette* appears to have been founded with at least two more modern sources in mind—one of them, London's *Police Gazette*, was government-sponsored and earned a tip of the hat from Wilkes in the first issue of his *National Police Gazette*. The idea of the London paper was to act as an agent of law enforcement, specifically for the purpose of offering details of crimes in order to catch criminals. The second source was *Cleave's Weekly Police Gazette*, also British, which was printed for working men and had content that suggested its purpose was to right wrongs in the justice system. New York's *Police Gazette*, then, served a sort of dual purpose: espousing the authority of law enforcement while championing equal rights for lower classes, including the public's right to know.[46]

In 1857, the *National Police Gazette* was sold to ex-New York City Police Chief George Washington Matsell, but it would be another twenty or thirty years before it would reach its heyday under Fox, boasting a circulation of as much as 500,000 before tabloids began copying its format and appearing daily.[47] In its earlier days, however, circulation reached about 20,000, when recruiting stations for government soldiers were among the major subscribers. But it valued a quality of writing not often found in "scandal sheets," and its fans included a large secondary readership at hotels and resorts, where it was consumed carefully over coffee or drinks. Readers supposedly included Martin Van Buren and John C. Calhoun.[48]

The first number of the *Gazette* appeared in the fall of 1845, and its publication cost a life, an ear, and two fingers. On the evening of October 11 a regular of Jonas Burks's saloon on Delancey Street entered and ordered a double noggin of gin and calamus. Burks, who was so well known for the drink that his saloon was known as Gin and Calamus Hall, obliged. The customer began waving around a copy of the new issue of the *National Police Gazette*, which carried the opening installment of a series called "Lives of the Felons," about Robert Sutton, a.k.a. "Bob the Wheeler," who was infamous in criminal, political, and pugilistic circles. Sutton was in jail at that time for the murder of the brother of his fifth wife, and Burks remarked that Bob the Wheeler deserved to be hanged. From across the bar a bottle was thrown at him, possibly by one of Bob the Wheeler's twelve sons, and crushed Burks's tall beaver hat. A melee ensued, and although Burks managed to inflict damage on the bottle-thrower, Burks lost an ear and two fingers, and a brawl participant, Croucher Collins, was killed.[49]

Two weeks later, the *Gazette* was all too happy to proclaim that the fight had had a positive affect on the sales of its first issue. "But the editors of this weekly will not feel adequately repaid until it has irritated all of New York's vermin to public battle where by they shall destroy themselves."[50]

Under Wilkes and Camp, the *Gazette* gained popularity as a major chronicler of crime news. Even before the penny press, newspapers reported about crimes, but it was the competition between the penny dailies that began to popularize the practice widely. American papers had paid less attention to crime than the British, and as late as 1824 the *Niles' Weekly Register* noted that most reports of crimes were found in "street literature" such as almanacs or pamphlets.[51] With the increasing reporting about crimes, and with Bennett's success at increasing the *Herald*'s regular circulation from 4,000 to 15,000 during the Jewett affair, the marketplace revealed a powerful incentive: the attraction of readers to crime news. The *Gazette* tapped into this knowledge and by its second month in business it was reporting a circulation of 15,000. Wilkes, who was responsible for editorial matters, began each issue with this description of priorities: "We offer this week a most interesting record of horrid murders, outrageous robberies, bold forgeries, astounding burglaries, hideous rapes, vulgar seductions, and recent exploits of pickpockets and hotel thieves in various parts of the country."[52]

Thus, here was a publication that made few pretensions of covering business or politics, and it was praised even by the *Herald*, the *Tribune*, and the *Sun*, and was imitated by such weeklies as the *Clipper*, the *Sunday News*, and the *New York Mercury*.[53] But Wilkes soon grew tired of focusing on crime news all the time. He railed against blue laws, prize fighting (a stance that for the *Gazette* would become an irony in thirty years), high rents, and hard-to-find city streets and addresses. According to Wilkes, the latter problem had caused an unfortunate *Gazette* reporter to arrive at the wrong address in search of a story, only to be beaten by the startled residents so badly that he spent two weeks in the hospital.[54]

Historian Schiller offers, for modern readers, a valuable assessment of *Gazette* content in those early years. In the "Lives of the Felons" series, the causes, character, and consequences of crime were explored, and the rest of the publication included features that would remain remarkably similar for more than eighty years. A large illustration adorned page 1. The inside pages had trial reports, shorts on offenses around the country, and what amounted to an editorial page offering unsigned opinion pieces. It rapidly gained a reputation for truthfulness and was praised for its credibility by such newspapers as the New Haven *Democrat*, Providence *Herald*, and Louisville *Daily Democrat*. A key characteristic was that because of its orientation—crime, not politics—it claimed a commitment to fact and not party loyalty. In keeping with this spirit, it went out of its way to assure readers that it checked facts.[55]

The *Gazette* trumpeted this mission of fact in early 1847 when it printed an "annual Address of the Carriers of the *National Police Gazette* to Their Patrons" on January 9:

> To read these deeds, and feel and know
> That they have been and must be so,
> . . .
> What mischiefs dire! what murders black!
> What corpses lie along your track!
> What fiendish rapes! what beastly acts
> Stand ranged in rows of stubborn facts![56]

The *Gazette* used this litany of fact to build a "philosophy of crime" (i.e., what it considered a science of crime). In addition, early technology in the form of the daguerreotype, which was a photograph but could not be reproduced in newsprint until later with halftone technology involving an engraver, gave powerful visual "proof" of criminal activity. *Gazette* artists created their drawings from daguerreotypes, an apparently "real" starting point that allowed great artistic leeway (later seized upon quite zealously by Fox and his illustrators). Thus, the *Gazette* practiced a method of journalism that, if examined cursorily, appears contradictory—it gleefully exposed the seamy and the seedy while condemning the very activities it sensationalized. But its amplification of moral failings was a self-serving nod to the world of fact—it offered "true-life" portraits of crime while claiming to make criminals fear the real and public consequences of their actions. As Schiller put it, "Our modern Eyewitness News is actually almost a century and a half old."[57]

The *Gazette*'s success gave it an air of credibility, so that it became an authority in and of itself. "Empirical fact-finding backed by lavish expenditure provided the access to the criminal world that, in turn, justified the *Police Gazette*'s claim to specialized competence and authority," Schiller wrote.[58] In an account of one murder, the *Gazette* noted that a killer had ripped open the belly of the victim before dumping it into the Mississippi River. The *Gazette* helpfully explained in a footnote, "This is the invariable practice of river pirates and assassins, to conceal the bodies of their victims. It prevents the decaying corpse from collecting those gaseous humors which would bring it to the surface."[59]

Another method of securing authenticity for the *Gazette* was its use of a language that conveyed its writers' and editors' savvy on pertinent subjects. Schiller said the *Gazette* used illustrations, diaries, official sources, transcripts, and criminal slang in this manner, by displaying "professional expertise" in strategic ways.[60] In addition, the *Gazette* equated its mass circulation—its very popularity—with a certain power to speak for the people who read it. In these early years it established traditions that would define it for decades, as it fought against political inequalities, public corruption, and unequal justice on property rights as a result of state decree.[61] Lawyers, as part of the system, were certainly not immune to criticism; they were vulnerable to corruption because of their role as mediators. On November 29, 1845, an unknown *Gazette* writer commented, "To hear some men at the bar, you would suppose that if they were held up by the feet the words would run out of their mouth by mere force of gravity, for a week at a time, without troubling their brains at all."[62]

This championing role for the *Gazette* becomes important in the consideration of its position on matters of class, central to its notions of masculinities. Schiller pointed out, "Because class was generally viewed as a political rather than as a social product, the *Police Gazette* attempted a powerful remedial role through publicity and exposure, to redress the political corruption that led to permanent class divisions."[63] During this period the working class was arguably more threatened by class divisions than by sex or race (though racial divisions would become increasingly important), so it was forced to defend itself against economic injustices, invasions, and depreciations. But the defensive assertions often took the form of reactions to *others*, whether they were sexist, racist, or classist in nature. The expressions of (white male) masculinities in the form of racism or certain portrayals of women (and men, including criminals) amounted to such defenses, and the rhetoric of *vox populi* was a powerful weapon in this battle. In 1846, the *Gazette* noted of the gentle classes: "They must beware how they help precipitate a reckoning between the two extremes, whose terrible realities may be too fearful for the contemplation."[64]

Thus, the *Gazette* favored reform to solve inequities, but it was not in open opposition to government or to law enforcement. It contended, said Schiller, that the failure to reform could result in a drastic fall into the brutish, Hobbesian state of nature. And the activities of the felons that the *Gazette* highlighted contributed to the dangerous breakdown of civilization. This fear, it may be said, was what guided *Gazette* coverage.

In a content analysis of the portrayals of the "felons" in the *Gazette* from 1845 to 1850, Schiller found the following:

1. All were white males (because blacks and women posed only external threats to the system, while white men posed an inside threat).
2. Most were mature, professional criminals.
3. Half were English, and not one was a native New Yorker. This is an interesting finding because it did not reflect the reality that increasing numbers of native New Yorkers were committing crimes. This shows an emphasis on the deviant activities of the "outsider," a key characteristic in the *Gazette*'s expressions of masculinities.
4. Crime was defined overwhelmingly as an act against an individual's right of property. This unlawful enrichment allowed criminals to advance into other class categories, making "distinctions between the rogue, the speculator and the banker difficult."[65] Later, as will be shown from a content analysis of *Gazette* illustrations during the Fox era, greater emphasis was placed on other kinds of crime, more directly highlighting the threats to masculinities as well as the responses that the threats created.
5. The attack on the natural right of property was not counterbalanced by the state's corrupt defense of property. In effect, the *Gazette* argued, the state was helpless to punish the ills it had produced; justice was incompetent and criminals were getting away with their misdeeds.[66]

Schiller reproduced a table, which appeared in the *Gazette* on February 28, 1846, showing the felons' self-reported causes of crime. Some of the major reasons were as follows:

Intemperance	150
No conscience	84
For gain	64
Evil Associations	195
Innocent (as they assert)	165
Weak principles	31
Sudden Temptation	24

The overall portrait of the "Lives of the Felons" was rather alarming. Schiller wrote,

> The dimensions of criminality appeared to be coextensive with American society itself; individual delinquents and a corrupt state were locked in a foul embrace, spawning a cycle of escalating depredation and disorganization. Only the *Police Gazette*, by its account, with the press as a whole, stood above these Hobbesian waters, where big fish chased little fish, looking back at the receding shoreline of an ideal republic and forward to an emerging landscape of liberal reform.[67]

The *Gazette* would become a leader in many of these agenda-setting frames concerning crime news, but there is another crucial element to its role in journalism history. During these years the *Gazette* developed a practice, which would survive for decades, of creating a national constituency of readers as well as writers. As shown by Wilkes's claims, the *Gazette* tried to distinguish itself from the dailies by offering news from "various parts of the country," something that many other New York publications did not emphasize. In this effort, Wilkes hired stringers and paid readers who would send stories or tips from their cities or towns to the *Gazette*'s offices, where they would be edited for publication. It was the national (and international, under Fox) nature of the *Gazette* that earned it its surviving, legendary status as a purveyor of popular American culture.

One event that helped spur this national reciprocation—the publishing of items outside of New York and the readership of the *Gazette* in other regions—again involved Bob the Wheeler (Robert Sutton). After his release from jail following the fight at Gin and Calumus Hall, he gathered some of his cronies, including Dingdong Kelly, John J. Betterton the Blockman, the "resurrectionist" (grave robber) James Downer, and a few others. The men went to the *Gazette*, determined to make Wilkes pay for what had been written about Sutton. The battle that followed was reported by the *Herald*, the *Sun*, and the *Tribune*. Three people—the ressurrectionist and two bystanders who became involved in the fighting—were killed, and many others were hospitalized. More than two hundred people were involved in the fight at its peak, but none of the *Gazette*'s editorial staff was injured. The publicity from the brawl, though, helped the *Gazette* in its reputation and spurred expansion efforts, and it soon established agents in towns as distant as New Orleans, St. Louis, and Quebec City. The *Gazette*'s readers became its agents, to a large extent, and many were its distributors. These early agents began introducing the weekly into what would be its home for three quarters of a century—the male-dominated barbershops of America. "Read the *Police Gazette?*"—"No, I shave myself" was a popular vaudeville joke of the era. Later, it would be a common item in saloons, another type of gathering place dominated by men.

The rise of the saloons was part demand, part economic accident. The higher concentration of populations in cities and a flood of immigration contributed to an increase in unionization and the growth of male gathering places. That meant more saloons, lodges, corner taverns, and union halls (which often *were* saloons), which helped foster a common identity and diversions among men of common interests and class.

As historians Elizabeth Pleck and Joseph Pleck wrote, economic forces during this era had major influences on the patterns of interaction between men and women, leading to changing professional and domestic roles and influencing perceptions of gender and class. At the beginning of the Civil War, 60 percent of all working-class men labored in agricultural fields; sixty years later, only a third were farmers. Simultaneously, the percentage of men working in manufacturing and construction—city jobs, primarily—rose from 18 percent in 1860 to 31 percent in 1920.[68] Mines and factories became dominated by men; at the same time, administrative jobs in chemistry, accounting, or engineering helped exploit the skills of a new male middle class. A developing business sense contributed to the belief in the power of reason and action, traits attributed almost exclusively to men. New businesses challenged the agrarian patriarchy, and in the nineteenth century many male roles fundamentally changed as men worked in offices and factories. Meanwhile, literacy was on the increase, making more and more people part of the popular culture. "That century," historian Peter N. Stearns wrote in 1979, "and the early part of our own, saw the most concerted efforts to adapt existing male traditions and even to hark back to earlier images of the fighting and hunting male."[69] By 1901, five-and-a-half million men belonged to lodges, which provided places for activities such as joking, drinking, parades, picnics, and sporting events. By 1897, licensed liquor dealers in the United States numbered over 215,000, and another 50,000 sellers of drink were unlicensed. Shortly after the turn of the century New York had 10,000 licensed saloons, 1 for every 515 residents; Houston had 1 for every 298 people; San Francisco had 1 for every 218. Meanwhile, adult annual per capita consumption of beer rose from 2.7 gallons in 1850 to 29.53 gallons a year from 1911 to 1915.[70] Yet the appeal of the saloon went beyond the alcoholic. The taverns served as gathering places for men of like minds, professions, and ethnic identities.

During this period industrialization helped fuel migration to cities from farm communities, but immigration also contributed to cities' sectional splintering that attracted different immigrant populations. That made neighborhood saloons, for many, homes away from home. Jon M. Kingsdale wrote,

> Many workingmen thought of and treated the corner saloon as their own private club rather than as a public institution. They used it as a mailing address; leaving and picking up messages, and meeting friends there; depositing money with, or borrowing from the saloon-keeper. Workingmen played cards, musical instruments and games, ate, sang and even slept there.[71]

Thus, as might be expected, the economic changes had consequences beyond the merely economic. Men were breadwinners and providers, to be sure, but they also continued to develop separate spheres in which to prove themselves. Stearns noted, "People reacted to a new economic and social structure . . . by providing themselves with gender measurements of self-worth."[72]

Economics also changed the domestic arena, where men no longer were dominant. In the absence of men who were at work in factories or businesses, women took over the task of ordering the family and attending to domestic duties. This created a sense among some men of the necessity to educate their young sons in the ways of maleness. Unlike in the agrarian community, wrote Stearns, boys were raised by their mothers, and, increasingly, they became exposed to female teachers. In addition, those women who were not full-time mothers entered the workforce, which amounted to another challenge to men.

The forces were complex and were certainly not uniform, but in many cases they created a sense of an identity crisis, many scholars argued. Stearns wrote,

> Many men adjusted with relative ease, but there was a self-conscious assertiveness about nineteenth-century manhood that deserves notice. A good bit of masculinity was vicarious now, the male bosom swelled with pride in reading about a frontier hero or a distant victory over some dusky tribe.[73]

For the *Gazette*, the alliance with saloon keepers began fortuitously. In the winter of 1846, Wilkes later recalled, he was told by one of his reporters that a prominent man had been on a three-day drunken binge in a Walker Street house. Wilkes did not consider this a news story, saying it was the man's own business, but then he got word that the famed temperance advocate John B. Gough had been reported missing by his family. They feared that he had been murdered by his foes, the rum dealers. Wilkes had no fondness for Gough; it was reported that on a night they had met earlier, Gough insisted on praying for Wilkes, but Wilkes told him not to bother. Yet Gough insisted. "Pray for yourself," Wilkes shouted. "You've been a drunkard most of your life, and I've never taken a drink. Also, you've been in jail more than I have."[74]

Sensing that Gough's disappearance might mean that he was murdered or being held captive by the purveyors of alcohol, Wilkes and his ace reporter, Andrew Frost, who had been the subject of Wilkes's rant about street signs when Frost was beaten for showing up at a wrong address, went to Walker Street to investigate. Wilkes wrote luridly,

> There we found him, John B. Gough, the mere shadow of a man, pacing the floor with tottering and uncertain steps. He was pale as ashes; (his eyes glared with a preternatural luster), his limbs trembled, and his fitful and wandering state that evinced his mind was as much shattered as his body. Beside him stood two terror-stricken wretches in the shape of women, and on the table of this den of infamy sat the curse of the inebriate. The pompous horror had dissolved from its huge proportions and had shrunk into a very vulgar and revolting common place. The man was drunk.[75]

The story went on in much the same vein for several columns, finally noting that the police were called and Gough was returned to his family.

The item caused a national uproar. Temperance advocates claimed that Gough was framed or that he had never been at the scene in question. Gough said he had been drugged by a man, whose name he could not recall, who had offered him what was ostensibly raspberry soda. The Boston *Star* said the *Gazette* was the enemy not only of temperance but also of religion itself, and some called for the mayor to investigate a possible conspiracy to hurt the cause of temperance.[76]

The *Gazette* responded with a lengthy article detailing Gough's whereabouts before the drunken spree, quoting not anonymous sources as it often did but instead naming as witnesses to Gough's activities a New York dentist, Joel G. Candee, and a deputy U.S. marshal. The *Gazette* intimated that Gough had followed a prostitute to the building, and said it was a house of ill-repute. It called readers' attention to "two other drunken sprees of the drunken apostle" and denied that the articles were being published with any personal bitterness toward Gough:

> Take one look back through his whole history, and the mind reels back sickened and disgusted with the spectacle. We first find him a mere brute wallowing in the mire and degradation of continual drunkenness; next a temperance apostle and member of a church, who, notwithstanding his solemn vows and pledges before the altar of God, and his sacred pledges before man, returns back to his vomit, and seeks solace for his forced abstemiousness in the secret orgies and caresses of drunken prostitutes. A beast in the commencement, next a mountebank and a hypocrite; and a wretch and villain in the last. And he must remain so branded until he can translate a brothel into an honest dwelling and make a holy sanctuary of a harlot's bosom. . . . We do not consider the letter of Mr. Bates [who had written to defend Gough and attest to his whereabouts on dates that the *Gazette* had said Gough was elsewhere] as any testimony at all, for though it represents the writer as traveling with his wife (whom he had married the day before) and in company with Gough from the 4th to the 7th of August, inclusive, it says he was not out of the company of Bates for a single hour in the whole four days. This was a very extraordinary way of passing the honeymoon, to say the least.[77]

Gough threatened a lawsuit, but *Gazette* editors scoffed at the idea. In print, Wilkes gave Gough a month to file the suit before speaking out again. A month later, no lawsuit had been filed. "We shall be fair, even to Mr. Gough. We generously extend the time for filing the suit another week. Hurry, Mr. Gough!" Again, nothing happened. So, Wilkes said, he was instructing his partner Enoch Camp to file suit against Wilkes: "He has nominated us as a liar. We wish to be rid of the imputation."[78]

The efforts of a well-known temperance advocate, B.F. Goodhue, eventually defused the affair. He said he had investigated the Gough matter to the fullest extent possible and found support for the *Gazette*'s account of the episode. He wrote a 3,500-word letter to the *Gazette* (three columns long) and it ran under the headlines,

THE LIAR'S DOOM!
statement of
Mr. B.F. Goodhue,
The celebrated temperance missionary,

Of the Drunkenness, Debaucheries,
and Blasphemies of
John B. Gough,
with an exposure of the forgeries and
other vile and villainous practices which
have been resorted to by his unprincipled
associates, to sustain him in his infamy[79]

Gough backed down, and after the episode, because the *Gazette* had found itself on the side opposing the "proper" classes, some considered the journal to be the friend of the lower-class elements of the city. But Wilkes was careful to distance himself from any lower-class elements that were not law-abiding, sometimes equating wretched conditions with crime. At every turn, he blasted criminals and "pirates" and called for the closing of all of the city's alleys, including Murder Alley, Blood Alley, and Midnight Alley, "to safeguard our womanhood."[80]

Wilkes also decried crime that took place behind closed doors. In 1846 he denounced the "execrable butchery" of a famous female abortionist named Ann Restell:

> Females are daily, nay, hourly, missing from our midst who never return. Where do they go? What becomes of them? Does funeral bell ever peal a note for their passage? Does funeral train ever leave her door? Do friends ever gather round the melancholy grave? No! An obscure hole in the earth; a consignment to the savage skill of the dissecting knife, or a splash in the cold wave, with the scream of the night blast for a requiem, is the only death service bestowed upon her victims. Witness this, ye shores of Hudson! Witness this, Hoboken beach!

Then, he hinted that Restell may have been responsible for one of the most publicized unsolved crimes of the 1840s, the murder of Mary Rogers.[81]

Rogers died on July 25, 1842, and her murder was never solved, but suspicion lingered on Restell for more than thirty years. Even as an elderly woman in the 1870s she was unable to escape the disapproving stares of society. When the weather was nice, she would step out of her dignified quarters at Fifth Avenue and Fifty-second Street, get into her carriage at the bow of her liveried coachmen, and take a ride for shopping or sightseeing. No sooner had the coachman jostled the reins, however, when a group of young boys would often scurry up to the carriage and shout, "Your house is built on babies' skulls!"[82]

The taunt was figurative, for by then she was known as a pricey abortionist—the worth of her estate at her suicide in 1878 was more than $1 million. But in the early 1840s she had managed to keep her business mostly a secret. Rogers's death changed all that.

Rogers, a clerk at John Anderson's cigar counter whose beauty was the main attraction for many of the young male patrons, had told her fiance, Daniel Payn, that she was going to visit a relative on a July afternoon in 1842. She never made it, and a week later her mutilated body was found at Weekhawken Heights. Edgar Allen Poe wrote a thinly disguised short story that told the story of the crime (and his solution to it) called "The Mystery of Marie Roget." Poe, who placed the crime in Paris instead of New York, blamed Mary's killing on an unwanted pregnancy.[83] Rogers was last seen not far from the Restell house on Greenwich Street, and rumors circulated for years that she had been killed in a botched abortion. Several months after her death, her fiance committed suicide with an overdose of laudanum.

The *Gazette* ran several inflammatory accounts of Restell's activities, and noted with approval that a "mob" had gathered outside her house in protest:

> Curses loud and deep upon Restell and her coadjuters [*sic*] were rife amid the crowd, and cries of "Haul her out!" "Where is Mary Applegate's child?" [Applegate had filed a complaint saying Mme. Restell had taken her child.] Where's the thousand children murdered in this house?" "Throw her into the dock!" "Hanging is too good for the monster!" "Who murdered Mary Rogers?" and other inflammatory exclamations of a like nature were continually uprising from the excited multitude. . . . We do not envy the feelings of the wretched woman during the existence of the threatened outbreak, for, although at some distance from the scene, yet, she very well knew what was going forward, being made acquainted at short intervals with the position of affairs. We trust from the expression of yesterday, Madame Restell is now convinced of the necessity of immediately closing her unlawful business; otherwise there seems to be a most fearful certainty that *the end is not yet.*[84]

More than a quarter century later, when Mrs. Restell committed suicide, her crimes were again publicized by the *Gazette*. Though many at the time believed she became suicidal because of charges of immorality leveled against her by crusader Anthony Comstock, the *Gazette* in 1878 hinted that she had killed herself because she faced an investigation for poisoning her husband in order to collect the proceeds from his will.[85]

For Wilkes, any murder involving scandal, sex, or society was the lifeblood of the *Gazette*. But even as he sensationalized crime he assailed criminals. These crusades led to frequent assaults on the cellar where the *Gazette* was published, but the most serious came after the publication of a rather innocuous-appearing page-three item in 1850: "Thirty dollars reward is offered by the mayor of Baltimore for information on the murderers of Jason Johnson. This must be a political gesture or else a distortion of fact. The reward should go to those public benefactors who removed Jason Johnson."[86]

Allies of Jason Johnson did not appreciate the item, and they stormed the *Gazette* offices, where battle-savvy editors beat them up and bashed in two people's skulls. That was not the end of it; in a few days a band of about fifty mobsters, including gangsters Nobby McChester, Country McCloskey, Deaf Martin, Stewart Sharpless of Albany, and two "Amazons" known as Lizzie the Poor Beauty and Donkey Dora Cole, stormed the office and destroyed it. Wilkes, a friend of his named Belcher, and the reporter Frost were all sent to the hospital, where Frost later died. Five of the attackers were also killed.[87]

The *Gazette* limped along even after the attack, but it was barely alive after the Financial Panic of 1857 left Wilkes in financial straights.[88] He surrendered the *Gazette* to George W. Matsell, the former New York City police chief, who proved to be an uninspired editor. The *Gazette* lost circulation and was unloaded in 1872 to two engravers, who named Herbert R. Mooney editor. The journal still lost money, but by the end of 1874, those who ran the *Gazette* made a decision to hire an enterprising new Irish immigrant as the business manager. Two years later Richard Kyle Fox would engineer a takeover of the *Gazette* and change the history of journalism.

2

An Illustrated
Journal of Sporting and
Sensational Events

When I see a young man coming from the tame life of the country and
going down in city ruin, I am not surprised.
                                    —Rev. T. DeWitt Talmage, 1878

As Christmas of 1874 approached, an issue of the *National Police
Gazette* contained several items that the editors considered worthy of
their readers' attention. One was a front-page illustrated spread of
"How Thanksgiving Day and Eve Was Kept" showing men, women,
and children celebrating, a large turkey, wine, and a gob of meat on a
platter labeled "Hash." Another was a short editorial headlined "A
Shocking Outrage" that recounted a recent New York *Herald* story
about a "poor Irish girl" who had caught a cold on a boat while cross-
ing Lake Champlain en route to New York City, only to have
Commissioners of Charities and Corrections officials misdiagnose her
hives as "smallpox pustules." After being quarantined with smallpox
victims, she "managed to crawl to the Board of Health" but lan-
guished there without proper treatment for several days until, finally,
to end her own misery, she took poison. According to the *Gazette*
account, she was then awaiting death. Another item, on page 3 of the
issue, was headlined "A Negro Monster/Life in a Mud-Hole" and
had been clipped from the *Nashville* (Tennessee) *Banner* and sent in
by a reader. It concerned a black man who "lives in a nude state, in a
mud-hole, to cure what he calls 'blood fever.' " The full item was not
reproduced, but the *Gazette* correspondent who sent it in said the
man had confronted his wife and daughters, only to be scared off by
the waving of the correspondent's ax.[1] And so on the copy went under
headlines that hinted at the subject matter: "Sunday at the Tombs,"
"A Monstrous Crime," "Youthful Depravity," and "A Romantic
Elopement."

But there was something new in this issue, something that might not have caught the eye of many readers, a small item at the bottom of page 2. It was a billing for a numbers game that encouraged readers to guess which number the *Gazette* business manager would select from an accompanying published table of sixty-four numbers. A different table was to be published each week for four straight weeks; if a reader guessed the four numbers that were picked over the four weeks, he would win $100. If no one won, whoever picked three of the numbers would win, and so on. In addition, several prizes were offered for those who guessed closest to the sum total of the four numbers picked. The business manager choosing the numbers was the newly hired Richard Kyle Fox, and the numbers game was his invention.[2] For readers of the *Gazette* this was just a hint of what was to come. For nearly half a century, he would come up with hundreds of ingenious prizes, promotions, and awards designed to boost *Gazette* sales and publicity. It worked well, perhaps beyond Fox's wildest expectations—he would become rich and famous and would become legendary for his promotion of sports and games.

That Fox was listed in the *Gazette* flag as business manager by December of 1874 is worth noting because many accounts of his life contend that he did not begin working for the *Gazette* until 1875. Indeed, the *Gazette*'s own account of his career, written more than a decade after it began, says he arrived in New York City in September of 1874 and spent several months working elsewhere before landing a job at the *Gazette*. However, this is not consistent with Fox's own stories or with the December 1874 masthead.

As he got older, Fox would tell many tales recounting his stewardship of the *Gazette*, and one of the most colorful concerned the day that he said he arrived at old Castle Garden in New York City on July 12, 1874. When Fox and his wife, the former Annie Scott, stepped off the ship, he said, he found himself in the middle of an ongoing conflict between Catholics and Protestants.[3]

No sooner had they disembarked than a large, whiskered man approached them and asked from where they came. When Fox replied that he had come from Belfast, the man gave him a history—already well known to Fox—of the Orangemen, a Protestant Irish society that had been established in 1795 to maintain the Protestant ascendancy in Ireland following demands for Catholic emancipation.[4] Although he was Irish Protestant, Fox, who had arrived in America with only $3, told the man that he was more interested in finding a job than in joining the demonstration that day. But he offered to join anyway if the man could find him a boardinghouse that would take them in on credit. He found out that the man had recruited several hundred others like him.[5]

Fox remembered later that he got in a fistfight that afternoon,[6] was injured, and was tended to by a man named O'Brien. But when O'Brien found out that Fox was Protestant, he smashed a window, only to cut his arm. After Fox helped nurse his wounds, the man took him to the *Commercial Bulletin*, a business journal, where he was hired to sell advertising.[7]

Because of his background, Fox was well suited to enter the world of New York publishing. He was born in Belfast on August 12, 1846, to a carpenter and mason, James Fox, and his wife, Mary (Kyle), the daughter of Presbyterian minister Henry Kyle. When he was twelve, Fox got a job at the *Banner of Ulster*, where he worked for four years, and out of his earnings he paid two shillings a week for his schooling. For another twelve years, he worked for the *Belfast News Letter*, a leading Irish newspaper. He married Annie Scott of Belfast in 1869, and five years later, with barely enough money for passage, came to America.[8]

After he had found his first job, Fox began saving money immediately, and within months he was working as business manager for the *Police Gazette*. After about two months, he was owed about $1,000 in advertising commissions, but when the journal had no money to pay him, he assumed a one-third interest in it. Later, in 1876, the same problem came up again, with Fox being owed $5,000. This time in repayment for the debts, he assumed full ownership and became the *Gazette*'s "owner and proprietor," as he phrased it on the masthead. Thus, the Richard K. Fox *Gazette* was born—and it did not take long for it to assume his personality.[9]

To spice up the *Gazette*, Fox hired the English barrister Bracebridge Hemyng, who had already quit the law because he gained fame and fortune as the writer of the Jack Harkaway stories, and Samuel A. MacKeever, who became famous while writing for the *Gazette* under such names as Paul Prowler, Colonel Lynx, and the Old Rounder. For the lavish, woodcut illustrations that would adorn the *Gazette*, Fox assembled well-known artists such as George G. White, Charles Kendrick, and Phil Cusachs. The talent served him well, but it was not without its incentives; Fox hired dozens of writers, locked them in an office on weekends, gave them four bottles of whiskey, and released them Monday morning after paying them $10 for their efforts. A retired pugilist named Gipman Matthews was hired by Fox to stand guard at the door to make sure that the writers did not escape before doing their work.[10]

During these formative years of the Fox era, stories about grisly crimes and unusual sports abounded, under columns such as "Vice's Varieties," "Divers Demoniacisms," and "Memorable Maulings," which was about historic fistfights in the early 1800s. On May 11, 1878, Fox rolled out the first of his sixteen-page issues, heralding what he called a "new era in illustrated journalism."[11] A week later, he devoted a column to the congratulations on the new issue that he said were pouring in from all over the country.

The *Gazette* reflected a general interest among men in sporting and other leisure-time activities. For example, in September 1878, the popular Harry Hill's saloon—where Fox would, as legend has it, later be snubbed by boxer John L. Sullivan—changed its *Gazette* advertisement from a simple announcement of a public tavern to a more elaborate description, calling itself the "Gentleman's Sporting Theatre" featuring vaudeville, "Edison's phonograph," and "new faces every week."[12] A couple of weeks later, on the front page, Fox featured a perfect combination of titillation and sport—a woodcut showing a group of swimsuited women in a rowing contest.[13] Of course, features about women, along with the coverage of crime and sports and games, would eventually become one of the signatures of the Fox *Gazette*. In 1879, he announced the inauguration of the "dramatic department" devoted to coverage of the theater (and more specifically, of the comings and goings of actresses and showgirls).

The four years following Fox's 1876 takeover foreshadowed what would become, over the next two decades, the typical *Gazette* that is remembered even today for its ribald irreverence. This was the *Gazette* that became the subject of jokes and references in popular culture, such as Sheriff Andy Taylor's remark in an old episode of *The Andy Griffith Show* that his deputy Barney Fife liked to look at the *Gazette* pictures, and Irving Berlin's song, "The Girl on the Police Gazette."[14]

Fox also demonstrated his marketing genius during these years. He announced the formation of "*Gazette* clubs" that enabled those who formed subscription clubs to save on the price. Those with six members or more received copies of the complete works of Shakespeare: "The edition is a full quarto giving every syllable of the immortal bard's words, including his grand poems as well as his plays," the announcement read. The magnificent volume was printed on tinted paper, bound in a brown, crimson, blue, olive, and "grass green" cover, and had gold lettering and ornamentation.[15]

This was an early form of self-promotion—it was an effort to gain subscribers, to be sure, but it also was a way of offering to *Gazette* readers something different from the average fare, thus enabling the publication to crow about that distinction later. This kind of sometimes vulgar self-promotion ("THERE IS NO OTHER" substitute for the *Gazette*, Fox repeatedly reminded readers on page 2 of his publication during the 1870s, 1880s, and 1890s)[16] brought scorn from more traditional practitioners of journalism. Just as the *Gazette*'s yellow-journalist New York cousins—the *Journal* and the *World*—boasted about their journalistic accomplishments, so too did Fox ceaselessly trumpet his, and the *Gazette*'s, triumphs. The hearty self-congratulations were one reason that yellow journalism is a pejorative term, and it is a reason that Fox and his *Gazette* have been marginalized in histories of journalism.[17]

This brings up the question as to what type of publication Fox's *Gazette* really was. It cannot be classified as part of the yellow journalism of the era, though it shared many of the defining characteristics of yellow journalism as identified by media historian Frank Luther Mott: an emphasis on "crime news, scandal and gossip, divorces and sex, and stress upon the reporting of disasters and sports."[18] He also added other distinguishing techniques of the yellow journals: "scare-heads," with large type, often in red ink, touting excitement often about relatively unimportant topics, thus imparting a "shrill falsity to the entire make-up"; frequent use of pictures, including faked pictures; frauds, including faked interviews and stories; Sunday supplements, including color comics; and sympathy with the "underdog."[19] To these characteristics historian W. Joseph Campbell added the following:

1. "frequent use of multicolumn headlines" that often crossed the front page;
2. a wide variety of content on page 1, "including news of politics, war, international diplomacy, sports, and society";
3. "generous and imaginative use of illustrations";
4. "bold and experimental layouts, including those in which one report and illustration would dominate the front page";
5. a frequent reliance on anonymous sources;
6 "a penchant for self-promotion, to call attention to the paper's accomplishments."[20]

Fox's *Gazette* met many of these defining characteristics, but not all of them; for example, his front pages never contained stories but always were dominated by the *Gazette* flag and a giant woodcut, often sexually suggestive in nature. Sometimes, but not always, a headline was included on the front page to hint at a leading story inside.

In addition, while Fox's writers sometimes reported on politics, they often did it in a humorous or condescending way and rarely in any detail, and any content about international diplomacy was often accompanied by scornful comment. The *Gazette* also did not meet the most common assumption about the yellow journals—that they were daily newspapers. Finally, Fox took over and remade the *Gazette* well before what many historians consider to be the beginning of "yellow journalism" (the term first came into use in about 1896).[21] In fact, it could be argued that Fox—along with the era's journalistic purveyors of gossip, crime and sports—helped pave the way for yellow journalism's heyday from 1896 to 1900.

So if the *Gazette* was not a yellow journal, what was it? Mott classified it as a magazine[22] and its weekly appearance, tabloid format, and illustrated front page certainly qualify it as such. In fact, it is often compared to today's tabloids[23] and can be said to have helped create the atmosphere that gave rise to the yellow press and led to tabloid-style reporting and layout today. Historian Sam G. Riley wrote,

> The *Police Gazette* was not quite a magazine and not quite a newspaper, much like today's *National Enquirer* and its several competitors. Such periodicals are produced on newsprint in tabloid format, yet they certainly do not report news in the manner of an ordinary newspaper. They are, therefore, often classified as nonnewspaper periodicals.[24]

But the *Gazette* was not merely a "nonnewspaper periodical" that existed to fill some void in the marketplace; it was a first cousin to the New York newspapers of its day. Like the other publications, the *Gazette* catered to an immigrant population with limited literacy skills (thus its focus on the timeless topics that also were covered in the *World*, the *Journal*, and the *Tribune*—sex, crime, violence, farce, and tragedy[25]). To fully understand the *Gazette*, then, one must consider its competitors in the mass marketplace that was New York City.

The 1870s were remarkable for many reasons, not the least of which was the rapid increase in publications available almost anywhere. The total number of American newspapers reached 7,000 by 1880, double what it had been ten years before.[26] At the same time, newspapers became more dependent on mass circulation and thus independent from party partisanship, a key reason that more emphasis was placed on human interest stories and less on politics, a trend reflected in the *Gazette*. The four large New York dailies at this time were the *Herald*, the *Sun*, the *Tribune*, and the *Times*, but the *Herald* and the *Sun* led the others in circulation, writing, and prestige, at least among the mass readership.

James Gordon Bennett Jr. assumed the helm of the *Herald* upon his father's death in 1872; he had been managing editor of the newspaper since 1866, when he turned twenty-five and his father assumed a reduced role at the paper. An angry obituary on Bennett Sr. in the *Evening Post* said he had vulgarized the press, but the *World* called him the "Columbus, the Luther, and the Napoleon of modern journalism."[27] Those proved to be difficult footsteps to follow. The rakish Bennett Jr. ran the *Herald* from Paris, visiting New York only occasionally. But he was successful for a time and the newspaper held its own even under advances from Charles A. Dana's *Sun*. The younger Bennett proved adept at journalistic stunts, making them staples of the day. The first and greatest of these was the expedition of Henry M. Stanley to Africa in an effort to find David Livingstone.

Stanley, an Englishman who was born John Rowlands but adopted the name of a benefactor named Henry Morton Stanley when the latter died, first wrote for newspapers during the Civil War. He eventually persuaded Bennett to hire him as a writer for the *Herald*, and he covered a conflict involving King Theodore of Abyssinia in 1868. Livingstone was an explorer and a missionary who had gone to Africa in an attempt to find the sources of the Nile and the Congo, and he had written widely of his adventures, much to the fascination of American and European readers. But by late 1871 he had not been heard from in three years. Stanley gave credit to the idea of finding Livingstone to Bennett; he was given generous newspaper funds to accomplish the task and in December 1871 had formed an expedition from Zanzibar that included 6 white men, 150 animals, and 30 armed natives.[28] It took two months, but Stanley did indeed find Livingstone, in the village of Ujiji on Lake Tanganyiki, after hearing a rumor that a white man was staying there. His article of the encounter ended with what would become a catchphrase for more than a century:

> Doffing my helmet, I bowed and said in an inquiring tone, "Dr. Livingstone, I presume?"
>
> Smiling cordially, he lifted his cap, and answered briefly, "Yes."[29]

Bennett Jr.'s fascination with such encounters was perhaps reflected in his taste for sports and a life of leisure. He was raised largely in Paris, where he developed a reputation as a playboy and enjoyed life sometimes to excess; he was known to drink but not to hold his liquor well.[30] While at the *Herald*, Bennett began publishing an afternoon edition, the *Evening Telegram*, which focused on crime and other sensational stories that had first graced the *Herald*. Bennett introduced polo to the United States, was a participant in the first transatlantic yacht race, and he became such an active yachtsman that he won the nickname "Commodore." Bennett also backed ballooning and automobile racing, and organized frequent sporting events, awarding prize money and trophies to boost publicity. All of these promotional efforts were adopted and expanded by Fox during his stewardship of the *Gazette*.

As part of his journalistic enterprise, Bennett financed explorations over the years, including sending a ship, the *Pandora*, in 1875 to find the Northwest Passage and explorer George Washington De Long to reach the North Pole (which ended in the deaths of De Long and his crew in 1881).[31]

A journalistic hoax was another notable event in Bennett's career. In 1874, the *Herald* said that animals had somehow escaped from the Central Park Zoo and were loose in the city, mauling and killing people. The article carried a disclaimer at the end saying that it was not true, but the disclaimer went largely unnoticed and the story panicked many New Yorkers. The article explained that its purpose was to point out that better precautions were needed to prevent such a disaster from actually happening.[32]

The *Herald*'s circulation averaged 100,000 in the mid-1870s, occasionally reaching as high as 150,000, and surpassed the New York *Sun* in 1876. From Paris Bennett was in control of the *Herald*, cabling instructions daily, making final decisions concerning hiring and firing, and sometimes summoning editors to see him. In one case he fired a group of employees that an editor told him were indispensable to their jobs in New York and thus were unable to make the demanded trip to Paris.[33] In 1883, Bennett and mining magnate John Mackay established the Commercial Cable Company, which laid transatlantic, European, and North American communications cables, allowing the *Herald* to attain preeminence in foreign news coverage. In 1885, the *Herald* achieved its highest circulation of 190,500, but it was soon eclipsed by Joseph Pulitzer's New York *World*.[34]

During this era, Charles A. Dana, who was editor of the *Sun*, promoted a literary quality to the writing. The *Sun* also adopted a more modern approach to news, with an emphasis on brevity, accuracy, and wit. Dana's managing editor was Amos Jay Cummings, who relied on human interest—not simply on the sensational or the salacious but also on the amusing or the touching. More than ever before, the *Sun* became a newspaper of the people. Dana also campaigned against Boss Tweed and the Tammany gang, who had passed a city charter that enabled them to enrich themselves off the public payroll.

Dana joined the utopian Brook Farm community in New England in 1840, lecturing in the school and editing the newspaper, *The Harbinger*. He eventually became city editor of the New York *Tribune* and traveled overseas, sending dispatches to Horace Greeley. He broke with Greeley over whether the Southern states had a right to secede, with Dana (who had served in 1864–65 as an assistant secretary of war under Stanton and had spent time on the front sending dispatches to Lincoln and his aides) arguing that they had no such right. Dana resigned in 1862 but purchased the *Sun* five years later.[35]

Dana would rule the *Sun* for thirty years, adhering to a maxim that he pronounced in an 1888 speech to the Wisconsin Editorial Association in Milwaukee: "Get the news, get all the news, get nothing but the news."[36] In keeping with the rivalrous spirit of the age, he mercilessly attacked Bennett and the *Herald*. After Livingstone was found, Dana published a letter from a man who cast doubts on Stanley's discovery. He claimed that Stanley was a liar and a forgerer, but the letter writer added that he was not sure whether Livingstone had actually been found. Eventually, Dana brought the *Sun*'s circulation to more than 100,000, and the *Sun* style helped revolutionize journalism by turning away from the florid approach to news.[37]

The status of daily journalism in New York City during the post–Civil War era gives a partial picture of how reporting was practiced. The period even gave a glimpse of what was to come when the first tabloid— as it was called by Simon Michael Bessie—rolled off the presses in New York City in 1872. The *Daily Graphic* featured four editions a day, depicted crime scenes and disasters, and even carried drawings that were little more than scenes dreamed up by illustrators— much like those in Fox's publication. One such drawing was under the title "Terrors of the Telephone" and showed a man shouting into a hideous device connected by wire to a smiling Chinese man, an irritated Irishman, a distracted Englishman, a dignified Bostonian, and a naked Fiji Islander.[38] The *Daily Graphic* folded after seven years.

As daily journalism flourished, an extraordinary development of non-daily periodical journalism—a "mania of magazine starting," as it was described by Mott—led to creation of publications that some would consider more direct relatives to Fox and the *Gazette*.[39] In 1865 the nation boasted 700 magazines; by 1885 the number had soared to 3,300.[40] At the same time, individual circulations were growing. A "story paper" (as publications such as the *Gazette* were called), the *New York Weekly*, claimed 350,000 readers in 1874, and others such as the *New York Ledger* and the *Youth's Companion* also said their readers numbered in the hundreds of thousands.[41] This rapid growth created fierce competition and, as has been noted, led to promotions, prizes, and gimmicks to attract readers. One type of successful promotion was the "premium," bonus prizes such as works of art, tools, pictures, books, and bells, and so on, which were given to subscribers. Magazines, which were helped by the growth of advertising, improved distribution methods, and mass marketing, also got a boost from the Postal Act of 1879, which gave publications discounted mail rates to ease circulation costs. The bill was enacted by Congress to facilitate magazines' role in contributing to literacy and a sense of nationhood.[42] In addition, many magazines used subscription clubs to boost sales. The expansion of news dealerships, also relied upon by Fox's *Gazette*, began to grow during this period as well. News dealers got up to ten cents on thirty-five cent magazines such as *Harper's* and *Scribner's*.[43]

Without question, New York City was the center of America's publishing world. Part of the reason was the city's position as a world trade center, but it was also the size and character of the city that mattered. The corruption of the city government and the shenanigans of individuals walking the streets attracted notice from all over the country. New York's crime was excellent fodder for publications such as the *Gazette*, with conflicting themes of temptation and reform. "When I see a young man coming from the tame life of the country and going down in city ruin, I am not surprised," said Rev. T. DeWitt Talmage. "My only surprise is that any escape, considering the allurements."[44] Those were many. The *Nation* estimated there were 6,000 prostitutes in New York by 1867, with 773 houses of ill repute. Meanwhile, *Harper's Weekly* reported there were more than 9,000 saloons in operation.[45]

The various kinds of magazines that flourished, which amounted to the first explorations of niche markets, are familiar even to readers today. Legal periodicals, insurance journals, medical periodicals, and agricultural publications, as well as publications dealing with scientific inquiry, railroads, education and curriculum, and music and entertainment, all grew and prospered. As noted in *News in the Land of Freedom*:

> The press won readers throughout the nineteenth century because Americans on the make had no better tool than the newspaper, with its ads, prices current, and advice on markets. Magazines were a gallery for

the clothing, home furnishings, and tools that women and men prized. Most newspapers carried the mother's milk of politics: stories of party strikes, the speeches of leaders, the hints about jobs or favors to be won. There were many other lures in the nation's press: agricultural information, fiction and sensational reports, religious news. . . . The periodicals of the United States served every taste.[46]

With so many publications developing, editors were forced to find ways to promote their products, and in many cases they were successful. With increased circulation came more advertising revenues; by the mid-1850s, circuses, which needed publicity to attract crowds as they traveled from city to city, had become important sources of advertising revenue for newspapers and other publications. The great circus owner Hackaliah Bailey had developed an 1815 tour featuring the first elephant to come to the United States, "Old Bet," which eventually led to the creation of advertising, free publicity, and press agents. Other types of attractions, such as Wild West shows and vaudeville, also used advertising and promotion to boost attendance. In the 1880s Buffalo Bill Cody used tales of his exploits, many of them fictional, to promote his image as a brave and heroic figure of the Western frontier. Cody, P.T. Barnum, and other showmen employed press agents to make contacts with newspapers and seek publicity. Advertising, both paid and unpaid, blossomed. Advertising agencies were formed after the Civil War, and many of them sponsored staged or pseudo events to promote wares. In 1892, for example, Sapolio Soap manufacturers sent a sloop to Spain to commemorate the 400th anniversary of Columbus's trip to the Americas.[47]

Fox has been called a genius for his promotional skills, but he was also fortunate; his efforts at publicity fit in with the trends of the age. Public relations developed during this period as a profession and as a sophisticated tool for attracting the public's attention to entertainment, products, or services. Using the same kinds of promotional efforts as public relations practitioners, Fox came to be an organizer and publicizer of events—boxing matches and others—that created publicity for his magazine and boosted his circulation. This new and quickly growing tradition of press agentry had patterns that were, as noted by public relations historian Scott M. Cutlip, "drawn, cut and stitched by the greatest showman and press agent of all time—that 'Prince of Humbug,' that mightiest of mountebanks, Phineas Taylor Barnum."[48] Born in 1810 in Bethel, Connecticut, he helped begin the age of showmanship in 1835 when he toured with and displayed a woman he absurdly claimed was George Washington's nurse.[49]

Barnum later propelled the career of singer Jenny Lind, who by the mid-1800s was one of the first megastars of American pop culture. He was a tireless inventor of stunts and events, and he used newspapers to publicize them. He also believed in the value of free publicity over paid advertisements.

Promotional activities and publicity-seeking events were also common among publishers. In 1895, the *Chicago Times Herald* staged a highly publicized race to promote the new automobile. Other newspapers sponsored rowing contests or essay contests.[50] As noted by Cutlip:

> [The] last two decades of the nineteenth century brought discernible beginnings of today's public relations practice in the United States . . . The fundamental force in setting the stage of public relations in the twentieth century was the frenzied and bold development development of industry, railroads and utilities in the United States' post-Civil War years.[51]

These forces, along with urbanization and immigration, were the same that helped give rise to the modern newspaper. During these years there was a scramble for advertising and circulation supremacy, widespread mechanical innovations to improve printing, higher capitalization costs and larger payrolls, and more difficult labor relations problems.[52]

A philosophy grew that education could lead the nation out of the excesses of capitalism. The fear and isolation brought about by the expansion of industry in the late nineteenth century also spawned the belief that a brighter future awaited, and that an informed citizenry, educated partly through honorable public relations by reformed corporations, could help make a better world. Social historian Stuart Ewen suggested that some utopianists' ideals were similar to that of a "nineteenth century publicist," Karl Marx, but others' hope for change rested on public opinion and public relations, not on class warfare.[53]

For America's publishers, the real war involved the fight for readers. Many of the promotional stunts by newspapers and magazines were journalistic in nature and would stop at little in the quest. Twelve years after Stanley found Livingstone in Central Africa, Joseph Pulitzer's *World* sent Elizabeth Cochrane, known under her byline as Nellie Bly, around the world to determine if she could beat Phileas Fogg's time in Jules Verne's *Around the World in Eighty Days*. She sailed on the *Augusta Victoria* on November 14, 1889, at 9:40 in the morning, but the beginning was inauspicious; when someone asked if she ever got seasick, the very thought of it made her rush to the ship's railing, and, as she put it delicately, she "gave vent to my feelings."[54]

Bly, who was twenty-five at the time although she had sworn on her passport application that she was twenty-two, claimed the idea for the journey was hers. When *World* editors said they thought it was a good idea but would have to send a man so a chaperone would not be needed, she threatened to go to an opposing newspaper and beat the *World*'s would-be male reporter in the race. Her dispatches from abroad were colorful but not always timely, and on many days the editors at the *World* waited in vain to hear from her. But the newspaper came up with other ways to stir interest. First they printed other newspapers' comments about her feats, and then they came up with the "Nellie Bly Guessing Match," allowing readers to guess her final global travel time. The grand prize was a trip to Europe. As Bly biographer Brooke Kroeger put it, "Demands for ballots poured in, and the newspaper found a whole new way to generate copy in the absence of news. By December 2, some 100,000 readers had sent back the guessing ballots, and the stories of contest entrants droned on for days. Pity the rewrite desk."[55] One reader penned a prediction in verse:

> Nellie Bly is flying high
> On the China Sea;
> With her goes the hope of one
> Who wants to see Paree;
> She'll get here in 74,
> Sure as she's alive,
> Hours 12, minutes 10 and seconds 25.

By the end of December, the *World*'s circulation topped 270,000. It also published a Nellie Bly game, a board game completed through the rolling of dice. On Bly's arrival in San Francisco, the *World*'s January 22 edition predicted victory: "M. Jules Verne Outdone," said the headline. Bly did not let it down. She finished the journey to New York in seventy-two days, and Verne cabled his congratulations.[56]

As the rage for contests and competition grew, it was no surprise that newspapers and magazines also seized upon the growth of sports as a way to boost circulation. Horse racing and yachting were two of the favorites—the successful defense of the America's cup brought an interest in yachting that one writer compared to the hysteria over Barnum's Jenny Lind—but baseball and football also were growing in popularity and were covered extensively.[57]

Fox seized upon promotions like no other, and boxing, because of its emphasis on brawn as well as science and "art," was a perfect vehicle for an editor to exploit in a world seeking new definitions for manliness. He was one of the first to sponsor ring matches with belts, cash, and other prizes awarded to the winners. He also would use these skills to gain publicity for other *Gazette*-backed sporting endeavors, such as shooting, canoeing, and archery. Over the objections of some, he would use pulp as a pulpit to fight against laws banning prizefighting.

Increased leisure time, along with the greater desire for entertainment spurred by the rapid growth of the mass media, helped put the spectacle in spectator sports—boxing, baseball, racing, yachting, bowling, and tennis, along with bicycling, baseball, golf, croquet, and football.[58] One of the biggest sporting events of the era came in 1882, when John L. Sullivan defeated Paddy Ryan in nine rounds on February 7; it helped lead to the creation of the modern sporting spectacle as a media event as well as to a general celebration of manhood. It was covered by the *Police Gazette*, the *Clipper*, and *Day's Doings*, among many others.[59]

But Fox did not stop at ordinary sports. He gave *Police Gazette* belts to dancers, rat catchers, drinkers, oyster openers, bridge jumpers, and even great steeple climbers. Fox's portrait adorned the championship belt he gave to Billy Wells, "champion of allowing his head to be pounded through an iron block by means of a sledge hammer."[60] Barbers (or "tonsorialists," as they were called in weekly *Gazette* profiles), those great friends of Fox's circulation managers, also were rewarded. One champion haircutter gave a professional haircut in thirty seconds, resulting in a frightened but satisfied customer.[61] Barbers all over the country also became minor celebrities, as Fox ran their pictures in weekly issues, profiling them with glowing tributes. One historian has compared the *Gazette*'s promotionalism to the staged competitions of the "battles of the network stars" seen in the late twentieth century.[62]

By 1880, Fox had, tellingly, redesigned the flag of the *Police Gazette*. Gone, along with the already-stodgy era, was the previous slogan, "The only criminal journal in the United States." Instead, he increased the size of the pages and added a huge banner announcing the name, "The National Police Gazette", with its new slogan, "An Illustrated Journal of Sporting and Sensational Events." The slogan would change again a few years later to emphasize sporting coverage even more.[63]

The pictures in the *Gazette* were, for Fox, another sensational promotion in an era of sensational promotions. The *Gazette* often boasted that these elaborate and ornamental illustrations were suitable for framing. They were certainly suitable for gazing, as an entire generation—in reality, two or three generations—of men and boys became enamored of the intricate drawings of raving beauties, heinous crimes, and brute strength. Indeed, these drawings became Fox's most effective public relations. Anecdotally, it is apparent that much of the *Gazette*'s impact on its readers came through its etchings; the salacious nature (by nineteenth-century standards) of these portrayals suggests their ability to shock, amaze, repulse, and titillate. It is because of the cultural and historical impact of *Gazette* illustrations, along with their ability to convey as well as reflect frames of readers, that the quantification of *Gazette* illustrations was chosen as the means for guiding the body of this study of Fox, his *Gazette*, and their making of modern masculinities.

Many scholars have noted that images are among the most powerful of framing devices; Paul Messaris and Linus Abraham pointed out that they have such a potent impact because they are thought to be more "real" than words. Although the nuances of the point have been debated by psychologists, generally it may be said that pictures constitute a largely analogical system of communication, while words are almost completely arbitrary. Thus, the meanings of words are social conventions or agreements, while (in the norm) the relationship between images and their meanings are thought to be based on analogous similarities that are apparent upon sight. Therefore, when illustrations are used in media content, the framing effect may be hidden while it remains powerful. "Precisely because . . . [the frame] can make images appear more natural, more closely linked to reality than words are, it can also inveigle viewers into overlooking the fact that all images are human-made, artificial constructions," Messaris and Abraham wrote in 2001.[64] For *Gazette* readers, that meant that often they may have chosen to believe more readily what they saw rather than what they read.

For the purposes of this study, the subject matter of *Gazette* illustrations was quantified over the twenty-seven-year period of 1879–1906, covering the prime years of Fox's stewardship until the *Gazette* began to change the nature of its illustrations.[65] In addition, issues beyond these years were examined qualitatively. A sampling procedure was used in which an issue was chosen randomly for content analysis in each month of each year.[66]

The results show that for more than two decades, the *Gazette* displayed a relative consistency in sports and sexual/theatrical portrayals, with depictions of crime dropping dramatically after the beginning of the twentieth century (see table 2.1). One reason for the latter was the improvement in picture production; with halftone technology the use of photographs became more common, and Fox did not choose to continue to use illustrations to depict criminal acts that his illustrators had often imagined in the past. But he was consistent in his promotion of masculinities, for decades showing showgirls and boxers in provocative portraits and poses. These quantitative findings give support to the analysis that follows—an examination of the way Fox and the *Gazette* covered the world from illustrated portrayals of sport, crime, and sex, and how these portrayals described emerging trends and conflicts of masculinities in Victorian and post-Victorian America.

Table 2.1 Average number of inside pages per issue of portrayals of sports, crime, and sex

Year	N	Sports	Crimes	Sex	All illustrations
1879	9[a]	.800	3.06	.90	5.85
1880	12	.458	1.79	2.36	5.75
1881	12	.650	1.99	1.93	5.62
1882	12	1.16	2.04	1.22[b]	5.58
1883	12	.825	2.38	1.40	5.95
1884	12	2.22	2.03	1.03	6.19
1885	12	1.63	2.23	1.70	6.90
1886	12	2.03	2.10	1.70	7.68
1887	12	2.00	3.10[b]	.783[b]	7.05
1888	12	1.73	3.25[b]	1.63	7.90
1889	12	2.06	2.14	1.32	7.08
1890	12	1.88	2.70	1.40	7.93
1891	6	2.25	2.75	2.05	8.65
1892	8	1.08	3.18	2.34	6.78
1893	12	1.38	3.45	2.63	7.65
1894	10	2.30	2.03	2.88	7.63
1895	8	2.15	0.75	2.78	7.50
1896	7	2.65[b]	1.70	3.30	7.90
1897	6	1.53	2.47	3.53	8.13
1899	10	2.52[b]	1.58	1.60	7.62
1900	6	2.95[b]	0.30[b]	2.53	8.25
1901	12	3.95[b]	0.70	2.58	8.18
1902	12	4.22[b]	0.76	2.46	8.11
1903	12	4.52[b]	0.72	2.92	8.33
1904	12	5.20[b]	0.00[b]	1.80	8.20
1905	12	6.00[b]	0.00[b]	1.17	7.88
1906	12	5.60[b]	0.00[b]	1.45	7.05
Totals	278	2.40	1.79	1.98	7.27

Notes: [a] Not all issues were available for each year. N = the number of copies examined in each year. Data for 1898 not available.
[b] Tukey HSD post hoc for analysis of variance shows significant differences at the .01 level in averages of inside illustrations comparing 1880 to these years.

3

THIS WICKED WORLD

Of all the women of the Cleopatra type, since the days of the Egyptian queen herself, the universe has produced none more remarkable than Bella Starr, the Bandit Queen.
—Richard K. Fox, *Bella Starr, The Bandit Queen*

They made the Police Gazette, *a periodical of note.*
—From the 2002 movie "Gangs of New York"

Estelle Cowell, of Savannah, New York, who was a pretty, single twenty-three-year-old in the fall of 1881, decided on the evening of November 10 to knit by the farmhouse stove and have a bit of cider with one of the hired hands. Five weeks later, the *National Police Gazette* ran a short item, on page 11, about what happened to Cowell that night, headlined, "Outraged By a Farm Hand." The quarter-column story about the forced assignation of Miss Cowell was just below a much larger story about the reasons behind the assassination six months before of U.S. President James A. Garfield, in which assassin Charles Julius Guiteau supposedly "Gives an Authentic History of his Wretched Life."[1]

On page 2 of the same issue, Richard K. Fox or one of his editors remarked in the editorial column, "What a beautiful chance the Brooklyn Bridge will offer for sensational suicides! All our artists are sharpening their pencils in anticipation."[2] This was prescient—Fox's writers and artists would within a couple of years cover several aerial jumpers who would find the Brooklyn Bridge to be a suitable launching pad if not for suicide, then at least for publicity stunts.

These mixtures of crimes and sensation in the *Gazette* served a specific journalistic purpose for Fox. A qualitative and quantitative review of the types of crimes illustrated in the *Gazette* shows that they broadly fell into one of three categories—the daily "ordinary" outrages; the sensational or scandalous crimes involving particularly heinous acts of the well-to-do or well-known as either victims or perpetrators; and the legendary exploits of outlaw heroes. All of these types of crimes served functions for Fox's readers in the context of late-nineteenth-century America. They were methods of defining deviance, of exposing hypocrisy, and of romanticizing a myth of justice and experience outside the confines of the law and civilized society.

During periods of social and civil development and upheaval, as was found in the late nineteenth century, many people saw their lives and worldviews disrupted. The types of crimes highlighted in the *Gazette* served to directly or indirectly reinforce traditional views by illustrating deviance, exposing injustices, and mocking the frauds of those who did not belong to the threatened underclasses. In a real sense, these stories showed what it was like to be an outlaw as well as an upstanding citizen. Fox was castigated by rivals as well as by others for printing such stories, but he was defiant in his mission. In an 1892 editorial, he called his publication a "newspaper in the real sense of the word" because it "prints the news of the week, but eliminates the filth":

> In that respect it has the advantage of the daily newspapers. But it never publishes anything that could give offense to the most punctilious person. Of a necessity it prints the offenses committed against the laws of society and State by men and women, but then the POLICE GAZETTE is a newspaper. It is needful for the public morals that the violators of the laws of man should be condemned and held up to public scorn and ridicule. Were their offenses overlooked crime would become rampant, society rotten, and virtue would be at a premium. It is the fear of public condemnation that keeps many in the straight and narrow path. The electric light of the press holds them in check. If they sin in the dark and their offense is known only to themselves, they continue to pose before society as models of virtue. But on the other hand, if their crime is made known they are punished and society is benefited. It is not the function of the newspaper to excite the appetite for scandal, but to expose all frauds and shams with a view of correcting them. Such is the mission of the POLICE GAZETTE.[3]

It might have come as a surprise to a reader in the 1890s that Fox was holding himself up as a protector of society's virtues. But he used his crime coverage in ways even more subtle than that. In addition to illustrating the dredges of crime—the run-of-the-mill murders, suicides, assaults, opium abuses, and star-crossed elopements ending in robbing sprees—he also elevated the scandalous and sensational criminals. For example, Garfield's assassin Guiteau, the "Whitechapel fiend" (known better today as Jack the Ripper), author Oscar Wilde, and the Rev. H. Ward Beecher were all favorite fodder for *Gazette* writers over the years.

In 1889 the hysteria over Jack the Ripper, which reached its peak the year before, was revived when prostitute Alice McKenzie was found dead at Castle Alley near Whitechapel Road; she was the Ripper's eighth victim. The *Gazette* called the crime "one of the most dastardly and barefaced ever committed even in London, the scene of many brutal and historic crimes." The attending physician, Dr. Bagster Phillips, noted that the killer undoubtedly had knowledge of anatomy because her mutilations appeared to be the work of an expert. In its account, which appears to be taken from other publications, the *Gazette* used some of its familiar sensational language of description:

> As the woman lay there it became evident that "Jack the Ripper" had departed slightly from his previous methods. . . . It was clearly evident, however, both from the appearance of the skin and the character of the cut, that the knife had been plunged into the left side of the neck and then drawn backwards toward the back of the neck and the operator. The blow was a heavy one, and the blade severed both the jugular vein and the cartoid artery, but the knife did not break the skin on the other side. It had been pressed toward the hand as it was drawn out, the gash running toward the left ear. This shows clearly two things—the first being that the man stood behind her. The second is a bit of evidence that may turn out to be very important. It is that the murderer is left-handed; no right-handed man could, by any possibility, have made the wound that appeared. When she was taken to the mortuary and closely examined the discovery was made that only the bluntness of the knife had prevented her from being as horribly dismembered as all the other victims.[4]

The Ripper case is cited by many historians as an example of the early brand of reportorial sensationalism, with its merger of a new mass medium and public hysteria signaling the beginning of modern coverage of crime and criminality.[5] For the *Gazette*, Jack the Ripper was a "fiend," a deviant, whose evil deeds were deplored, yet amplified, in the publication's columns. This kind of amplification mixed with condemnation is a common feature of news accounts of deviant behavior, and it was found repeatedly in the *Gazette*. This amounts to the telling of crime tales as a sort of art form—Thomas de Quincey expounded on the characteristics of more skillfully committed murders in "On Murder Considered as One of the Fine Arts" in 1827: he wrote that a criminal must be more than an ordinary thug for his or her actions to gain the rightful glorification of the news media.[6]

De Quincey's romanticism notwithstanding, the *Gazette* reveled in ordinary thuggery, although it elevated it to heroic levels. As historian Elliot J. Gorn noted, throughout the 1870s and 1880s (and, one might add, through most of the 1890s), "crimes of violence, the more bizarre and blood-soaked the better, were the journal's lifeblood." Regular *Gazette* columns included "Vice's Varieties," "Lives of the Poisoners," "Crooked Capers: Scrapes and Scandals of All Sorts and From All Quarters," "Homicidal Horrors," "Noose Notes" (on lynchings), "Crimes of the Clergy," "Glimpses of Gotham" (by Paul Prowler, the pseudonym for the journalist Samuel MacKeever), and, one of the most famous, "This Wicked World: A Few Samples of Man's Duplicity and Woman's Worse Than Weakness."[7]

Not every item concerned a crime, of course; sometimes the columns simply highlighted the bizarre. The July 9, 1887, entry of "This Wicked World," for example, carried a description of a Cincinnati bank fraud, but it also—in much more detail—described another, more horrid, happening in Cincinnati, involving a man living on Vine Street Hill who had been mournfully keeping watch over the corpse of his infant son. The grieving father finally fell asleep, only to be roused by a sound and the startling sight of the young baby moving in his crib. When the father approached, a large rat jumped out of the crib. Upon inspection he found that the rat had been feeding on the baby's brain, having eaten a hole in the back of his head.[8]

Crimes, however, were the primary reason for these columns' existence, and the notion of justice for criminals was a key part of the Fox equation. In this sense, reports on lynchings provided frequent means of highlighting what passed for justice, often with racial underpinnings. A single issue from 1882, for example, contained the following items:

A "joke" on page 2:

Southern niggers have lately taken such a fancy to white meat that Judge Lynch is decorating all the groves with them. Pretty soon every tree will have its nigger, and all varieties will bear cocoanuts [*sic*] and wool.

A crime short on page 10:

Butler Durham, a darkey aged 19, at Oberlin, O. . . . . made a desperate attempt to outrage a young white girl named Libbie Porter, aged 17. She fought him furiously, however, till several white men came to her rescue. They lost their grip on him, he made for the woods and it took a large party three days to run down the desperate youngster. He was lodged in jail. A few degrees farther south or west he would now be lodged in in the angels' boarding house, breathless from having been yanked up the golden stairs by the rapid transit means of a rope around the neck.

A crime short on page 10:

Chung Hing, a Chinese laundryman of Denver, was a person of distinction among the heathens, but he paid the penalty. He was made the treasurer of a Chinese society and got $200 of its funds in his keeping. Some of his countrymen who knew this chopped him all to pieces . . . and got away with the money. The Chinaman is dead, the society is "busted" and Judge Lynch is furious because he cannot get his hands on the murderer.[9]

Some historians have concluded that because the *Gazette* printed items like these, Fox was a racist or a "good hater."[10] But the truth is more complicated, particularly when his career is viewed as a whole. By 1893, on his editorial page Fox was condemning the torture and lynching of a black man who had committed one of the most horrendous crimes imaginable: the rape and murder of a baby (white) girl. The accused man, Henry Smith, "a big negro," had been burned alive, while hanging, before 20,000 people in Paris, Texas, after his eyes had been gouged out by hot pokers. The editorial called the scene a "horrible" one that "should never again be witnessed in any civilized community." The column, which appeared below Fox's name on an item advertising a Spanish version of the *Police Gazette*, added, "It would have been more creditable to the State of Texas had Smith been allowed to expiate his crime in a legal and less barbarous way."[11] In 1887, in a startling account of an act similar to that which prompted the 1960s Civil Rights demonstrations, the *Gazette* came out in defense of two black men who had refused to move to the rear of a train in Georgia, and in 1895, it carried a nearly full-page story condemning the "white cap" (Ku Klux Klan) "reign of terror" in Georgia. This remarkable piece, which qualifies as an early example of investigative journalism, criticized authorities for being unable to stop "some of the blackest crimes in the history of the State" because of official corruption and rampant KKK membership.[12] Fox did allow some racist sentiment in the *Gazette*, but he also frequently called for color-blind justice. He reserved some of his greatest contempt for Chinese immigrants—an 1885 editorial demanded that the "petting of lustful, leprous, opium-smoking, child-seducing, air-polluting, blood-poisoning Canton and Hong-Kong coolies by American women must be ended fiercely and sharply by American men." But the same editorial defended black men as worthy of respect:

> The American negro is . . . the fellow-citizen, the fellow-sovereign, of the American white man. A bloody war and a constitutional amendment have advanced him to political equality with the American white man. Often American white blood flows in the American negro's veins. . . . He has fought shoulder to shoulder with our sons. He worships our God. He obeys, sometimes enforces, our laws. He was born on American soil, and when he dies he is buried as an American Christian in an American grave.[13]

Thus, it is apparent that the *Gazette* allowed for a variety of voices on race. Likewise, crime coverage took on many frames.

The stories of crime and criminals in all their varieties—from the craven, corrupt bureaucrat, to a "naughty, naughty parson" (from an item about a seventy-year-old who adopted a twenty-year-old as his daughter only to take her as his wife[14]), to the brazen "masher" or assaulter of women—provided a convenient method for Fox to claim a high road while pandering to sensation. This was one way he promoted masculinities—he idealized the form while he sensationalized the deviations. After claiming that a million or more people, presumably through pass-along readership, had read a recent issue of the *Gazette*, a March 1889 editorial explained,

> There is a notion prevalent among a large class of people that the publication of criminal doings has a deleterious effect on the morals of the masses. Some even go so far as to claim that this class of news stimulates crime—in other words, that the desire, or rather thirst, for notoriety—actuates many to become criminals. The POLICE GAZETTE has, very naturally, always stoutly contended that this view of the subject was entirely erroneous, and it is glad to see that other prominent journals from throughout the country treat the matter from the same standpoint.

The item then quoted approvingly from the Des Moines (Iowa) *Leader*, saying that journalism's glare helped deter would-be criminals.[15]

In a content analysis of the illustrations during the peak of the Fox era, crimes were categorized as either murder, robbery, sexual assault, nonsexual assault, defense by women against men, fighting between women, lynching, gambling, or "other." Tellingly, over the Fox years, excluding the murder category, women fighting men or fighting back against men was the most frequently depicted act of violence, with an average of nearly one-third of a page of such illustrations per issue from 1879 to 1906. Next was fighting between women, with an average of more than a quarter of a page of such illustrations per issue (see table 3.1). This suggests a heavy emphasis on the activities of women as aggressors or defenders, a finding that fits in with the notion of the *Gazette* as a chronicler of threats and reactions to masculinities. The complex treatment of women—not just as sex objects but as physically and psychologically strong creatures—demonstrates the emerging mass of messages of the period. Women were moving out of the traditional roles of frontier housewife and farmhand into more challenging avocations, including sports, hunting, demonstrating, and, yes, brawling and standing up for themselves (figure 3.1). The *Gazette's* illustrations sometimes highlighted amusement or titillation in these activities—the pictures of women scrapping or competing often included ruffled petticoats, skimpy sporting outfits or cutlines winking at their cat-fighting (figure 3.2). But often, particularly as the years went by, these activities were presented with a straight face, as a sort of matter-of-fact record of the new activities of modern women. This information served the male readership well, as men sought to

Table 3.1 Average number of inside pages per issue of portrayals of certain crimes at five-year intervals

Year	FDM	FFF	MSF
1880	.150	.020	.117
1885	.350	.000	.100
1890	.140	.275	.050
1895	.075	.175	.050
1900	.000	.167	.000
1905	.000	.000	.000
T. (1879–1906)	.29	.261	.096

Year	Murder	Nonsexual assault	Robbery
1880	.34	.192	.133
1885	.3	.350	.225
1890	.86	.300	.050
1895	.35	.050	.000
1900	.08	.050	.000
1905	.00	.000	.000
T. (1879–1906)	.414	.168	.143

Notes: FDM = Females defending themselves against males.
FFF = Female fighting females.
MSF = Males sexually assaulting females.

64

PUNISHED HER HUSBAND'S CHARMER.

WHAT A NEWARK, NEW JERSEY, YOUNG WOMAN GOT FOR FLIRTING WITH A MARRIED MAN.

Figure 3.1

RICHARD K. FOX, Editor and Proprietor.

NEW YORK, SATURDAY, JANUARY 26, 1884.

VOLUME XLIII.—No. 331. Price Ten Cents.

WAR IN THE WINGS.

TWO OF THE VESTALS EMPLOYED BY THE KIRALFYS TO RAISE THE DRAMA TO THE LEVEL OF A FINE ART, HAVE A FALLING-OUT AND SETTLE IT LIKE LITTLE MEN; AT THE BROOKLYN ACADEMY OF MUSIC.

Figure 3.2

acclimate themselves to the changing sex roles of the late nineteenth century.

As the Fox years progressed, crime became less of an emphasis in *Gazette* illustrations. The number of inside pages featuring some sort of illustrated crime dropped from an average of two or three pages (per issue) through most of the 1880s and 1890s to less than a page after 1900, finally dropping to no crime illustrations at all from 1904 through 1906. Because it becomes cumbersome to discuss findings of significant differences in individual years, it is more useful to consider the correlation between the year and *Gazette* coverage. Here, the significance was clear: as the years went by, there was a decrease in illustrated crime coverage. Further, illustrated sports coverage increased at a significant level as the years went by, while the coverage of sex or provocative portrayals remained fairly constant, with no significant correlation between date and sex coverage.[16]

Some reasons for this have been discussed: reliance on halftone technology after the turn of the century prohibited the kind of freewheeling and imaginative "artists' renditions" of crimes found in earlier years; in addition, group shots of sporting or other types of clubs became popular after the turn of the century as Fox found ways to put as many faces in his journal as possible. Fox still emphasized crime in the written word, but the cutback in the illustrations depicting crime had a significant effect on the *feel* of the *Gazette*. In the later years it was much more easily identified as a sporting and theatrical journal; the "sins of New York" as far as the criminal element was concerned did not seem to carry as much impact as they did in the gaslight era, and the shock had departed the pink shocker. Fox may have made a miscalculation, however. As will be discussed later, much has been written about the *Gazette*'s decline—that it succumbed to prohibition, new hairstyles, or simply died of old age—but many historians have ignored this change in content as a possible factor. Crime and criminal activity have always had a fascination for the public, and Fox recognized this early on. But the replacement of the woodcut may have hindered *Gazette* editors' ability to illustrate crimes in an attention-getting way, and, without realizing it, Fox may have let the *Gazette*'s claim to be a leader in sensationalism die with the woodcut. However, for more than two decades, the *Gazette* set the standard for crime coverage, even into the yellow journalism era of Pulitzer and Hearst, who adopted "circus extremes" in all types of coverage, including crime.[17]

To be sure, conscious reinforcement of a particular worldview probably was not the specific aim of Fox's *Gazette*. It would be a disservice to "read" a specific meaning into any column of the publication's content. On the other hand, to gain a better under-standing of why the *Gazette* was so successful and so appealing to a particular class of consumers—mostly men of the lower or middle class—it is necessary to examine the historical forces that were at work in the era. And during this period there is one key idea that ties together the journalistic (and reader) fascination with these types of crimes with the disrupted lives and work of men. It concerns, as we have discussed, the masculinities of the newly created industrial age. Fox may not have known it, but he was a practitioner of structured action.

If, as criminologist James Messerschmidt wrote, structured action theory "emphasizes the construction of gender as a situated social and interactional accomplishment," and "sex category and its meaning are given concrete expression by the specific social relations and historical context in which they are embedded,"[18] then it may be said that the mass media of a specific time and place help to construct these rela-tions and contexts. This process may be referred to as the framing of structured action. With regard to crime portrayals, the news and entertainment media act as constructors of society's pictures of crime and deviance and how to react to them. One may say that the *Gazette* participated in this construction, but for a complete understanding it is necessary to examine modern interpretations.

Over the past few years the term "cultural criminology" has taken a prominent position in the fields of criminology, sociology, and criminal justice. As explained by criminal justice professors Jeff Ferrell and Neil Websdale, editors of *Making Trouble: Cultural Constructions of Crime, Deviance, and Control*, the field of cultural criminology "explores the convergence of cultural and criminal processes in con-temporary social life."[19] More specifically, it refers to the increasing attention being paid to popular cultural constructions—particularly mass media constructions—of crime and crime control. In the authors' collection of fourteen essays, it was argued that the interrela-tionships between media and crime occur at a variety of levels, from policing to interaction to audience. Indeed, as the editors noted, "policing can in fact hardly be understood apart from its interpenetra-tion with media at all levels."[20] But as is also clear from mass commu-nication research, the media's influence works beyond just portrayals involving real-life police and criminals; "media constructions of crime and crime control emerge out of an alliance of convenience between media institutions and criminal justice agencies . . . and in turn serve to both trivialize and dramatize the meaning of crime."[21] This alliance of reporters and police existed from the early days of modern journalism, as editors sought information that was relatively easy to obtain (through police channels) and that also dealt with an aspect of society familiar to all, crime and crime control.

Crime coverage serves a variety of purposes, as noted by news historian Mitchell Stephens. It may

> assist in the apprehension of a criminal. In publicizing the punishment that is meted out, it can help deter other potential criminals. And in making the public aware of both crime and punishment, it can help clarify the lines of acceptable behavior [by defining deviance] within a society. Political bonds are also strengthened when a particularly despicable act unites a people in a great chorus of moral outrage.[22]

Depictions of deviance, in crime news or in other coverage, imply a depiction of the extraordinary, and distortion of crime news can have implications beyond the media, giving a picture of society that may not be in keeping with actual reality.[23] In a comprehensive study of deviance in crime news, David Pritchard and Karen D. Hughes identified four types of deviance: statistical deviance, status deviance, cultural deviance, and normative deviance. Statistical deviance is the extent to which something is unusual; status deviance is the extent to which a person or group is different in class; and cultural deviance is the extent to which an act is considered to be unhealthy, unclean, or perverted. Those involved in illegal activities (such as rape, sexual promiscuity, murder, or drug use) are said to be culturally deviant. Since news about crime helps an audience define the moral centers of its cultures, this suggests that the greater a crime's cultural deviance, the more newsworthy the crime. Finally, normative deviance exists when an act violates formal norms. While simply breaking a law may violate formal norms, Pritchard and Hughes argued that there are gradations of violations and thus, gradations of normative deviance. They concluded that status deviance and cultural deviance, when considered together, provide a sufficient explanation for evaluations of newsworthiness.[24]

More broadly, crimes give readers intimate glimpses into the lives of others; they provide a human interest element, and they give reporters and editors a sensational gateway through which to shout to readers. In the case of the *National Police Gazette*, crimes also served as a method of identifying, constructing, and protecting masculinities. This social construction of gender in connection with crimes is not unique to the *Gazette*, of course. Many social scientists argue that the "vamp-virgin" dichotomy in news coverage of sex crimes—that the victim was either a vamp who probably deserved rape or a virgin who was so innocent that she fell into it—leads to victim blaming and an indirect justification of hypermasculinity.[25]

There is no question that sex or sexual activity, along with class, is a frequent element in reporting of crimes. As Stephens remarked,

> The crimes that have most intrigued the readers of modern American newspapers appear to have had four qualities in common beyond mere heinousness: a woman or child as victim or suspect; a highborn or well known victim or suspect; some doubt about the guilt of the suspect; and intimations of promiscuous behavior by the victim or suspect.[26]

When one considers these elements of crime—deviance and sensation among classes—along with a *Gazette* audience found in "every self-respecting barber shop, billiard parlor, barroom and bagnio throughout the republic," as historian Peter Lyon described Fox's common circulation points, the character of the publication's masculine identification and construction becomes inescapable. The outlaw hero—the challenger of class and convention—was the jewel in this masculine criminal crown.

By 1889, a few years after Estelle Cowell was raped, Fox was on his way to selling a quarter of a million copies of a book called *Bella Starr, The Bandit Queen, or The Female Jesse James. A Full and Authentic History of the Dashing Female Highwayman, with Copious Extracts from Her Journal. Handsomely and Profusely Illustrated*. The contents of this book were not serialized by Fox in the *Gazette*, as were other accounts of thuggery and banditry; instead, they were published on their own as a separate edition. Fox, undoubtedly, was not the author of the volume, but it carried no credited author; instead it merely said it was "published by Richard K. Fox, New York, 1889."[27] It cost twenty-five cents, so Fox collected more than $60,000 in gross proceeds from the book. (In one biographical entry, Fox is credited as "author" of seventeen books, but authorship was fuzzy both in the *Gazette* columns and in the *Gazette*'s external publications. Most of these books "by" Fox were on sports and games or outlaws,[28] but he did not play games and knew almost nothing of the rules of the most common sports.)[29]

The creation of the myth of the rough-and-ready hero—even from the lives of murderous criminals—is not surprising for the period. Few remember it today, but Theodore Roosevelt, early in his career as a New York legislator in the 1880s, was ridiculed as a dandy of questionable manhood; one newspaper rather suggestively said he was "given to sucking the knob of an ivory cane."[30] He quickly realized what was needed to transform himself. Five years later he was running for mayor of New York as a cowboy, and he fashioned himself as a chiseled character carved out by his rugged sojourn in Dakota territory. Noting Roosevelt's re-creation of himself, historians Matthew Bass, Laura McCall, and Dee Garceau remarked,

> When Roosevelt left his elegant and refined home for the bustling world of late-nineteenth century politics, he relinquished his father's [Victorian] emblems of proper masculine behavior and embraced a newer ideal that stressed physical prowess, the masculine primitive, and a delicate linkage between white supremacy and male dominance.[31]

Roosevelt recognized that his times called for a masculine-flavored public relations machine. As noted by Bass et al., "Unstable economic conditions, the emergence of giant industrial combinations," and a dullness of existence in factories and cities defined the era and demanded that politicians respond to the prevailing currents in this America:

> Working-class and immigrant men competed with middle-class men for control of the political arena. Women publicly challenged men to quit alcohol and give them the vote. In reaction to the growing sentimentalization and feminization of American culture, beleaguered men responded with muscular Christianity, the strenuous life, and pseudo-scientific theories that stressed the mental and physical superiority of white males. The rugged, individualistic maverick of the West became a fashionable antidote to urban malaise.[32]

It is not at all unexpected, then, to find that at least some of these mavericks were the quasi-fictional heroic criminals of the territories. Lyon said that many of the myths of the adventures of these heroes arise from the memories of old-timers, who in turn were recalling what they had read about the criminals in the *Police Gazette*, probably in a barroom or barbershop with other men sharing the tales. Since the *Gazette*'s accounts were full of embellishment, so were the recollections: "Their memories were all faithful transcripts of the *Gazette*'s nonsense. Its editor's classic formula for manufacturing heroes had so effectively rotted the minds of his readers that they could never thereafter disentangle fiction from fact."[33]

Lyon, whose jocular style hints at a certain tongue-in-cheek approach, said that his "analysis" of the *Gazette*'s treatment of outlaw heroes revealed that Fox had a formula for outlaw features that had ten ingredients, "like a Chinese soup";

1. The hero's accuracy with any weapon is prodigious.
2. He is a nonpareil of bravery and courage.
3. He is courteous to all women, regardless of rank, station, age, or physical charm.
4. He is gentle, modest, and unassuming.
5. He is handsome, sometimes even pretty, so that he seems even feminine in appearance; but withal he is of course very masculine, and exceedingly attractive to women.
6. He is blue-eyed. His piercing blue eyes turn gray as steel (or flint) when he is aroused; his associates would have been well advised to keep a color chart handy, so that they might have dived for a storm-cellar when the blue turned to tattle-tale gray.
7. He was driven to a life of outlawry and crime by having quite properly defended a loved one from an intolerable affront—with lethal consequences. Thereafter, however,
8. He shields the widow and orphan, robbing only the banker or railroad monopolist.
9. His death comes about by means of betrayal or treachery, but
10. It is rarely a conclusive death, since he keeps bobbing up later on, in other places, for many years. It is, indeed, arguable whether he is dead yet.[34]

In general, this is an accurate characterization because it shows how Fox combined the heroic/criminal elements of gallantry, cunning, and chivalry, all critical attributes of the men of the lost frontier who were rapidly being displaced in the fin de siecle's industrial world of selfishness, ambiguity, and greed. There is one slight over generalization in Lyon's description, however: one of Fox's most important archetypes of the Western outlaw hero was a woman. Although Lyon remarked drolly that the Fox hero was sometimes so good-looking as to be feminine in appearance, he was referring not to women as heroes but to "pretty boys" who were nevertheless attractive to all women. Still, Fox's most famous outlaw heroine of the West illustrated Lyon's points just as well as the men did. For Fox found in Belle Starr a woman who could demonstrate many of the same masculinities as Jesse James. But she offered a twist for readers, because her sex provided certain contrasts that made the story all the more sensational and loaded with references to gender.

Myra Belle Shirley was born near Carthage, Missouri, in 1848, but she grew up in Dallas, Texas. Shortly after the Civil War she had a daughter with Cole Younger and a son by Jim Reed, who was killed in 1874 (Belle supposedly refused to identify Reed's body to prevent collection of a reward). She later took up with a man named Bluford (Blue) Duck, one of the many male admirers she gained during frequent episodes of horse rustling. At one point Duck borrowed $2,000 from Belle, and then lost it in a crooked poker game at Fort Dodge, Kansas; Belle supposedly headed straight for the hall and took her money, plus another $5,000, at gunpoint. In 1880, she married a Cherokee outlaw, Sam Starr, thus acquiring the name that would go down in history. Starr, too, was killed, by an Indian police officer, and Belle married a Creek, Jim July. A short time after that marriage, in 1889, she was ambushed by someone with a shotgun near Fort Smith, Arkansas.

Who killed Belle Starr? No one is sure. A neighbor was a suspect, and so was her son, Edward, with whom some biographers have speculated with glee that she had an incestuous relationship. July may also have been the culprit.[35] Whoever shot her, it was in death that she was immortalized. The *Gazette* ran an illustration showing her dying in her saddle,[36] and on February 6, 1889, on the front page of the *New York Times*, the following item appeared bearing a Fort Smith dateline:

> Word has been received from . . . Indian Territory, that Belle Starr was killed there Sunday night . . . .
> Belle Starr was the most desperate woman that ever figured on the borders. She married Cole Younger directly after the war, but left him and joined a band of outlaws that operated in the Indian Territory. She had been arrested for murder and robbery a score of times, but always managed to escape.[37]

Starr biographer Glenn Shirley, in a book chapter entitled "From Richard K. Fox to 20th Century-Fox," remarked that following this account, Starr soon became a household word. She had been known as a frontier anomaly, a bandit queen, but now, Shirley noted, she became a household word. She had been known as a frontier anomaly, a bandit queen, but now, Shirley noted, she was

> a sex-crazed hellion with the morals of an alley cat, a harborer and consort of horse and cattle thieves, a petty blackmailer who dabbled in every crime from murder to the dark sin of incest, a female Robin Hood

who robbed the rich to feed the poor, an exhibitionistic and clever she-devil on horseback and leader of the most blood-thirsty band of cutthroats in the American West.[38]

Word about Belle reached Fox, perhaps partly through the *Times'* story but also probably through word from the region itself, where Fox had many agents, including freelancer Alton B. Meyers, who was the *Gazette*'s Southwest representative. Shirley recounted one version of the *Gazette* latching onto the story when a hungry Meyers, who was lingering on the wood sidewalks of Fort Smith's Garrison Avenue with seven cents in his pockets, came across an old-timer reading the *Fort Smith Elevator*'s account of Starr's killing. After the man told Meyers that Starr had been killed, Meyers became enamored at the sound of her name—"a more romantic sound than even Sam Bass, Jesse James, or Billy the Kid."

"Who was Belle Starr?" he asked.

"Oh, hell," the old man spat and snorted, "just a nutty old whore who imagined she was a bandit queen."

Belle Starr! A *bandit queen*! Meyers practically ran to the telegraph office. Within hours he had a cash advance, a hotel room, a full stomach, and a ream of writing paper. Apparently, Belle's son and daughter and her mother, who had arrived from Texas, refused to divulge any family history likely to bring discredit upon themselves, so Meyers had to resort to less-reliable information among her acquaintances. Court records, easily available, were consulted carelessly. Few of the names, dates, or essential facts were correct. Alleged excerpts from Belle's letters and diary—a gag used by most writers of the yellow-journalism school to make their work appear authentic—were pure fabrication.[39]

So Meyers sent Fox a dispatch, and the result became a "dime novel" (it actually cost twenty-five cents) that purported to be true:

Of all the women of the Cleopatra type, since the days of the Egyptian queen herself, the universe has produced none more remarkable than Bella Starr, the Bandit Queen. Her character was a combination of the very worst as well as some of the very best traits of her sex. She was more amorous than Anthony's mistress; more relentless than Pharaoh's daughter, and braver than Joan of Arc. Of her it may well be said that Mother Nature was indulging in one of her rarest freaks, when she produced such a novel specimen of womankind. Bella was not only well educated, but gifted with uncommon musical and literary talents, which were almost thrown away through the bias of her nomadic and lawless disposition, which early isolated her from civilized life, except at intervals, when in a strange country, and under an assumed name, she brightened the social circle for a week or a month, and then was, perhaps, lost forever.[40]

Fox's account of Starr's life and feats became a leading source for many of the error-filled, tear-jerking, florid, and lurid biographies to follow, but Shirley argued that its most significant contribution may have been to the field of criminology. In 1895, six years after Starr's death, an Italian criminologist and professor of psychiatry and criminal anthropology, Caesar Lombroso, published a volume called *The Female Offender*, in which he apparently used material taken from Fox's *Bella Starr, Bandit Queen*. Lombroso, born in 1835 in Verona, is perhaps best known for two other works, 1876's *The Criminal Man* and 1899's *Crime, its Causes and Remedies*. In connection with the theories advanced in these books, he became renowned worldwide for his studies in the field of characterology, which was the relation between mental and physical characteristics. He argued that physical characteristics such as enormous jaws, strong canines, prominent zygomae,[41] "and strongly developed orbital arches . . . are common to carnivores and savages, who tear and devour raw flesh" and are also found in predatory criminals.[42] (Interestingly, two years after *The Criminal Man* appeared, the *Gazette* ran an item under the headline " 'Nigger Sam's' Brain," which described the results of an autopsy of a black man, Sam Steenbergh, who was executed on April 19, 1878, at Fonda, New York, for the murder of eleven people. His brain weighed fifty-nine ounces—which was rather large—and was confined by a skull with a circumference of twenty-three and a half inches. The story said his brain was marred with inflammations, "which has been deemed in some criminal cases affecting mental action, and is a very interesting scientific inquiry."[43])

Later, Lombroso modified the theory of characterology somewhat, saying that disease or environmental factors also caused individuals to commit crimes, but his views remain important not necessarily for their specifics but because they helped establish the "positive school" of criminology. It is significant because it attempted to search for causes of crime, whether biological, sociological, or psychological, which was the antithesis of the eighteenth-century classical theory that people freely chose to participate in crime to maximize pleasure and reduce pain.

In *The Female Offender*, Lombroso commented on Starr as a sort of case study illustrating the atavistic characteristics exhibited by barbarous women. Where did Lombroso get his material about her life? Shirley believed that it was probably from Fox's book or from Charles Victor Crosnier de Varigny, an Italian "stringer" in New York who supplied copy to Rome and Milan newspapers from publications such as the *World*, the *Herald*, the *Police Gazette*, and the *Police News*. Like Fox's reporters, de Varigny lifted his material, often adding embellishments from publications, and his account of Starr has many of the same "facts" as Fox's book. It is clear that Lombroso bought the ludicrous notion that Starr had written a diary (Fox, as noted, claimed his volume contained "copious extracts from her journal," but in fact it carried mere fancy disguised as her journal).[44] Lombroso wrote:

> The born [female] criminal is rarely inclined to write much. We know but of three instances among them of memoirs; those of Madame Lafarge,[45] of X. [another case study], and of Bell-Star, while male criminals are greatly addicted to these egotistic outpourings. Madame Lafarge, the woman X., and Bell-Star, particularly the last, were certainly endowed with superior intelligence, but among male criminals even those whose mental equipment is less than mediocre, there have been many who wrote memoirs.[46]

In Lombroso's view, the mannish, hawk-faced Starr exhibited a female version of hypermasculinity—a hyperfemininity—that was dangerous and seductive. In short, she had characteristics that one might expect of a female who regressed to the uncivilized state of womanhood: dominant, daring, and sex-starved.

> In general the moral physiognomy of the born female criminal approximates strongly to that of the male. The atavistic dimunition of secondary sexual characters which is to be observed in the anthropology of the subject, shows itself once again in the psychology of the female criminal, who is excessively erotic, weak in maternal feeling, inclined to dissipation, astute and audacious, and dominates weaker beings sometimes by suggestion, at others by muscular force; while her love of violent exercise, her vices, and even her dress, increase her resemblance to the sterner sex. Added to these virile characteristics are often the worst qualities of woman: namely, an excessive desire for revenge, cunning, cruelty, love of dress, and untruthfulness, forming a combination of evil tendencies which often results in a type of extraordinary wickedness. . . . A typical example of these extraordinary women is presented by Bell-Star, the female brigand, who a few years ago terrorised all Texas. Her education had been the sort to develop her natural qualities; for, being the daughter of a guerrilla chief who had fought on the

side of the South in the war of 1861–65, she had grown up in the midst of fighting, and when only ten years old, already used the lasso, the revolver, the carbine, and the bowie knife in a way to excite the enthusiasm of her ferocious companions.[47]

These details, probably all false, were in Fox's account, as were Lombroso's claims that "Bell-Star" was a "Napoleon in petticoats" who had as many lovers as there were desperados in four states. Fox's account remained an important source for many other authors. Samuel W. Harman, who was a professional juryman in the court of the original famed "hanging Judge" Isaac C. Parker of Fort Smith, Arkansas, based an 1898 book about Starr on Fox's text. By 1941, Starr was ripe for the silver screen. Irving Cummings directed "Belle Starr, The Bandit Queen" for 20th Century-Fox, basing it loosely on a book by Burton Rascoe. The movie turned the heroine, played by Gene Tierney, into a Scarlett O'Hara-like character who was killed while saving Sam Starr from an ambush.[48]

The Fox book is filled with descriptions of a "Bella" who is clever, difficult to figure, and a master of disguise, at various times appearing as a young man or a wrinkled grandmother. The book refers to her as the "heroine" of the story and credits her with returning stolen goods if the victim happened to be particularly kind or a man of God. In one story, she disguises herself as a young man and shares a bed, for lack of other accommodations, with a judge from Dallas who had boasted to friends that "I'd know Myra . . . if those fiery eyes of hers were set in the head of a cabbage. Yes, she's a wild one, but she cannot fool me, ha! ha! ha!"[49] Of course, Myra (Bella) does fool him, and sleeps in his bed with him, and the next morning cannot resist rubbing it in. Still disguised as a young man, she wakes the judge and tells him that the Bandit Queen is waiting for him outside:

> Our heroine was on the porch awaiting [the judge] who descended with a cautious step, till he reached the door. Looking out and seeing nothing of "his own dear Myra," as he had called her . . . he broke out with the following remarks:
>
> "Young man, it ill becomes you to play practical jokes on your elders. I was particularly anxious for sleep this morning, and you—"
>
> "Wait a moment, judge," said she. "Just step as far as the gate and you'll see the Bandit Queen."
>
> Bella opened the gate, and laying one hand on the withers of her horse, vaulted into the saddle.
>
> "Where? Where is she?" asked the judge.

"Look right into my face. Look well. I am Bella . . . and you—well, you are a consummate old fool. Your own self-conceit will damn you without the devil's help. . . . Go home and tell your friends that you have had the honor and glory of sleeping with the Bandit Queen." With these words Bella put spurs to her horse and struck westward like a blue streak.[50]

Like other publishers who celebrated the feats of Western outlaws, Fox couched his coverage of villains in disapproving language while providing readers with a hint of their bravado. For example, the *Gazette* noted that on the morning of October 5, 1892, at Coffeyville, Kansas, "six men, wearing broad-brimmed hats, mounted on magnificent horses and carrying Winchesters on their shoulders and with belts well filled with cartridges, rode straight into the business portion of town."[51] After robbing the two banks in the town, the group rode out, only to be met by a posse armed also with Winchester rifles, and following a "sharp but brief fight," five of the robbers were killed. Four of the posse also were killed. This marked the end of the famous train- and bank-robbing brothers known as the Dalton Gang, former deputy marshals who for a time found crime to be a more lucrative profession.[52]

The *Gazette* was often disapproving of criminal deeds while sensationalizing them; this pattern was found in its winks and nods at the activities of Jesse James and the Hatfields and the McCoys, for example. In 1882, Fox was proud to boast that he had received a letter from James, the "harlequin bandit" who had purportedly been dead:

We have received a communication from the grave. From a veritable corpse. Yes, a dead man. Not only a dead man but a dead man who has been riddled to hash by bullets and slashed to ribbons with bowie knives. That is, if we can believe the newspapers. The alleged corpse that has written us is none other than the remains or the ghost or what is left of the much-killed Jesse James, the terror of Missouri.

This famous bandit, train robber and desperado has been killed so often, however, in newspaper reports and has turned up safe and sound thereafter, that the people of Kansas have lost faith in death.[53]

James's "deaths," the *Gazette* reported, had a cycle to them: he was rumored killed, then would resurrect himself, turn up on another train, "clean out the express packages and the passengers and then hie him away to the setting sun with many merry cuss words on his lips and his thumb pivoted on his nose and his fingers agitated in insulting suggestions to the minions of the law."[54] The railroad companies became so tired of the game that they pooled $7,000 for his capture or corpse. Then every "clerk who had a holiday and every tenderfoot who was out west selling tape and shoelaces shouldered his little gun and went out to capture or slaughter the famous bandit." James supposedly connived with a fellow gang member, who offered proof of his death to authorities and then was awarded the money and promptly split it with James. In another instance, a deputy claimed James had been captured in a shootout with officers at a log cabin in Kansas, in which seven officers had been killed. James turned up a few days later, "safe and sound and as saucy as ever." Moreover, the *Gazette* noted proudly, he kept up with the *Police Gazette* regularly, and it published a "photographic *fac simile*" of a stream-of-consciousness handwritten letter by James:

Mr Fox I write to you this that Sheriff's Detectives & Scouts have been after me but it is of no use when I want to give up my job I will so people let me alone,

Yours Truly,
Jesse James

Added the *Gazette:*

As Mr. James by his own avowal will not be brought to justice until he is good and ready and as the authorities will only enrich him by offering rewards for his slaughter, the wise course would be for Missourians to Boycott him, so to speak. Let them depopulate the State so he may have no one to kill; let them stop all the railroads so that he may have no chance to rob. Then when he grows weary of living alone he may, like Robinson Crusoe, have a hankering after civilization and may of his own volition come in and go cheerily to his dungeon cell as a variation to the monotony of his lonesome life. That is the only way to fix it. Jesse James says so himself and surely he ought to know. It is plain anyhow that he is the most knowing person in Missouri as far as we've got.[55]

Fox was not the creator of the James myth, but he bought into it. As the letter to Fox suggests, James was not afraid to cultivate relationships with editors and publishers, and James biographer T.J. Stiles suggested that he used such communications because he understood the nature of myth creation and wanted to take part in the making of his own legend. James formed a lasting friendship with *Kansas City Times* editor John Newman Edwards, and in June 1870 James published a letter in the newspaper in which he called on secessionist sympathizers to have sympathy with him. He admitted to being a "bushwhacker," or Confederate guerrilla fighter, during the Civil War, but said he had lived peaceably since the war. Stiles presented a portrait of James that might lead some to conclude that he had simply moved from the casual killing of wartime to the casual killing of peacetime, with the primary difference being that in the peacetime killings, he sought money more often than he sought to make political statements. Yet, for Stiles, the beginnings of the James myth could be traced to his association with causes greater than mere banditry. It was a time in which Horace Greeley was touted as a presidential candidate by another editor, Peter Donan, a rabid rebel who headed the *Lexington Caucasian*, who had railed against the "yankonigger bayonet amendments" to the Constitution attempting to force a modicum of civil rights for blacks in the defeated South. James thus had a ready fan base for political bloodshed.[56]

A classic James crime came during this political uproar, the robbery of the second annual Industrial Exposition in Kansas City in 1872. Thousands paid fifty cents to attend the gathering of the most important and exciting of Missouri's harvest-time county fairs with visitors traveling from as far as Iowa, Illinois, and Texas.

At sunset on September 26, the fourth day of the fair, three men on horseback, wearing masks of checkered cloth, approached the Twelfth Street gate. One of them casually grabbed the gate cash box as the others brandished weapons at the startled crowd; when a clerk resisted, a gun was fired and a bullet struck a small girl in the leg. After seizing the cashbox, the bandits rode off into the woods, $978 richer—if they had arrived half an hour earlier, before the booth's funds had been collected by the fair's treasurer, the haul would have been closer to $12,000.[57]

Edwards spared no ink in recounting the daring-do. As Stiles put it, "The frothing editor devoted most of the article to high-pitched hyperbole."[58] Edwards wrote: "It was one of those exhibitions of superb daring that chills the blood and transfixes the muscles of the looker-on with a mingling of amazement, admiration, and horror."[59] He called on the public to "revere" the bandits—language that, as Stiles noted, was not entirely unheard of because many newspapers described banditry as a "daring" act conducted with "cool audacity." But the level of Edwards's admiration led Stiles to conclude that he must have known James was behind the robbery. He would follow the account with a famous editorial, "The Chivalry of Crime," in which Edwards romanticized bandits and outlaws as "chivalric; poetic; superb," and belonging to another, more heroic, age: "The nineteenth century with its Sybaritic civilization is not the social soil for men who might have sat with Arthur at the Round table, ridden at tourney with Sir Launcelot or worn the colors of Guinevere."[60]

The ralliers to Confederate manhood had found themselves a hero, and James added to the adulation when he endorsed Greeley for president.[61] It was a fortuitous combination of circumstances. For the creation of the James myth, Stiles gave credit to James's "missives to the press," his poetically alliterative name, his promotion of himself as a Robin Hood, and his decision to serve up his life as a symbol for manliness and the Confederacy.[62] It did not hurt that he lived in an era in need of new manly heroes. For the *Gazette*—an outlawish as well as outlandish publication in a real sense—James was a hero *because* of his outlaw status and his willingness to spit in the face of convention; at least according to his own letters, he had a bold, rough-and-ready quality that was to be admired among the timid, challenged men of the city.

But while James might have been seen as another of Fox's friendly readers who just happened to be a boastful brigand, not all criminals were treated so cheerfully. Fox also ran a column called "Deeds of the Lawless/Robbers, Desperados and Ruffians of all Sorts on the Rampage" that appeared occasionally (coincidentally, next to Jesse James's letter in April 1882), that was not nearly as kind to other robbers, murderers, and thieves. Such contradictions in accounts of criminal activities during this period were not uncommon; James may have been lionized as an "American Robin Hood" who symbolically captured American ideals of individuality and cleverness, but not everyone embraced him as a representative of cherished values. As a contemporary remarked: "What language can furnish the vocabulary which contains enough lurid words, wild synonyms, ensanguinary adjectives, and murderous verbs to do justice to this horrible monster; this insatiable vampire who has drank enough blood to print, in red, an entire edition of this narrative."[63] Indeed, sociologist Paul Kooistra noted, "virtually every criminal who has been labeled as a hero has also been cast in the role of a villain."[64] But neither role is entirely accurate, as he pointed out, "We should not be surprised at the varying and even contradictory themes that are offered as explanations for the popularity of the heroic criminal. Tales of notorious criminals will hold different meanings for different audiences."[65]

The outlaw, therefore, serves as a myth and by definition is thus the product of an ambiguous portrait. Thus, said the French anthropologist Claude Levi-Strauss, one should be careful about placing a myth into one particular meaning because, "The diversity of sequences and themes is a fundamental attribute of mythic thought. . . . Unconcerned with neat beginnings and clear goals, mythic thought does not effect complete courses; it always has something more to achieve."[66]

The historian Lyon, who often viewed *Gazette* content with a wink, did not care much in this instance for the *Gazette*'s brand of hero-making. Noting that James's mischievous charm was celebrated in the *Gazette*, he further pointed out that James murdered two unarmed bank officers—not because they offered any resistance but because they were cowering at his feet. He regarded with contempt any type of myth creation that may gloss over cruelty and bloodshed. In Fox's publication he identified a legacy that he believed was misleading and vulgar:

> Television in particular would seem to have inherited the august mantle of *The National Police Gazette*. The parallels between the two mass media are striking. The *Gazette* preached each week a superficial, meretricious ethic; so do the televised entertainments that deal with the West. The *Gazette*'s editor was not concerned with the facts of the matters his journal reported but only with the number of his readers; the producers of the televised entertainments fill his shoes precisely. He was successful; so, as Nielsen is their judge, are they. He worked out a formula for populating the American pantheon; so have they. It is the master's recipe, only slightly sauced to make the stew more palatable for those who had instilled in them the democratic ethos. Thus, on television the hero must protect such underdogs as the Mexican, the Indian, and the Chinese from the acquisitive Anglo-Saxon upperdog, a behavior which, in terms of historical fact, is ludicrously fanciful . . . .
>
> And even granting the assumption that the purveyors of this sludge are concerned not with history but with legend, what a shameful and ghastly legend it is! to be despised, if not on the sufficient grounds of its ugly violence, then on the grounds of its even uglier vulgarity.
>
> The moral, of course, is that crime, when commercially exploited, *does* pay, and the more sadistic the better. The Wild, Wild West, as exploited by irresponsible men—from Richard K. Fox of the *The National Police Gazette* to the television producers of today—who care not a hang for the truth of history so long as they can count their audiences in the scores of millions, have created for the world an enduring image of America.
>
> Over it there hangs the stink of evil.[67]

Multiple meanings are not confined to the tales of heroic criminals, of course; they also apply to the criminals whose deeds become notorious because of the fame or class of the perpetrators or victims before the crime was committed. Two sensational cases covered by the *Gazette* illustrated these meanings in the context of the issues of masculinities discussed in this book: the cases of Beecher and Wilde.

Scandal and disgrace were favorite themes of Fox's *Gazette*; a popular column was "Crimes of the Clergy," in which the hypocrisy of clergymen was gleefully exposed. The *Gazette* remarked casually in a July 1880 editorial that the summer had seen numerous ministerial scandals (duly reported upon, in detail, in its pages). The editorialist, Fox or one of his writers, said it would be nice "to know just when and where the latter-day clergyman is going to stop in his reckless career of lechery."[68]

One of the most famous clergymen to face the ridicule of the *Gazette* was Rev. H. Ward Beecher, the son of Lyman Beecher and the brother of *Uncle Tom's Cabin* author Harriet Beecher Stowe. He was known for his remarkable oratorical skills, ready wit, and, on some subjects, progressive outlook. Born in 1813 in Litchfield, Connecticutt, he was an abolitionist, a proponent of women's suffrage, and a supporter of the theory of evolution. He graduated from Amherst in 1834, later attending Lane Theological Seminary in Cincinnati. By 1847 he had moved to the "City of Churches"—Brooklyn, New York—where he would achieve his greatest renown.

What would become known as the Beecher-Tilton scandal, which lasted for years, first came to the public eye in 1872 when women's rights advocate Victoria Woodhull published an article accusing Beecher of adultery with Elizabeth Tilton, the wife of Theodore Tilton. Both Tiltons were members of Beecher's Plymouth Church, and Theodore Tilton, a journalist and author, was editor of the journal the *Independent*. The scandal played out in the press because both Tiltons and Beecher all wrote letters to newspaper editors advancing their positions. Mrs. Tilton confessed, recanted, and then confessed again, all in the public arena.

Beecher directed a Plymouth Church committee to investigate the matter, and he was exonerated by the committee, which was made up of his close supporters. Subsequently, Tilton brought suit against Beecher, and the trial in 1875 became a national sensation. At the end of the six-month trial, the jury could not come to an agreement, and the result meant that Beecher effectively won. In the following year, a second church committee again exonerated Beecher; in 1878 Elizabeth Tilton, in another reversal, publicly admitted to the affair and was dismissed from Plymouth Church.[69]

In an editorial in the same issue that told of Mrs. Tilton having a friend deliver her latest confession of sin to the *Gazette*, the *Gazette* lamented the entire episode:

> It is a pity . . . that a community already sickened and fatigued of the
> whole affair could not have been spared this renewed and purposeless
> infliction, but the return of the spasm was an inevitable concomitant of
> the moral disease generated in the morbific atmosphere of the City of
> Churches and will have to be endured with whatever equanimity can be
> commanded, no matter of how little avail it may be deemed by a long
> suffering public.[70]

But that did not stop the magazine from publishing a lengthy article
on Mrs. Tilton's latest turnabout; apparently the temptation to again
hold Beecher up to public scrutiny was too great. The succession of
headlines read,

Badgered Beecher.

—

Plymouth Church Experiences
Another Throe of the Great
Moral Earthquake.

——

Mrs. Tilton Tells Again.

——

This Time she Swears it is so, for she
Cannot Tell a Lie, and she did it—
with her Little Hatch-it.

——

The Biggest Cackle on Record.[71]

The Beecher story was perfect for the *Gazette*—it illustrated the
failings of the upper classes, the hypocrisy of the clergy, the humor and
limitations of sensationalism, and the complexities of being a man in
the late nineteenth century. Then Fox would find an even wilder story.
    Dr. William Wilde, the father of Oscar Wilde, wrote twenty books
and had an international reputation as the author of the standard text-
book on aural surgery. But he was also well known for his peculiarities;
George Bernard Shaw said he was "Beyond Soap and Water, as his
Nietzchean son was Beyond Good and Evil."[72] A popular joke in
Dublin society was, "Why are Sir William Wilde's nails black?" The
answer: "Because he scratches himself." Sir William was, like his son,
felled by a sexual scandal; Mary Travers, the daughter of a professor at
Trinity College, accused him of violating her after chloroforming her

in 1854. But she was in fact his mistress, and no force was involved. After he attempted to end the affair, she published a pamphlet, which she attributed to Lady Wilde, claiming that he seduced patients in his office. A jury did not believe her to be a victim, and when she sued Sir William, she was awarded one farthing, about a quarter of a cent. But the case ruined Sir William Wilde's career.[73]

Oscar Wilde, born in Dublin in 1854, was a brilliant young student and writer who had a thirst for the spotlight. In 1884 he married a beautiful woman, Constance Lloyd, whose hand came with the considerable sum of £800 a year. But two years later he began experimenting with homosexuality, and in 1891 he met the young man who would change his life, Lord Alfred Douglas, the twenty-one-year-old son of Henry Sholto Douglas, the eighth Marquess of Queensberry, who developed boxing's Queensberry rules.[74] Alfred Douglas was, by all accounts, a beautiful man, attractive to men and women alike. Wilde was taken with him and began writing him letters that would later be used against him. The two were careless in their activities—they once were unexpectedly visited by the local clergyman, who found them naked in a garden. Even though Wilde told the clergyman, "You have come just in time to enjoy a perfectly Greek scene," the clergyman decided to skip that act of the play; he fled and rumors spread.[75] But by February 1895, with Wilde's most remarkable literary successes flourishing and two weeks after *The Importance of Being Earnest* opened to smashing reviews in London, the Marquess of Queensberry left at his club a fateful note for Wilde: "For Oscar Wilde, posing as a somdomite [*sic*]." The misspelling was, for one Wilde biographer, a sort of Freudian slip for a repressed age: "In Victorian society nearly everyone knew the behavior and the behavers to exist, but to utter a name for it or even spell it was really too much. Queensberry tried and got it famously wrong on the insulting calling card he left for Oscar at the Albemarle Club."[76]

Friends advised Wilde to ignore the insult, but, encouraged by Lord Alfred, he would have none of it. He sued the Marquess for libel, an error that was to cost him dearly. For one thing, the Marquess had merely accused Wilde of *posing* as a sodomite, an easier charge to prove than the actual act. Secondly Wilde made the grievous error of many plaintiffs; by suing Queensberry, he was in effect putting himself on trial, in this case for homosexuality. After the libel suit failed, Wilde was arrested, since Queensberry's accusations had been proved justified. In two trials (the first ended in a hung jury), Wilde was questioned at length about his fondness for young men and his supposed celebration of indecency in his literary work.[77]

One might have expected the *National Police Gazette* to offer lurid, and vivid, details of Wilde's transgressions, but as Wilde biographer Gary Schmidgall put it, the deeds were considered too repulsive for the press of the era to describe in any detail. It noted that Wilde was found guilty of immoral conduct, "but the evidence is such that it cannot be reproduced here." The *Gazette* confined itself to a sort of celebration of the tyranny of heterosexuality, reveling in the humiliation of Wilde. It reported that one letter that Wilde wrote to Lord Douglas was read in court:

> My Own Dear Boy—Your sonnet is quite lovely and it is a marvel that those red roseleaf lips of yours should be made no less for the music of song than for the madness of kissing. Your slim gilt soul walks between passion and poetry. I know that Hyacinthus, whom Apollo loved so madly, was you in Greek days. Why are you alone in London and when do you go to Salisbury? Do go there and cool your hands in the gray twilight of gothic things and come here whenever you like. It is a lovely place;. it only lacks you, but go to Salisbury first. Always with undying love, yours.
>
>   Oscar.[78]

Following Wilde's conviction, the *Gazette* led with the specter of his fall from grace:

> At last, after a career that had been, up to a certain point, brilliant as well as successful, Oscar Wilde, aesthete, author and poet, has been convicted of a series of revolting and unnatural crimes, dragged down from the heighth at which he had placed himself, and thrust into a prison cell.[79]

As did many authors, the writer of the *Gazette* account (no byline was given) treated Wilde's life as an obvious source for the author's fiction. One *Gazette* story quoted from a portion of *The Picture of Dorian Gray*, Wilde's morality tale about aging and the price of vanity, in which Hallward asks Gray: "Why is it, Dorian, when I am away from you and I hear all these hideous things that people are whispering about you I don't know what to say? Why is it that a man like the Duke of Berwick leaves the room of a club when you enter it?" The *Gazette* writer remarked of Wilde, "Never was humiliation and fall so complete. He was sentenced to two years at hard labor, which means a great deal more in England than it does in America."[80]

Wilde was jailed at Pentonville Prison, where he spent several hours a day for a month on the treadmill. He also was confined for twenty-three hours a day in a small, badly ventilated cell (in May 1895 the *Gazette* ran a fanciful picture of Wilde in his cell surrounded by female admirers, much to his apparent disdain). During his only hour outside, in the exercise yard, he was not permitted to speak to others or he would be confined for seventy-two hours in a dark cell (which happened to him more than once). Within a few days of his imprisonment his books stopped selling and his plays closed. His personal possessions were sold off at outrageous prices—one original Whistler fetched a shilling, or about twenty-five cents.

> His breakfasts are as plain and rude as were ever dignified by the name—cocoa and bread. His noon dinners are scarcely better, and a specimen meal consists of bacon and beans and potatoes.
>
> His month on the treadmill is a sort of initiation for him—simply a foretaste of what hard labor really is, and after it has been concluded he will be put to some kind of legitimate work, and something which will be profitable to the prison; perhaps bag making, tailoring or picking oakum . . .
>
> At the end of two years Oscar Wilde will have earned the princely sum of $2.50, which he can have all at once if he wants it.[81]

The prosecution of Wilde was selective, of course. Many authors have noted that charges were never brought against the men who consorted with him. In that sense he was made an example, not just of the dangers of homosexuality, but of the dangers of flaunting homosexuality in the "face" of the patrician class. For Fox, Wilde also served as an example of the decadence of the aesthetes and aristocracy, many of whom considered Fox to be a champion of the vulgar. It was as if Fox was determined to show where the vulgarity really was—in the hypocrisy and greed of the ruling class. His subscribers might have enjoyed their beer and wine and showgirls and prizefights, but they were law-abiding men who still could find something to admire in the spunk of Starr or the "remarkable nerve" of Billy the Kid.[82] The real men, to Fox, were those who were honest about their choices. That is probably one reason that the *Gazette* lampooned the madman who shot President Garfield. To Fox and his editors, Charles J. Guiteau was like a lot of hypocritical criminals; he was not crazy—he was just a malicious actor trying to hide his guile.

The felled president was repeatedly eulogized during his sufferings following his shooting (he lingered from July 2, 1881, until September 19). He was a self-made man, rising from the poverty of his Ohio boyhood to a Civil War commission as a brigadier general and then to Congress and the presidency. He was, reported Charles Rosenberg in his book about Guiteau's trial, "strong and tenacious, a punishing fighter when insulted, though no bully." The public biographies of Garfield reported somewhat contradictory claims, Rosenberg noted: he was "ceaselessly ambitious, yet humble and modest; scholarly and methodical, yet courageous and astonishingly vigorous; pious and uxorious, yet competent in the harsh acts of the soldier." Rosenberg wrote that Garfield's traits were quite different from those attributed to Andrew Jackson, the "western fighting cock" who acted with primal instinct and nerve. Rosenberg said,

> The construction of such public myths is hardly a random process, and the contrast between the popular images of Jackson and Garfield may well reflect the need of an increasingly stable and institutionalized society to articulate new and more appropriate ideals of behavior.[83]

On the other hand, Guiteau, born in 1841 as the son of a pious and stern bank cashier and county clerk in Freeport, Illinois, was portrayed in *Gazette* accounts and elsewhere as the deluded product of indolence, vanity, and deceit. Not motivated to murder because he was a "disgruntled office seeker" as he was to be portrayed in some popular histories, Guiteau was mentally ill and deranged, and he said he killed the president because he was told by God to do so. But the *Gazette*, like many in the press of the time, was skeptical of his claimed insanity, preferring to contend that his crime was the result of living a "wretched life." In the last sentence of the story just above the account of Cowell's rape, the *Gazette* said merely of Guiteau's defense that at his Washington trial his counsel "called several unimportant witnesses to prove Guiteau's insanity."[84] His trial antics were regarded with a certain disdain, but they were presented in the *Gazette* so as to reflect Guiteau's calculating manner, not his madness:

> For two hours the counsel and the prisoner kept up their war of words, and Guiteau manifested much cunning in detecting the traps that were prepared for him in the examination.
>
> On Friday morning Guiteau announced to the court that he would answer no more questions going over old ground, and when Judge Porter addressed him, coolly took up a newspaper and began to read. He was finally prevailed on to reply, but was very snappish with Porter, whose habit of pointing his finger was very offensive to the prisoner. Being pressed for an answer to the question why if he was inspired by the Deity he did not shoot the President on the 18th of June when he was at the depot with Mrs. Garfield, he replied:
>
> "It depended on whether I had a suitable opportunity. If your head is so thick that you can't get the idea in, I won't try to pound it in. Don't ask your questions in a mean, sickly sort of way."

The prisoner was very "cranky" throughout the last day's examination, which he concluded by shouting at the counsel:

"I feel remorse for what I did so far as my personal feelings are concerned, but my duty to the Lord and American people overcame my personal feelings. If the Lord had not inspired the act it would not have been done!"[85]

In an editorial page item, Fox or one of his writers remarked that "Guiteau outdid himself as a 'crank'. . . . 'The assassin manifested great cunning in parrying the counsel's questions, and gave every evidence that if he be mad, indeed, there is much 'method in his madness.' "[86]

Apparently he elected to continue his acts of delusion up to his death. After having sent for his shoes to be shined on the morning of his execution, Guiteau was hanged at noon on June 30, 1882. He had eaten a hearty breakfast and supper and composed a poem in which he proclaimed (and read before his hanging), "I am going to the Lordy, I am so glad. . . . I saved my party and my land,/ Glory Hallelujah! But they have murdered me for it/And that is the reason I am going to the Lordy,/ Glory Hallelujah! Glory Hallelujah!"[87]

For journalistic purposes the sensation of the Guiteau story contrasted nicely with the rather mundane assault upon the honor of Estelle Cowell.

On the night of the "outrage," the *Gazette*'s account said, the owner of the house and his wife, Estelle Cowell's sister, had gone to a wedding. After drawing some cider from the cellar, Smith asked Cowell to play the organ for him. She demurred, saying she was too busy with her knitting.

"You can play well enough for me," he told her. She did not like the look of him and wanted to leave the house and seek refuge with neighbors across the road. But, "The ruffianly farm hand placed himself before the door and stopped her." He asked where she was going. She said she was going outside to remove some clothes from the grass. " 'Oh no you don't!' he cried; and thereupon he threw a cord about her neck, put his hand over her mouth and dragged her out of the house."

She broke the cord but the man then used a handkerchief to tie around her throat. "She lost consciousness, and the villain, after taking her to an orchard a hundred feet away, gratified his lust and then fled." He was later captured.[88]

The assassination of Garfield and the rape of Cowell were quite different kinds of crimes. But they were perfect stories for the *Gazette*— they illustrated the actions of evil men by framing those actions as the product of callous calculations. They were both cautionary tales offered to a jaundiced public. In a rational age every crime had its reason; Guiteau was no madman, and the nondescript farmhand named Joe Smith had been driven by simple lust.

The *Gazette*'s reporting on crimes and sensations covered the same clashes of class, gender, and race that marked the era. Fox may have considered these events as a sort of roadmap to danger, disaster, deviance—and deliverance. But his deliverance was not of the religious sort, but of what he regarded as the truth, the facts notwithstanding. Fox and his *Gazette* offered tales that served as illustrations—and illustrations that served as tales—of wrongs and rights of a society caught up in sexual, economic, political, racial, and ethnic whirlwinds. Making sense of it all was sometimes difficult to do. But for a few moments, the men who went to barbershops and saloons and hotels and newsstands and picked up a copy of the *Gazette* had a piece of entertainment that helped them—if not to make sense of it all, then to at least give them a chance to take it all in. In those moments they were a *community* of men who might chuckle at outlaws, cheer at fisticuffs, raise eyebrows at homosexuals, sneer at patrician hypocrites, gasp at rapists, rankle at blacks and Asians, or flush at showgirls. At the same time they might seek a new medicine for baldness or impotence, or consider buying a new book on card tricks or billiards. In other words, they might have had many diverse interests, but there was no doubt that they were men of the *Police Gazette*.

4

MASCULINITIES AND THE
MANLY ARTS

From his childhood he has been a great admirer of athletic sports and proved to be very clever with his mawleys. He displayed great agility as a wrestler and at the age of 19 was able to handle any of his comrades in a rough-and-tumble scrap.
—*National Police Gazette*, 1881 on fighter Paddy Ryan

If crime was one way for the *Gazette* to demonstrate some of the rights and wrongs of male behavior, then sports (and pseudo-sports) became its way of purveying male fantasies. The thrills of competition, the masculinities of athleticism, the fervor of spectatorship—all of these were specific images in the *Gazette*'s reflections of American manhood. And no sport served these purposes better than boxing.

Pugilism, wrote historian Elliott J. Gorn, was an almost perfect metaphor for the entire trend of masculine awareness during the nineteenth century; it was not just two men facing off in the ring, it was a "profession" with terminology that suggested a retaking of an "art" that men had lost as they became more urbanized and domesticated. Its practice was called a "science" and "craft," suggesting that men could *learn* to be more masculine in an age in which threats to masculinity were common. Working-class immigrants, particularly the Irish, used the sport as a signal of defiance and independence. Sociologist Michael Kimmel, in his studies of masculinities, has, like Gorn, connected boxing to the lower class' expressions of masculine prowess.[1] The *Gazette*, in interpreting, illustrating, and protecting masculinities for a generation of men, was in an ideal position to seize on the popularity of boxing. Its male readers were drilled with the knowledge that men not only had to be strong to win at boxing but also smart. Fox did not invent the term "plucky pugilist," but the phrase was often used in his writers' columns. Not only was boxing popular among the men who frequented taverns, where the *Gazette* was widely read, but matches were often held in the taverns (or sporting houses, as they were often called). Thus, boxing was a good way for participants to directly display manliness and for participants to show knowledge through informed wagering and speculation. Boxing also fit in with the health craze of the age, and it was mischievous; it was illegal in many jurisdictions and legal only for "exhibition purposes" in many others. In addition, pictures of boxers gave Fox a good excuse to repeatedly show men shirtless, often with fisticuffs raised. Boxers were both heroes and outlaws, men of both brawn and brain—in short, boxing amounted to a decisive way to answer challenges to dominant masculinities in the late nineteenth century.

As many historians have noted, the creation of a working-class man who was not bound to agriculture led to greater pursuits, both in leisure and in profession, of sporting activities. This applied to both the working class as well as to the middle class; meanwhile, many upper-class men enjoyed the spectator role, even through gambling at the local club. Sports not only served to emphasize some class differences, but they also bonded men to men and fathers to sons. "In fact," wrote historian Peter Stearns, "sports, enjoyed as either participant or spectator, increasingly became if not the real world, at least the best world, because they so clearly confirmed the male identity."[2]

In addition, physical health became an important consideration for men, scientists, and the mass media. Some doctors were worried about the new disease of "neurasthenia"—the malady of middle-class men who were supposedly worried about business life and thus neglected their physical well-being. Homosexuality, which had long been punishable as criminal offense, was also being studied as a disease or deformity in the male body.

Meanwhile, popular images of the perfect male body were changing, according to historian Gail Bederman:

> In the 1860s, the middle class had seen the ideal male body as lean and wiry. By the 1890s, however, an ideal male body required physical bulk and well-defined muscles. . . . Middle-class men's new fascination with muscularity allowed strongmen Eugene Sandow and Bernard McFadden to make fortunes promoting themselves and marketing bodybuilding magazines like *Physical Culture*. By the 1890s, strenuous exercise and team sports had come to be seen as crucial to the development of powerful manhood. College football had become a national craze; and commentators like Theodore Roosevelt argued that football's ability to foster virility was worth even an occasional death on the playing field.[3]

The physical evolution of city life contributed to the development of organized sport and recreational activities. Urban areas, wrote social historian Steven Riess, helped lead to a mass of sporting activities, such as billiard halls and bowling alleys, ballparks, racetracks, sporting clubs, and professional teams. The cities were not merely passive geographic areas that provided audiences and participants—they were political entities that actively encouraged the creation of communities and identities that led to the growth of sports. Between 1830 and 1860, cities grew at astounding rates, increasing by more than 90 percent in population during the decade of the 1840s.[4]

Along with cities, sports became a way of life that set apart classes and ethnic groups as well as men and women. They were forces for order and methods for assertion of masculinity, and they helped influence landscapes by encouraging park construction as well as arena development. Riess argued that cities provided venues for working-class participatory sports, such as billiards or bowling. At the end of the nineteenth century 140 Chicago taverns had billiard tables; by 1909, half of that city's 7,600 saloons had pool tables.[5] Other sports were almost as ubiquitous; boxing, baseball, basketball, and bodybuilding provided outlets for ethnic men to assert their masculine prowess. Riess wrote, "The sport that probably best fit in with the urban slum environment was pugilism. Because boys and young men from different ethnic backgrounds were constantly getting into fights to protect their honor or their turf, self-defense was a very useful skill to learn."[6] Tied to the notion of ethnic identify was the concept of racial superiority in physical pursuits, which took the form of scientific racism and eugenicists' efforts to purify genes. This was a result of an imperial outlook, wrote cultural scholar John Beynon, that manifested itself in the pursuit of physical excellence as "proof" of (white) male superiority.[7]

Because industrialization had de-emphasized physical strength, a myth of "degeneracy" of masculinity developed. The response, wrote Beynon, was a "spectacular rise in popularity of a particular aspect of sport, namely physical training or 'physical culture.' "[8] In postbellum America, men also longed for the old barracks, the campfire, and the battlefield, wrote Pleck and Pleck. Life was seen as a physical battle, whether it involved resolute Indians still holding out on the plains, labor fights against management, or American interventions in Hawaii, Panama, the Philippines, Cuba, and Mexico.

All this love of soldiering served to initiate a cult of body building. . . . The rise of organized athletics was one feature of this cult. Whereas prior to the war college athletics had been discouraged, soon after it manly competition was encouraged.[9]

As shown previously, sex, crime, and sports were the staples of the illustrations featured in the *Gazette*. But Fox was too savvy to risk becoming committed to a formula that might bore his readers, so he varied the emphasis over the years. For example, over the nearly three decades studied in a content analysis conducted of *Gazette* illustrations in 1879–1906, the number of illustrations featuring sports was at first relatively small, with an average of less than a page for each sixteen-page issue. By the mid-1880s, however, Fox—having seen his circulation skyrocket with sporting, particularly boxing, coverage—sometimes featured two or more full pages of illustrations showing sporting activities[10] (see table 4.1).

By the end of the 1880s, sports were often a subtext—or a head-lining text—even when the *Gazette* featured a familiar woodcut on crime or sex. For example, in a cover woodcut that ran in October 1888, the *Gazette* depicted a young actress appearing in a production of "Mountain Park" at Green's Opera House in Vincennes, Indiana, as she suffered a torn gown when her father rushed backstage to confront the production manager. He demanded the proceeds of three nights' performances, but the manager, Mr. Pringle, refused, whereupon the actress's father, Mr. Sachs, clutched him by the throat and dragged him before the footlights. Three weeks later Mr. Sachs, Mr. Pringle, and Sachs' distressed, disheveled daughter won the equivalent of the nineteenth-century's fifteen minutes of fame—an appearance on the cover of the *National Police Gazette* (figure 4.1). The woodcut depicted a violent act—a fierce on-stage struggle between the two men, with one of them (Mr. Pringle) on his knees—but it also included the provocative motion of the gown flapping

Table 4.1 Average number of inside pages per issue of portrayals of boxing and bodybuilding at five-year intervals

Year	Boxing	Bodybuilding
1880	.208	.05
1885	.600	.125
1890	1.55[a]	.0
1895	.875	.05
1900	1.267[a]	.117
1905	2.757[a]	.986[a]
T.(1879–1906)	1.05	.283

Note: [a] Tukey HSD post hoc for analysis of variance shows significant differences at the .01 level in increased averages of inside illustrations comparing 1880 to these years.

DRAGGED BEFORE THE FOOTLIGHTS.
THE ALLEGED FRACAS BETWEEN MANAGER PRINGLE AND MR. SACHS AT VINCENNES, IND.

Figure 4.1

across the fleeing daughter. Above the illustration was a promotion for the inside coverage of the Jack McAuliffe–Mike Conley prizefight and the new Jake Kilrain song. For *Gazette* editors, who had in hand a nice cover showing boxing, an assault, and a showgirl (the neat journalistic hat trick of sport, crime, and sex), it made little difference that all that came of the matter was the arrest of the two men and the disbanding of the "Mountain Park" company. What really mattered was that there was action, there was boxing, there was crime, and there was theater—perfect ingredients for the *National Police Gazette* in 1888. This November 10 issue, which featured the fight in Vincennes, was similar to about half of all the others in that year because it included an assault and a boxing headline.

By the early 1900s sports became even more prominent, with five or six pages devoted to pictures of sports (see table 4.1). As shown before, illustrations showing criminal activity dropped. Crime coverage was heaviest in Fox's early years until the early 1890s, but then it began to taper off until, at the turn of the century, crime illustrations became rare. The *Gazette* still carried stories about crime, but the illustrations largely disappeared.[11] Perhaps not surprisingly, the most consistently placed illustrations over the years were those featuring sexually provocative activities, glamor shots of women, or theatrical "poses" with sexual undertones. These were the most common in the late 1890s, but pictorial content of a sexual nature never varied widely, and even in the twentieth century the glamor girls remained a key ingredient of the Fox formula. The *Gazette* carried significant differences in the number of boxing illustrations over the years, with that subject matter increasing to an average of more than two pages per issue by 1905. Bodybuilding and "beefcake" pictures (figure 4.2), often interchangeable with boxing portrayals, also increased[12] (see table 4.1).

It is clear that these ingredients were at least partly the result of sociological forces that were acting upon many aspects of the great changes in sex roles, city demographics, class lines, leisure time, and media competition in late-nineteenth-century America. Simply put, the *Gazette* content did not exist in a vacuum, and it was not simply a conductor of societal trends but was also the product of historical influences.

Media researchers Pamela J. Shoemaker and Stephen D. Reese developed a hierarchical model describing various forces that "tug, pull, squeeze, and ultimately form mass media content."[13] The model identified influences that act at five different levels to form media content—the influences of individuals' actions, media routines, organizational pressures, extramedia factors, and ideological sources.[14]

Figure 4.2

The innermost area of the Shoemaker and Reese model of concentric circles was defined as the realm of individuals. Here are the individuals who create news and entertainment (and other forms of content) for the media. Shoemaker and Reese considered the characteristics of reporters, line editors, copy editors, photographers, and others who contribute to the news process. These individuals often share certain demographic, educational, political, and socioeconomic traits that tend to influence the way that choices are made about content. Shoemaker and Reese argued that individuals' personal and professional backgrounds and beliefs can and do make a difference in the type of content that they produce.

Next, media routines were considered by Shoemaker and Reese in terms of such factors as gatekeeping, sourcing, journalistic professionalism, and news values. The routines are within the structure of the organization and contain a variety of potential influences, from the way a reporter approaches his beat to the social interaction and social control of the newsroom. Shoemaker and Reese contended that values such as prominence, proximity, conflict, human interest, timeliness, and the unusual may be said to be routines in news production because they are part and parcel of the newsgathering process.

Organizational influences enveloped routines at the next level of the Shoemaker-Reese model. These influences included policies, structures, and finances at the level of the media organization itself. The researchers argued that enforcement of these influences may or may not be overt, but they can become factors in content because among the media organization employees, there is an awareness that they exist.

Shoemaker and Reese next highlighted extramedia influences on content. These were defined by the authors as materials, events, and people who directly interact with message producers to shape content. Examples are press releases, publicity agents, press conferences, advertisers, and staged or pseudo events that sometimes provide raw materials for news and entertainment production.

Finally, the area encompassing the largest space in the model was summed up by Shoemaker and Reese as ideology. In a sense, ideology may be considered an extramedia factor, but Shoemaker and Reese, citing Raymond Williams,[15] defined it more broadly as a system of meanings that indirectly act on content by including the society's doctines, codes, worldview, or outlook. Ideology serves as an influencing factor not just in obvious ways but also in ways of social hegemony, defined as the means by which the ruling class maintains its dominance. For example, in a capitalist system, capitalism is the hegemonic model for society. Challenges to capitalist notions may be met with disdain or distrust; individuals or organizations that do not adhere to the elite's views may be treated differently in news accounts. Shoemaker and Reese also advanced the notion of deviance as a control mechanism. Deviance from norms (or the hegemonic conception of norms) may be highlighted in news accounts, and the news value of objectivity in these cases, said the authors, may be discarded.[16]

The content of Fox's *Gazette* may be examined through consideration of any or all of the influences discussed by Shoemaker and Reese. However, given the broad societal influences at work in this era, the ideological sphere of influences was chosen as a method of examining content of the Fox *Gazette*.

As has been discussed, defining features of late-nineteenth-century America included the reactions of men and women to rapid changes in their ways of life caused by aspects of modernity such as urbanization, industrialization, immigration, and changing sex roles. During this period people were adapting to new roles and expectations, and The *Gazette* was portraying both sides of the coin—the changing sex roles as well as the traditional notions of hegemonic masculinity that served many of its male readers in barbershops and saloons. The *Gazette*, subtly as well as overtly, acted in part as a sort of ideological and behavioral policeman for the world it covered.

For Shoemaker and Reese, a prime consideration of today's ideological atmosphere for U.S. news outlets was the dominance of the capitalist/private ownership system, and they maintained that much of today's content is shaped by an adherence to this dominance. For Fox and his late-nineteenth-century editors, dominant considerations included the growing interest in sports for men to watch and follow, the large numbers of women who broke barriers in provocative new ways, and the hedonism of the city and its redefinitions of the way of life of the American male. All of these forces may be considered as threats to masculinities or, on the other side of the coin, as responses to changing masculinities. Any medium has the power to define a situation that gives it an ideological power; for the *Gazette* it was how men were to react to the threatening, scurrilous, humorous, conflicting, and scary state of the rapidly changing world.

As Shoemaker and Reese noted, "One of the key functions performed by media is to maintain boundaries in a culture. To integrate societal interests, some views and values must be defined as within the bounds of acceptability, whereas others are read out of legitimacy."[17]

The *Gazette* acted as a method of social control for its readers by communicating deviant behavior, much of which threatened the status of males. As noted, a key point is that media do not act to marginalize deviant behavior through lack of coverage; instead, media often "play up" deviant behavior to emphasize its deviance. In fact, as Shoemaker and Reese point out, "News selection criteria themselves may be said to be based on dimensions of deviance, including the controversial, sensational, prominent, and unusual."[18] The *Gazette* sometimes thus acted as a control mechanism for "right" behavior (as it often pointed out). This is consistent with Shoemaker's and Reese's comment that in media coverage, "The normal is reaffirmed by being presented . . . in juxtaposition to the deviant," while those at the deviant margins of society compete for attention through "protests, strikes, or crime"[19] (or, it may be added after a review of *Gazette* pages, they also competed for attention by fighting, jumping off bridges, or showing their bloomers).

In advancing the argument that the *Gazette* represented and encouraged certain forms of masculinities, it is helpful to consider how masculinities are constructed and formed. As has been discussed, criminological studies include the "structured action theory" of crime causation—or, more accurately, of gender identification as a factor in crime causation—that emphasizes the construction of gender as a "situated social and interactional accomplishment."[20] Put more simply, gender is not merely a condition but also a construction and an act of construction. It is a creation that results from social practices that take place in historical, cultural, and social settings, and its creation also influences such settings and the practices within them. Sex categories may be defined, as well as manipulated and maintained, through social identifications and interactions associated with one's gender. But in a larger context one's sex, as well as what it means, is known and learned through the interplay of the specific social relations and historical context in which it is found. According to criminologist James W. Messerschmidt, in social settings we engage constantly in sex attribution, thus categorizing ourselves and others. "Doing gender" is more than adopting the social emblems of our sex—it systematically corroborates that identification through social interaction, he maintained. There is a plurality in our actions: We manipulate and change our activities to do gender in situational ways, and situations vary across time and across cultures.[21]

An important feature of this notion is accountability. People know that others may hold them accountable for their sexual identifications, so they change their conduct in relation to how such actions may be interpreted by others in different situations (or historical periods). So, according to Messerschmidt, at its heart doing gender is different in different situations, and it involves norms of perceptions that fit in with one's sex category in the specific situation in which one acts. It is an active accomplishment, it is reciprocal, it is self-regulating, and it is never finished. When people do gender, they do it under specific structures of society, under structured action.[22]

As we have seen, in Fox's America one structured action was the rise of the saloon. Another was the creation of the Boy Scouts. Another was the growth of cities. Another was the sporting world. Another was the assertion of new roles for women; and finally, another was the conduct of deviant criminals described as overrunning the cities. Media portrayals can, and do, have an important affect on gender identifications, and one argument here is that the *National Police Gazette*, along with other publications of the era, helped create notions of masculinity that endure even today by a "framing of structured action" that has already been mentioned.

Sociologist R.W. Connell attempted to tie together the notion of gendered power relationships (the relationships of labor, power, and sexuality). He wrote that these are gendered social structures, and they happen only through social action. We can change social structures, and they can change our perceptions (this is one reason we speak of masculinities and femininities in the plural, according to Connell). But there is, at any given time, a "hegemonic masculinity" that is a "configuration of gender practice which embodies the currently accepted answer to the problem of the legitimacy of patriarchy."[23] During Fox's heyday, this hegemonic masculinity was threatened, was changing, was fighting back, and was retreating all at the same time.

Connell's notion of hegemonic masculinity is defined as a "culturally idealized" form of masculinity in a given historical and social setting. Thus, it varies over time, in societies, and among institutions. It is the dominant masculinity and is the popularly glorified form, and it is built in relation to subordinated masculinities based on race, class, and sexual preferences. Connell defined two other kinds of masculinities, which he called oppositional masculinities, that are helpful in defining the hegemonic masculinities. One type is the subordinated masculinities, which he said includes the "gay," "wimps," "cream puff," "candy ass," and "nerds."[24] Oppositional masculinities may include the freaks or the "toughs."[25] (It is important to realize that these types, as well as others, may be represented and framed in the mass media, including, for the purposes of this discussion, in the *Gazette*.) In addition, he contended that those representing the hegemonic masculinities may be stereotyped as part of syndromes or types—that is, as jocks or strongmen—but he also pointed out that one may notice that a large number of men fit into the hegemonic model without being bodybuilders or boxers.

> This can be done by recognizing another relationship among groups of men, the relationship of complicity with the hegemonic project. Masculinities constructed in ways that realize the patriarchal dividend, without the tensions or risks of being the frontline troops of patriarchy, are complicit in this sense.
>
> It is tempting to treat them simply as a slacker version of hegemonic masculinity—the difference between the men who cheer football matches on TV and those who run out into the mud and the tackles themselves. But there is often something more definite and carefully crafted than that. Marriage, fatherhood and community life often involve extensive compromises with women rather than male domination or an uncontested display of authority. A great many men who draw the patriarchal dividend also respect their wives and mothers, are never violent towards women, do their accustomed share of the housework, bring home the family wage, and can easily convince themselves that feminists must be bra-burning extremists.[26]

Sociologists became interested in structured action, in part, as a way of explaining the causes of crime. But structured action theory is not considered a general theory of crime because masculinities and femininities vary so much from situation to situation. Still, studies suggest there is an importance in the role of gender in leading to crime, or to the creation of racial expectations, or to the requirements of class, or to the emphasis on the male sex role, or to other things that affect the conduct of our lives.[27] But students of the media may be more interested in structured action theory from the perspective of considering media outlets as creating or reinforcing factors in the structures—of framing—that lead to the gendered action.

This helps to explain why the *Gazette*'s crime portrayals—in addition to its sexual and sporting portrayals—fit in with the overall model of it as a purveyor of masculinities. In the *Gazette* pages the oppositional masculinity of a Jesse James might get a wink and a nod because of the romanticism of his role as a tough guy. But James was nevertheless portrayed as an example of an oppositional masculinity who did not abide by the rules and authorities of the mainstream patriarchal society. Also condemned in the *Gazette* was the cowardice of a "masher," or assaulter of a woman on a street corner. Messerschmidt noted that hegemonic masculinities emphasize, in varying degrees and in different situations, "authority, control, independence, competitive individualism, aggressiveness and the capacity for violence."[28] This type is always constructed and it may not be consistent. In some cases, in crime causation, violent men have "bought into" the connection of violence with hegemonic masculinity.

Challenges to hegemony exist in any diverse society, as America certainly was in the nineteenth century. When hegemonic masculinities are threatened, the threats can result in masculine "degradation" and may require a response. Messerschmidt noted that these challenges could arise from threats from peers, teachers, or others, or from an uneasiness that certain masculine goals may not be achievable. Thus, threats may cause movement toward masculine goals. Men and boys pursue gendered action strategies, he wrote, to reinforce their masculinities in keeping with dominant notions of hegemonic masculinity.[29] This same concept can be applied to society as a whole, particularly during the turbulent nineteenth century.

Framing of structured action can happen in ways that are subtle as well as overt. In November 1880, on page 2 of an issue Fox offered an engraving of a scene from an old international prizefight involving Heonan, the "Benecia Boy," and Englishman Tom Sayers:

This interesting picture represents the scene at the battle-ground at Farnborough, Eng., at the opening of the "mill," the two gladiators having just "put up their mawleys" for action. Grouped about the ring are four hundred of the leading sporting lights, at that time, of the world, every one of whom can be easily recognized, special attention having been given to the preservation of their countenances. "Cheek by jowl" with America's champion, and afterwards statesman, John Morrissey, are old Lord Palmerston, England's great premier; Lords, Dukes, Earls, Sportsmen of every nation and class, all shoulder to shoulder, spectators of the greatest exhibition of muscle, pluck and science of modern times. To every sporting man, and every one who admires courage and muscle, this picture will prove valuable and interesting. Connoisseurs in famous sporting pictures cannot fail to appreciate the gift, its original being very rare.

The presentation of this engraving is intended as a personal compliment to the loyal patrons of the *Police Gazette* who have contributed by their continued approval of its efforts to please by word and substance. To successfully reproduce a picture of this great battle will involve a large expenditure of money and skill; but the publisher will be amply compensated for the outlay by the knowledge that he enhances the merits of the *Police Gazette*, universally conceded by all to be the handsomest and best sporting and sensational journal in America.[30]

The engraving was meant for any who might purchase it, but it was particularly for display in taverns as well as barbershops—in other words, where the men were. Similarly, in March 1881, Fox offered an engraving of prizefighter Sayers and a opponent named Heenan, free to all who signed up for a $4 annual subscription to the *Gazette*, and it was "suitable for framing. No Saloon, Restaurant or Sporting House should be without it."[31]

This was simply another method for Fox to link his success to that of tavern patronage. It was by no means lost on him that the tavern served as a male haven away from the constraints of the home. The saloon was becoming one of the most popular gathering places for men—and an excellent source of circulation for the *Gazette*.

In 1901 (as well as in other years) Fox championed what he considered one of his best ideas—the *Police Gazette*'s "Bartender's medal." In this contest thousands of bartenders sent in their favorite drink recipes. The medal was won by bartender Peter F. Sindar, twenty-seven, of St. Paul, Minnesota, an amateur billiards player whose "Elk's Fizz" included whiskey, port wine, and the white of an egg.[32]

The *Gazette* said Fox was grateful for the interest:

> It is apropos here to thank the thousands of saloonmen and bartenders of the United Sates, for the deep interest they have manifested in the bartender's contest for 1901, and to assure them that the *Police Gazette* will always be at their service and devoted to their interests. A special feature will be made of the publication from week to week of recipes for new and novel drinks, and all portraits will be reproduced free of charge.[33]

Fox's repeated emphasis on alcohol is not surprising; the "cult of masculinity" in which boxers like John L. Sullivan flourished was "welded together by alcohol," as noted by Sullivan biographer Michael T. Isenberg.[34] Drinking, then, was another manly art. At the same time, in an act of conscience if not social control, Fox felt it was unseemly for any man to fall into the traps of the saloons, including addiction to alcohol, tobacco, or billiards: In 1881, an editorial remarked about an "an actual occurrence"[35] that illustrated the unfortunate effect of excise laws. These laws, enacted in 1857, required that any establishment selling alcohol was required to have sleeping quarters for at least three persons. The law was intended to keep drunks off the streets by making taverns double as "hotels," but the editorial claimed it merely promoted prostitution:

> Once inside the unholy precincts of the "hotel," the young man squanders his money in riotous dissipation, being ably assisted by his

fair friend, who carefully caters to his every taste, and when thoroughly "bled" he is thrown into the streets in a beastly state of intoxication.[36]

On its face this is a confounding example of *Gazette* content. Some historians, faced with the contradictions, have chosen to solve the problem by ignoring them. Fox has been described as a racist, sexist, and sensationalist—historian Gene Smith called Fox "a good hater"; boxing historian Gorn noted the racism and anti-Semitism in *Gazette* columns, finding its treatment of blacks particularly ugly.[37] But Fox would sometimes have his *Gazette* display egalitarian reserve. He hated weak men but often raved about strong women. He made fun of blacks but once insisted that lynchers of accused black criminals be brought to court to answer for their crimes. He could remark on the "beastly state of intoxication" while condemning the hypocrisy of those who would ban alcohol. One column warned of the "consequences of snuff chewing," noting that "the expectorations consequent upon the use of snuff produces an appetite for alcoholic stimulants."[38] Yet just below the item promoting the boxing engraving (for display in saloons) discussed above was a classic Fox diatribe against temperance advocates:

The glory of lager beer, ginger pop and soda slushes hath departed with the dog days, and now cometh the rampant, exhilarating, intoxicating, headaching hot scotch, rum whisky straight and good old "arf and arf." With the change of the seasons the mild rule of stomach-filling drinks gives way to old King Alcohol, the sweller of heads, the fuddler of reason, the forerunner of remorse, and, alas ! in the majority of cases, ruin and misery. His frisky subject, while bowing willingly to his rule, chafe at his will, knowing that he but lures to destroy.

With a consistency that would be admirable if the theories put forth were only supplemented by as much consistency in action, the enemies of old King Alcohol buckle on the armor and begin anew their warfare every time he resumes his winter throne. . . . On the platform, in the pulpit and through the medium of prosily-written tracts they attack his stronghold. So far these methods, while being considered good, have not proven very effective, especially the "tract" system of warfare. Before us is one of these documents, which states that in this "great and glorious country 60,000 people are marching to drunkards' graves." If this fact is authentic, it only goes to prove what has always been considered true of temperance reformers, that they are, to put it mildly, "harmless idiots." Fancy for a moment entrusting an important command of an army to a general who would follow up tactics of warfare that had proven disastrous every time they were put to use. But this is just what the generals of temperance reform do, and then have the brass to publish to the world. If tracts, appeals and "crusades" have resulted in accomplishing so little, why do their authors persist in following them up? That is a leading question, reader, but as we (modestly) assume to enlighten you on general matters, we will answer it. Nine-tenths of these reformers are humbugs, who follow their self-imposed duties just as you and I follow our regular occupations, and for the same purpose—to make money. The difference between ourselves and them is this: We are honest in our professions, assume nothing but what is legitimate, work openly and above board, using no mask, making no pretensions to piety or anything else outside of being human. They profess to be embodiments of philanthropy, piety and humanitarianism. . . . They spout tirades, hurl invectives and tell melting tales which make the angels weep o'er man's hypocrisy—and men who never drank before drink out of disgust and indignation. There is no sincerity in their efforts. Self and the almighty dollar is at the bottom of the whole business.

For these reasons 60,000 are annually marching to drunkards' graves.[39]

As has been shown, these varying stances were not contradictions but were consistent with the framing of structured action; a man might like to drink, but a true man did not lose control, and those who did were held up to as much scorn and ridicule as the weaklings who would not drink at all.

One wonders how the *Gazette* would have fared in a world empty of alcohol. Jon M. Kingsdale recounted the exponential growth of saloons in America's cities during this period, as "homes away from homes" for beleaguered men and as gathering places for male immigrants who often made certain pubs the center of Irish, German, Italian, or other ethnic communities. In addition, local saloons often served as union halls, because many other establishments or public buildings were not open to this sort of activity. This was during the rise of Progressivism, a key part of an attempt by some workers to retake male dignity in a changing workplace, and a chance for laborers to reassert themselves as idealized, hardworking heroes of ordinary life. Many saloons were for men only; some catered to the bourgeois, others to the lower working classes. When women were allowed in, it was often only because they were prostitutes. In addition, these corner saloons, ubiquitous in cities such as New York, Philadelphia, and Chicago, served as a sort of romantic gathering place for young boys. While the boys might not be allowed inside, they often gathered outside saloons, formed relationships with one another, and "hung out," as they watched their fathers drinking and doing much the same inside. The saloons, then, helped men of like minds and backgrounds form associations and relationships where they could talk about sports, politics, women, and work. They also served as a sort of reaction to women-influenced initiatives such as the temperance movement. While in many cases ethnic gathering places did not encourage assimilation of immigrants into the society outside the tavern walls, they did bring together men of like backgrounds, which was an important role in a rapidly changing world.[40]

So, by early 1881, with his circulation growing in taverns and barbershops, Fox had arrived at a formula that would emphasize the varying aspects of masculinity with provocative front-page images combined with a headline hinting at content about crime, sports, or sex. But it was clear which of these would soon be his primary emphasis, for Fox changed the slogan that appeared under the *Gazette* flag. It was, he announced weekly, "The Leading Illustrated Sporting Journal in America." A typical 1881 issue showed the kind of content that readers would find for years to come: two columns on "The American Prize Ring," the exploits of a champion skater Rudolph Goetz, a pictorial gallery of sporting heroes, including an equine master named Hiram W. Howe, and a full page of "sporting news" that included reports on billiards, walking contests, wrestling, oarsmen, scullers, and bird-shooting.[41] But it would be the sport of boxing—and the rise of a legendary champion whose exploits were celebrated in a widespread media spectacle that spanned the world—that would transform Fox's legacy as a publisher.

5

FOX AND SULLIVAN: THE BRAWL
THAT STARTED IT ALL?

The Fox may go to England
And the Fox may go to France,
But to beat John L., he can go to Hell,
And then he won't have a chance.
—Nineteenth-century schoolboy chant,
Edward Van Avery, 1930

Those who knew Richard Kyle Fox, and those who would write about him later, recognized that he was never above hearty self-congratulations, even to the point of creating his own legend. But no one is sure whether he or someone else was responsible for the near-perfect narrative that had him snubbed by boxing great John L. Sullivan on a rowdy night in a New York boxing-and-dance hall saloon. As the story goes, in early April 1881, Fox donned his Prince Albert coat and went to the famous Harry Hill's tavern on Houston Street to have a few drinks, smoke his ever-present cigar, and eat some roast beef. The bar and dance hall, with its trademark blue-and-red lantern outside, was well known among the sporting crowd of gentlemen; it was also a popular place for prostitutes and gamblers.[1] It was known to have been patronized by Oscar Wilde, Lillian Russell, Thomas A. Edison, P.T. Barnum (the building's landlord), and Diamond Jim Brady.[2] On that April evening, Fox was accompanied by his well-known sports editor, William E. Harding, and the two were given the royal treatment by the proprietor, Hill. But as they sat down, they noticed a crowd paying a great deal of attention to a man at another table. They realized at once that the man was Sullivan, the up-and-coming fighter from Boston.[3]

Sullivan had disposed of another fighter, Steve Taylor, a couple of nights earlier on the stage of the same room where the men were eating. Before that brief bout, Sullivan had made his usual boast of saying he would pay $50 to any man in the saloon who could last four rounds with him. Taylor took him up on the offer and lost in a single round. Sullivan apparently made quite a bit off the fight in wagers and generously paid Taylor $25 for agreeing to the offer.[4]

Like Fox, Sullivan was of Irish descent, but he was born in America on October 15, 1858, in a house near what is now Boston College. His mother said he had shown a propensity for strength at an early age; when he was not yet a year old, she said, he gave his aunt a black eye when she tried to pick him up.[5] By 1877, he had discovered a knack for fighting, and he firmly believed he could defeat all comers.[6]

Shortly after Fox and Harding sat down, Fox, in his brash manner, supposedly told Hill to tell Sullivan to come across the dance hall and meet him. Hill went over to the next table and delivered the message, but Sullivan, a known binge drinker who was surrounded by admirers and several empty glasses of champagne (or a stein of bourbon, depending on which account of the meeting is believed[7]), was in no mood to take orders from anyone. He told Hill to relay the message to Fox that if he wanted to meet him, then he had to come to his table.[8]

This scene, even if it did not happen exactly as legend has it, was a perfect setup for storytellers to come. It is repeated regularly in boxing lore; in a 2002 issue of *Sports Illustrated*, a writer claimed that the legendary 1889 Sullivan-Kilrain bout—considered one of the greatest prizefights ever—would never have happened had Fox (a driven showman who was the "Rupert Murdoch of his day") not been slighted by a drunken Sullivan on that night in Harry Hill's eight years earlier.[9] This claim may carry some weight because Fox was indeed, in 1881, embarking on the years of his greatest success, partly attributable to his insatiable ego and partly to his inarguable talent as a kingmaker. Somewhere over the next few years, Fox may have realized that he and Sullivan could be perfect foils. Fox, an egocentric media tycoon, helped create the first great American sports superstar; at the same time he would owe much of his success to a man he supposedly despised.

The historical context of the meeting between Fox and Sullivan is not in dispute. It was the golden age of American sport. Sociologist David B. Welky put the *Gazette* at the center of this era, crediting it with creating a "democracy of sport" by publishing sports histories and promoting participation by ordinary men and women. It also used sports as a tool to promote America's virtue by emphasizing fair play, encouraging fitness by attending to a higher physical and mental culture, advancing patriotism through international contests (such as yachting's America's Cup), and giving working-class men escape hatches and heroes during growing wealth gaps in the Gilded Age.[10]

This democratic urge was also apparent in Fox's attempt through the years, beginning in earnest in the 1890s, to build up a national interest in an annual "physical culture contest," with first place offering a gold medal worth $100. Young men between eighteen and twenty-five were to send in their pictures, with judges to determine who was the "physically supreme" specimen. These contests were open to all, with Fox boasting proudly there would be no color line in the contest of 1902.

John F. Kasson, a scholar on the development of physical fitness trends in the nineteenth century, wrote that (true or fictional) acts of physical strength and daring—such as those of strongman Eugene Sandow, Tarzan, or Harry Houdini—had the power to create legends and give a common interest to their fans. Thus, the

> appeal of Sandow, Houdini and Tarzan could unite followers of John L. Sullivan and Theodore Roosevelt; readers of newspapers as diverse as Richard Kyle Fox's *National Police Gazette*, Hearst and Pulitzer's metropolitan dailies, and the socialist *Masses*; admirers of Burt L. Standish's *Frank Merriwell at Yale* and Jack London's *The Call of the Wild*; and fans of the illustrator J.C. Leyendecker's Arrow Collar Man and the painter George Bellows's savage boxers.[11]

Houdini, ne Erich Weiss, served as a masculine symbol because of his ability to master the mysteries of the body, and he was celebrated for his incredible dexterity, stamina, and strength. For Kasson he was a symbol of freedom as well as what was possible, and he succeeded because he was able to challenge his body and the limits of his masculinity using the "synergy of inexpensive vaudeville entertainment, mass media information and newspaper and theatrical photography."[12] Further, figures like Sandow, Houdini, and Tarzan illuminated popular culture:

> They help us to understand more about how the shift to an advancing technological civilization was communicated to and apprehended by publics in North America and abroad. They tell us about how modernity was understood in terms of the body and how the white male body became a powerful symbol by which to dramatize modernity's impact and how to resist it. They reveal the degree to which thinking about masculinity in this period meant thinking about sexual and racial dominance as well. They also tell us that hopes and fears, aspirations and anxieties are often difficult to distinguish. Perhaps every dream is the sunny side of some nightmare; perhaps every cultural wish has a dark lining of fear.[13]

Sandow, an acrobat who first gained fame through acts of strength in appearances at English music halls, came to America in June 1893. His image was perfectly sculpted in the classical traditions of male muscular development that trace their origins to the very beginnings of Western culture. As Kasson noted, Sandow wore sandals and a loincloth, and in a famous 1894 picture by Benjamin J. Falk also wore a figleaf. His best-known stunt was his "human bridge," which he performed with his chest upraised and hand and feet on the floor as he supported a wooden platform. Three horses, with an advertised rate of £2,600, stepped on the platform and paused for about five seconds while he held the pose. "Starkly exposed as thoroughly publicized as he was, he became an icon of the hypermasculine who with his extraordinary muscular development literally embodied characteristics that many men and women believed were threatened by modern life," Kasson wrote.[14]

Some contradictions blurred Sandow's image. He claimed a regimen founded on medical science and sport, but he was essentially a vaudevillian and showman. His act was erotic to women and some men alike, but he never acknowledged it. He claimed to embody an ancient "heroic ideal of manhood that had been lost in the modern world, yet he turned his body into a commercial spectacle whose image was widely reproduced and sold."[15] Kasson maintained that Sullivan, too, was primarily an actor and showman, like Sandow and other masculine symbols of the era. Both were heralded as perfect specimens, and as if to prove the point both were examined by the nation's leader in physical education at that time, Dudley Sargent. Sullivan was pronounced not perfect—he was judged too specialized as a slugger. But Sargent proclaimed that Sandow was, indeed, perfect.[16]

Gazette coverage of Sandow came most notably in 1893, after he was shockingly horsewhipped by a woman on July 1 after he made a public appearance in New York. The *Gazette* offered gleeful coverage of the incident, which apparently happened after Sandow had refused to speak with the woman. Kasson pointed out that accounts of women beating up men were not unfamiliar to *Gazette* readers.

Accounts of women horsewhipping husbands, lovers and slanderers frequently emblazoned its pages, together with stories of (preferably young, ideally scantily clad) women, ranging from "plucky" to "insane," who punched, bit, stabbed, slashed, bludgeoned, and shot men. Plainly, these accounts aroused men, who found such gender-crossing punishments both provocative and disturbing.[17]

The woman who bested Sandow was called "Lurline, the Water Queen" in the printed accounts, but her real name was Sarah E. Swift. She claimed she had advanced money to train and develop Sandow and had helped him rig some strength contests by switching chains and coins that he had then broken.[18] Her story was symbolic of a larger truth. She became representative of the new kind of women who were not afraid to assert themselves, not content to behold men simply as protectors. For Kasson this also was reflected in *Gazette* advertisements that featured such touchy subjects as impotence and masturbation. Like Sandow's fall, Kasson wrote, "Such advertisements . . . suggest some of the deeper fears about manly power and virility, and the keen sense of shame that attended them."[19] In effect, the ads illuminated male inadequacies while advertising restorative powers for manliness, he wrote. Sandow, too, was a symbol of the inadequacy of ordinary men. Kasson reflected on the "phallic power of his muscles" as depicted in a *Police Gazette* illustration of January 27, 1894; the drawing of his chest being admired by women driven to fainting "set forth its own fantasy of phallic power and female response."[20]

This was the physical culture in which Fox and Sullivan found themselves; for both men, boxing was at the center of the ring. Arguments about its legality and morality aside, boxing had a concrete value to Fox. Through the 1880s and most of the 1890s, the *Gazette*'s circulation would be a healthy 150,000, but it spiked upward—sometimes dramatically—when he was able to whip up enough frenzy over various boxing matches. This circulation growth first came to Fox's attention in a big way in 1880, when coverage of the Paddy Ryan-Joe Goss match caused circulation to leap to more than 400,000.

Before Sullivan arrived on the scene, boxing was a thoroughly discredited activity. Bare-knuckle boxing, for which prizes were usually awarded, was illegal and often barbaric. In England a few rules had been adopted, but they still allowed such activities as kicking and scratching, and fighters often fought for hours until one of them could not stand. In 1835 the *Mirror* expressed "regret and alarm" that the "detestable" practice of prizefighting was gaining popularity in America.[21] Over the years, different groups emerged—those who supported the legal "amateur sparring," a "science" seen in sports clubs, and the more disreputable crowd who favored illegal prizefighting. But despite prohibitions in New York and elsewhere, prizefighting, with its allure of spectacle, took place (sometimes with police knowledge, sometimes without), and was described by Sullivan biographer Michael T. Isenberg as "most often involving a brace of

Irish Americans slugging each other before a motley assemblage sequestered at some remote site."[22]

Because of the circulation gains that largely resulted from his boxing coverage, Fox also was able to cash in, more and more, on advertising, eventually carrying two or more pages of classifieds that were testaments to masculinities. They offered impotence cures for "weak men," joke books, song books, racy pictures, cures for opium habits, wrinkle reducers, relief for ladies, syphilis cures, hangover relief, and restorative medicines to fight fits, depression, and "errors of youth" in the health-crazed age. Fox charged the remarkable rate of $1 per agate line, the same as such popular contemporary general-interest publications as *Leslie's Popular Monthly* and the *Ladies Home Journal.*[23]

Though all of Fox's greatest successes would come after that night at Harry Hill's, it is not difficult to imagine him even then flushed with the possibilities of fortune. As he was imbibing and enjoying himself, the room probably looked much as it was described in a *Gazette* account of a typical night at Harry Hill's: at center may have been a "young lady in a wig the color of 'yellow-jack molasses candy,' and a pair of pink tights," her singing displaying "her bosom lavishly," though the men would have tried to be gentlemanly enough not to notice. Boxers, sportsmen, and businessmen likely discussed coming fights. Fox was the center of some measure of attention at the club, which was no dive—indeed, a sign warned of improper conduct and implored, "Gentlemen will not smoke while dancing." Two years earlier the *Gazette* had run a full-page picture of the saloon showing women boxers, an orchestra, and inspired drinkers, and it tipped its hat to the club as the place for "young swells."[24] The young, dapper, mustachioed Fox was, no doubt, beginning to see himself as a powerful man and was supposedly taken aback by what he perceived as a personal affront by the young, husky fighter's refusal to come to his table. It might have been only natural for him to determine that the Bostonian should be taken down a notch—and over the next several years he would campaign far and wide for a worthy opponent for Sullivan.[25]

As noted earlier, in this crusade Fox would master the art of boxing promotion by becoming one of the first to sponsor ring matches with belts, cash, and other prizes awarded to the winners. He also would use these skills to gain publicity for other *Gazette*-backed sporting endeavors, such as shooting, canoeing, and archery. Over the objections of some, he would use pulp as a pulpit to fight against laws banning prizefighting. He would turn the *Gazette* into what its banner proclaimed it was: the "leading illustrated sporting journal in America."

And he did not stop at ordinary sports. He gave *Police Gazette* belts to dancers, rat catchers, drinkers, bridge jumpers, oyster openers, and even great steeple climbers. But his greatest achievements were in pugilism; upon his induction to the International Boxing Hall of Fame in 1997, Fox was credited with creating modern boxing.[26] During the period of 1881, when Sullivan and Fox met, through 1889, when Sullivan finally went into semiretirement after one of the most remarkable boxing records in history, perhaps no other one-two combination did more to popularize boxing—and bring it into modern respectability—than Fox and Sullivan. The *Gazette*'s boxing coverage began to take off in the early 1880s, with illustrations averaging about three-quarters of a page in 1882, increasing to more than a page in 1886, then varying somewhat until consistently amounting to a page or more from 1894 to 1906. At the same time, Fox increased coverage of bodybuilding or weightlifting, which were (at least conceptually) linked to boxing by the *Gazette*'s promotion of the quest for manliness and its regular depiction of shirtless, muscle-bound boxers next to muscle-bound bodybuilders. Even more of the bodybuilding illustrations occurred in the early part of the twentieth century. Interestingly, most of the cover art featuring boxing did not occur until after the twentieth century (for an exception, see figure 4.2), although Fox often used a boxing headline on his cover promoting inside coverage—nearly 30 percent of the headlines from 1879 to 1906 dealt with boxing (table 5.1), with the peak in 1889 at about 60 percent. Another 18 percent dealt with *Gazette* promotions for contests, which included bodybuilding as well as bartending competitions. These findings suggest what is apparent from the *Gazette* circulation patterns: that boxing, bodybuilding, and other contests were a good sales tool for Fox, although perhaps not visually striking enough for consistent cover art. The lurid and the sexy seemed to suit him better, and it fit the personality and later fed the historical remembrances of the *Gazette*. Headlines with more violent subject matter, including murder, rioting, and disaster, were also common. Headlines concerning showgirls, a topic probably better suited for pictures than words, made up 6.3 percent of the total (see table 5.1).[27]

Fox, of course, was not alone. During this era many newspapers and magazines seized upon the growth of sports as a way to boost circulation and self-promotion. Horse racing and yachting were two of the favorites—a successful defense of the America's cup brought an interest in yachting that one writer compared to the hysteria over Barnum's Jenny Lind, but baseball and football also were growing in popularity and were covered extensively.[28]

Table 5.1 Percent of subject matter of covers, 1879–1906
N = 278 (Total number of covers)

Sex	Males + females	61.7
	Females	30
	Males	8.3
Race	White	96.1
	Black	1.7
	Asian	1.7
	Hispanic	.4
Subject	Theater/glamour pose	24.8
	Other sexually provocative	20
	Drinking/carousing	15.7
	Fighting between women	7
	Defense by women	6.1
	Boxing	4
	Murder	3.5
Headlines (N = 198)[a]	Boxing	29.6
	Gazette promotions	18.2
	Murder	8.8
	Rioting	7.5
	Disaster	6.9
	Theatrical/showgirl	6.3
	Baseball	5.7

Note: [a] Total number of covers with headlines.

Sports historian John Rickards Betts summarized the growth of sporting publications as an outgrowth of changes in society:

> Organization, journalistic exploitation, commercialization, intercommunity competition, and sundry other developments increased rapidly after 1850 as the agrarian nature of sport gave way gradually to the influences of urbanization and industrialization.[29]

It was a simple formula. Urbanization increased the demand for spectator sports and facilities, and industrialization helped increase leisure time for the middle class and led to a demand for distractions for physical pursuits outside office or factory jobs. The YMCA's athletic clubs as well as neighborhood and regional gymnasiums, armories, and arenas gained attendance with better-built facilities and the installation of electric lights.[30] Betts noted,

> The rapid construction of college gymnasiums and the building of more luxurious clubhouses after the middle eighties stemmed in great

part from the superior appointments and more brilliant lighting available for athletic games, and much of the appeal of indoor sport [such as volleyball or basketball] was directly attributable to the revolution which electric lighting made in the night life of the metropolis.[31]

Betts credited William Randolph Hearst with creating the first sports section in 1895, with the use of Western writers, but for historian Frank Luther Mott an equally important development was Fox's assemblage of the first modern sports department in 1879.[32] But sporting coverage had been given a boost even earlier, in the 1830s, with the development of the Napier double-cylinder press, which enabled the printing of cheap and sensational papers focusing on horse racing, prizefights, and running in such publications as New York's *Sun* and the *Transcript*, and the Philadelphia *Public Ledger*. Also important were inventions such as the sewing machine, enabling mass production of uniforms, and standardization of equipment such as bicycles, pool tables, and fishing rods.[33]

Mott wrote that the sporting press owes its origins to William Trotter Porter, a Vermont journalist who went to New York City and began the *Spirit of the Times* in 1831. It covered rowing, horse racing, yachting cricket, and baseball. Following that publication were *The Whip*, *The Flash*, and *The Rake*, along with specialized publications focusing on billiards or chess. These sporting publications sometimes gave coverage to crime and sex, claiming that while they despised sensationalism, they were merely trying to help stamp out crime and other bad behavior. *Gazette* cofounder George Wilkes bought Porter's *Spirit of the Times* in 1856, changing it to *Wilkes's Spirit of the Times* and developing its reputation as a sporting publication. A year after the Civil War ended he sold the *Gazette* to former New York City police Chief George Washington Matsell; crushed by the parade of publications that were similar to it, Matsell sold out in 1872 to his engravers, who, as has been noted, later turned it over to Fox.[34]

The most important publication of the sporting period in the 1860s and early 1870s, Betts wrote, was the *New York Clipper*, begun by Frank Queen in 1853. It was a popularizer of baseball but also defended the prize ring, although some editors, such as Horace Greeley, derided boxing, calling it the sport of "the grog-shops and brothels and the low gaming hells." In the 1860s two leading sporting journals were George Wilkes's *Spirit of the Times* and the new *Turf, Field and Farm*, founded in 1865, which denounced pugilism. Betts concluded that sports were at first treated with caution by editors concerned with respectable journalism, but the *Gazette*, which wanted the "common man of the streets" in its circulation fold, ultimately realized its potential.[35] Historians Alan Nourie and Barbara Nourie credited Fox with foresight in having sports coverage eclipse even crime stories: "Soon [after Fox took over] the offices of the *Gazette* were the sports headquarters of the country and perhaps the world."[36]

This position of prominence may have given Fox an inflated view of the importance of his opinion about sports; he certainly pulled no punches in his promotion of boxing above all else. This led him to initially consider football, as practiced in the Ivy League, to be a more hypocritically physical sport than the "art" of boxing; thus, he disparaged it. In 1887 the *Gazette* covered but one football match, the game between Harvard and Yale on Thanksgiving. An accompanying illustration, wrote historian Michael Oriard, served as a "powerful visual rebuke to the claim that football was a 'scientific' game."[37] Oriard noted that the opening sentence of the *Gazette*'s account of the game served as a counterpoint to the coverage by the *World* and the *Herald*, by beginning with heroism but ending with ridicule:

> If the noble Roman who cheered as he saw the bloody coxcombs of distinguished gladiators, or the cavalier Spaniard who likes to see a countryman try to get at the bull before the bulls get at him, had taken a seat at the Polo Grounds Thanksgiving Day and seen but one act of getting a football on the ground and about twenty-two Yale and Harvard men in assorted positions on top of it, reminiscences of the stupid sports of old times would have driven him away to drown his mortification in Harlem beer.[38]

Oriard considered the *Gazette*'s opposition to football "genuine class anger." He wrote, "What galled was not brutality but class pretension" because the gentlemen sons at Harvard and Yale played football while belittling the brutality and stupidity of boxing, a sport aimed at a lower class.[39] In addition, the individual sports promoted by the *Gazette*, such as boxing, weightlifting, or even glass-eating or bridge-jumping, gave an entree into sport for lower-class men. That was something that the team-oriented college football, or baseball, could not provide as easily. Individual sports such as boxing provided members of immigrant groups a chance to become heroes within their own communities. In 1853, Jim Morrissey, a famed street brawler who was the son of Irish immigrants, won the American boxing championship, much to the pride of his followers. He later became lionized as a great fighter defending the Irish community against nativists in street fights with Butcher Bill Poole and the Bowery Boys.[40]

Oriard concluded that the development of football as an organized sport illustrated a nineteenth-century social movement that amounted to part class conflict, part masculine assertion. In this environment, the upper classes were sometimes defensive about their masculinities. In 1898 the *Chicago Tribune* defended the eastern establishment not as "dandies" but as the "swells" who went up San Juan Hill with Teddy Roosevelt in the Spanish-American War:

> They scoffed when we lined up with Teddy,
> They said we were dudes and all that;
> They imagined that "Cholly" and "Fweddie"
> Would faint at the drop of a hat.
> But let them look there in the ditches,
> Blood-stained by the swells in the van,
> And know that a chap may have riches,
> And still be a man![41]

To modern observers, the passions surrounding classifications of manliness might be difficult to understand. But this dispute, particularly involving whether football or boxing was the more humane and scientific pursuit worthy of male attention, involved class consciousness, medical science, and masculine diversions, all of which were at the heart of late-nineteenth-century American society. Fox was all too eager to point out the hypocrisy of those championing football while denouncing prizefighting.[42] Some, such as polemicist E.L. Godkin, consistently opposed brutality in all sports, but others drew a distinction between boxing and other sports because injury was its *intent*, while in other sports, injury was incidental.[43]

The *Gazette*'s coverage of football through the 1880s and 1890s was marked by "contemptuous irony and graphic accompaniment," noted Oriard; it ignored football altogether until 1874 when it ran a caption, dripping with irony, of a slugging brawl at a Princeton-Yale game: "Cheerful sport between the aesthetic young men of Princeton and Yale." An editorial added: "I saw more brutality, more punching, butting, yes, and kicking, between the Princeton bruisers and the Yale sluggers than in any glove contest that ever occurred in Madison Square Garden."[44]

Rather than having a negative effect on football, the *Gazette* observations may have actually helped the sport. "The Police

Gazette's promotion of prizefighting at the expense of college football asserted the rights of working men to their pleasures and recreations, against a double standard whose hypocrisy the Gazette persistently exposed," wrote Oriard. However,

> [e]ven if the *National Police Gazette* had enjoyed any cultural authority beyond the working-class masculine subculture of saloons and barbershops, its expose of football as no better than prizefighting might have contributed to the demise of football but could have had little effect on the legal status of prizefights. . . . By articulating a narrative of football as indistinguishable from prizefighting, it gave working-class males a share of the elite college game.[45]

Later, Oriard added,

> In mocking the pretensions of "gentlemen's" sport, the *Police Gazette* voiced the class antagonism of its readers. But the representation of football as a slugfest, and of its audience as the sort of sporting crowd that also patronized prizefights, cockfights, and dogfights, probably had another, unintended effect: making the game more attractive and accessible to working-class males for whom universities were alien institutions. In its campaign against football, the *Police Gazette* may have ironically helped broaden the college sport's audience.[46]

This distinction of class occurred in popular illustrations; depictions of crowds were different depending on who was being shown—the "sports" (in derbies) or the upper class (in top hats). These were "unambiguous symbols for different classes, for different audiences constructed in competing cultural narratives."[47] Oriard maintained that this was hardly surprising. The *Gazette*, after all, was offered at reduced rates to saloons and barbershops; these proprietors were *Gazette* heroes and had pictures of themselves in the publication. Other *Gazette* readers, including salesmen and laborers, frequented hotels and saloons, and the journal invited "sports" to send in pictures of themselves: "(long before Andy Warhol's time the *National Police Gazette* was offering ordinary Americans their fifteen minutes of celebrity)."[48] The publication offered writing that addressed readers as insiders, as part of a certain viewpoint and club, and, Oriard maintained, other daily press took up the multiple narratives, serving up larger-than-life gladiators, heroes who were violent as well as masculine. For example, the *Herald* and the *World* "embraced both sides of football's dialectic of manliness and class."[49]

As noted by sociologist Michael Kimmel, the increased attention to sports was not just simply because of growing opportunities for leisure in an industrialized age. Sports—and, by extension, a general health craze that included attention to bodybuilding and attempts to consume healthier mineral waters, spirits, and medications (many of which, as has been shown, were aimed at curing male ailments such as impotence or loss of hair, or male and female afflictions such as "neuralgia")—were a way to express and protect manliness and a competitive spirit. Nearly all sports saw a rapid increase in participation during this period, particularly such activities as baseball, college football, and boxing. Boxing was also a favorite sport of some ethnic groups, particularly the Irish, and Sullivan used that popularity to become what is often considered America's first super sports hero. As Kimmel pointed out, boxing was a catharsis for working-class men, many of whom had no sooner been cast into clerical and office work before they fought back in the prize ring.[50] It was, said Kimmel, a sort of proclamation announcing the return of the working-class artisan. Ernest Thompson Seton, who seized upon Englishman Robert Baden-Powell's ideas about scouting and helped form the Boy Scouts of America, remarked on boxing's popularity—and its opposition to "bookish" education—when he remarked, "What boy wouldn't rather be Sullivan than Darwin or Tolstoy?"[51]

As was Baden-Powell, Seton was worried that young men were becoming too feminized and he helped found the Boy Scouts of America specifically to address the problem. The slogan, "making big men of little boys," left no doubt about its purpose. As Daniel Beard noted in the Boy Scout manual,

> Wilderness is gone, the Buckskin man is gone, the painted Indian has hit the trail over the Great Divide, the hardships and privations of pioneer life which did so much to develop sterling manhood are now but a legend in history, and we must depend on the Boy Scout Movement to produce the MEN of the future.[52]

Founded in 1910, the Boy Scouts were in many ways an attempt to recapture the lost frontier (a development noted by historian Frederick Jackson Turner near the end of the nineteenth century) and to get men more involved in boys' lives. One concern was that boys had too much exposure to women. Fewer servants in middle- and working-class households meant that mothers became domestically dominant, and motherhood became sanctified. When the boys left home for school, they were met with even more women: four out of five elementary teachers were female by 1910, up from two out of three in 1870.[53] In addition, some working-class men did not spend as much time in the home as they had in an agrarian economy. And as these men looked around the workplace, they found that the women who did not have the income to remain full-time homemakers were taking clerical or office jobs, threatening their roles as breadwinners.[54]

Boys did not spend all their time at home with their mothers, of course. But schooling was not the answer: even the act of learning was considered sedentary and rather feminine. Because of urbanization, men who were raised on the frontier or on farms found themselves supporting their families in cities, where there were few opportunities to bind with nature. Scouting offered a way not just to teach physical activities, but also moral values, and rewards were linked to specific achievements, thus promoting individualism as well as pride and a competitive spirit. Kimmel noted that scouting advocate Robert Baden-Powell was an ideologue who saw hunting, fishing, and "bushcraft" as his way to push the virtues of the frontier. Scouts took an oath as a sort of rite of passage, reaffirming basic values of honesty, work and obedience.[55]

Generally speaking, these social movements can be seen as working throughout American society. Even capitalism became an expression of masculinity, according to sociologist R.W. Connell. It was not just that the "captains of industry" were American role models (who did their fighting in business affairs rather than on the frontier or in the ring), but the lower echelons of the capitalist workforce also were part of the masculine culture. He noted that America's popular heroes were gendered, and similar portrayals were found on both sides of the Atlantic: Paul Bunyan and Davy Crockett in America and Lawrence of Arabia in England. Connell, in this analysis, went a step further, claiming that empires themselves were gendered, along with the modern capitalist economy and its gendered division of power. He summed up history as a sort of gendered power struggle—from the New World's Conquistadors, to colonialism, to the growth of cities as centers of capitalism, to the rise of entrepreneurialism. In the development of modern societies, wrote Connell, there was a splitting apart of the old gentry masculinity, with its gradual displacement by new hegemonic forms, and the emergence of subordinated and marginalized masculinities. What followed were challenges to the gender order by women, the logic of gendered accumulation in capitalism, and the power of empire. In the nineteenth century, feminism rose as a form of mass politics, and there was a mobilization for women's rights, especially suffrage, in connection with the growth of the liberal state and its emphasis on civil rights. Women were active in reforms of morals and domestic customs, while violence was common in disputes among men. Even the creation of standing armies and officers' corps began to connect acts of violence to male rationality, Connell wrote. At the same time, the homosexual as a type became more clearly defined, thus preserving the hegemonic order through its definition of this "deviance." On the Western frontier, there was a contrast between the brawling fighter and the married (gentleman) farmer, according to Connell. Portrayals of masculine strength were part of James Fenimore Cooper's writings and Bill Cody's "Wild West Show," later leading to the creation of the Western as a film genre exemplifying masculine heroism.[56]

It was this atmosphere that set the stage for Fox to capitalize on the popularity of boxing. In 1878 he expanded the *Gazette* to sixteen pages, printed it on pink-tinted paper to attract attention, and sold it for a dime. To the network of barbershops and saloons he added hotels, in order to attract traveling businessmen. In 1879 he added a regular sports column. In 1880, astonished to see his circulation top 400,000 when he featured weekly coverage of the Joe Goss-Paddy Ryan fight, he vowed to make his journal the most important of the prize ring. On March 20, the sports editor, Harding, announced the formation of a sports department and invited submissions.[57] He subsequently cashed in by producing the voluminous *History of the American Prize Ring*.[58]

Harding was among those who covered the Goss-Ryan fight. The presses were busy for weeks after the match to satisfy demand from all over the United States and many places overseas. Goss and Ryan fought near Colliers, West Virginia, in June 1880, and after eighty-seven brutal and bloody rounds, Ryan emerged victorious. After that, the *Gazette* earned its nickname the "Barber's Bible" because of its ubiquitousness in barbershops, and Fox began giving out the trophies for which he became famous. Following the Ryan victory, Fox backed him and found Sullivan to be a worthy opponent.

One of the fights that impressed Sullivan's followers was on May 16, 1881, on a barge that had been towed by the *Sadie Ellis* to a dock on the Hudson River (the *Sadie Ellis* was later sunk by accident in a collision with the ferryboat *Seacaucus*, which was graphically illustrated in a *National Police Gazette* woodcut). That evening, aboard the barge to avoid authorities because the fight was illegal under an 1859 New York ordinance, Sullivan fought John Flood, a barrel-chested longshoreman. The Boston Strong Boy was so dominant that he became viewed with a certain sense of awe. The first blow of the fight sent Flood reeling, and after eight rounds Sullivan collected the winner-take-all stakes—$1,000. Sullivan contributed $10 to a collection for the beaten Flood after the fight, and the vanquished fighter received another $88 from sympathetic spectators.[59] The *Gazette* did not sponsor the fight, but it capitalized by publishing a woodcut of the scene aboard the barge, in what is believed to be the first artistic representation of Sullivan in action.

Following the Flood fight, it was apparent that a Sullivan-Ryan match was inevitable. Ryan, another Irish immigrant, was backed by Fox with a stake of $1,000. In those days, each fighter's camp posted a certain amount of money, and the winner was to take the entire purse. As the sport grew, boxing backers developed rules in order to silence some of the criticism—the twenty-nine London Prize Ring Rules, generally adopted in 1838, were among the first efforts to corral some of the violence. However, those rules allowed for bare-knuckled brawling, a practice later forbidden under the rules authored by the Englishman Henry Sholto Douglas, eighth Marquis of Queensberry. The 1866 Queensberry rules outlawed wrestling and grappling holds, required boxing gloves, and established three-minute rounds, with a minute of rest in between. Queensberry rules, slow to be uniformly adopted, usually designated a specific number of rounds, but fighters often agreed to fight beyond any set limit and would thus "fight to the finish."[60] By Sullivan's day, boxing was illegal in jurisdictions covered by the thirty-eight states, including New York, but the enforcement varied widely. Some states permitted boxing "exhibitions" or amateur boxing; others had penalties so minor that any prohibition was virtually meaningless. Fox lobbied for a change in attitudes; the *Police Gazette* lauded the sport as a "manly art" that promoted fitness as well as sharpness of mind and feet. A new era of legality dawned when Sullivan was defeated by "Gentleman Jim" Corbett in 1892 under the Queensberry rules, with gloves; that marked the end of bare-knuckle brawling and gave new legitimacy to the sport.[61]

For the Ryan-Sullivan fight, Fox was to ultimately guarantee half of the purse of $5,000, with Hill designated as the stakeholder. The attention given to the fight was unequaled; Fox trumped his competitors by offering weekly coverage of the training. The men met in Mississippi City, Mississippi, on February 7, 1882, even after the Mississippi Legislature heard of the planned fight and passed a bill banning prizefighting (the fight had been originally scheduled for New Orleans but was moved when Louisiana authorities threatened action). On January 28, a train left New York City carrying so many from New York that, according to the *Gazette*, "Gotham was depleted of her fancy element almost entirely." In defiance of the boxing ban, the men squared off in front of the Barnes Hotel in Mississippi City.[62]

In order to fully cover the fight, the *Gazette* added eight pages to its normal run of sixteen. Even the fighting colors of the men were described in minute detail—with Ryan's colors, the colors of the "*Police Gazette* champion"—said to represent America, Ireland and New York:

> On white silk is a border of red, white and blue, our national colors. In the center is an eagle standing on a globe, the latter colored blue and dotted with stars. Beneath is the inscription, "Paddy Ryan, Champion of America." The eagle holds a scroll with the inscription, "POLICE GAZETTE, New York, 1881." In the left hand corner is an Irish harp, which is an emblem of the Fenian Brotherhood. In the lower right-hand corner "Excelsior" represents the seal of New York.[63]

These colors were hung in the barber shops and saloons whose proprietors were regular subscribers to the *Gazette*. In the supplement available a week after the fight, an artist titled the great match "The Battle of the Giants," but only one giant emerged. Sullivan dispatched Ryan with "sledgehammer smashes."[64] The *Gazette* described the battle this way:

> Paddy was game throughout, and came up like the Trojan he is before the sledgehammer blows of his antagonist, getting in with vigor and a gameness that were declared admirable on all hands. He was making a gallant fight in every respect, but after the fifth round it was detected by his friends that Sullivan's blows were telling the more severely.[65]

Sullivan won by knockout in the ninth round. Fox offered Ryan $5,000 for another fight with Sullivan, and a rematch was eventually held almost three years later, with Sullivan winning again.[66] Although it was clear who Fox's favorite was, he could not have been all that unhappy with the first outcome. The *Gazette* noted in its pages that its special supplement on the fight had sold more than 300,000 copies, twice its normal run.[67]

Given the immense publicity that Sullivan afforded the sport of boxing, it was obvious that a win by Sullivan only served to set up the next big fight, which could be trumpeted in the *Gazette*. But when Sullivan was presented with the championship belt after the first fight, he refused to accept it, calling it a "dog collar."[68] Even though he knew Sullivan was probably good for the sport and thus good for the *Gazette*, Fox took offense at the comment, and he next brought in

British middleweight Tug Wilson to serve as an opponent. At first Sullivan said Wilson (a squat five-eight) was too small to fight, but eventually became convinced when enough prize money was put up. More than 5,000 people paid as much as $5 a seat, and it was the biggest crowd yet to come see Sullivan. The fight was held in Madison Square Garden on July 17, 1882, and Sullivan performed poorly. He failed to knock out Wilson, who used evasive maneuvers to keep Sullivan off balance. Wilson backpedaled, fell down intentionally or was knocked down nine times in the first round alone, but he avoided most of Sullivan's serious blows. It had been an obvious setup to beat the terms of the match—that a man could not "last" with Sullivan for four rounds. Fox crowed that Wilson had won $11,000, an absurdly high figure, and he and his group departed for Hill's saloon, where "the wine flowed like water."[69] An angry Sullivan accused his manager, Billy Madden, of double-crossing him, and the two parted ways but only temporarily.[70]

In many ways the early heyday for Fox and the *Gazette* was during this period, 1882–83. In 1883, Fox opened a new building with a view of the construction of the Brooklyn Bridge. On the bridge's grand opening, May 24, Fox threw a gigantic party, to which he invited some of the nation's most illustrious citizens, including the president, Chester A. Arthur, who declined to attend because of his busy schedule in attending the bridge opening. The fireworks, called by the *Gazette* "decorations on the exterior of the building," were said to be unequaled.[71] By the time the police were called because of the unruly crowd behavior in the building, which was filled to the rooftop, the guests were busy smashing several pieces of furniture.[72] This is perhaps not surprising; one item reported that in a single room of the publishing house—the religious editor's office, which was reserved for clergymen—guests consumed 180 bottles of Blue Grass whiskey, four baskets of champagne, a barrel of lager beer, and twenty-four bottles of Old Tom gin. They also ate four chicken sandwiches and two lobster salads. "The visiting clergymen were not hungry but somewhat thirsty," the article noted dryly, but it also pointed out that they behaved relatively well. Many wore slogans such as "The *Police Gazette* first—Our Country Next," "The Widow's Joy and the Poor Man's Friend—the *Police Gazette*," and "Three names which will never die—George Washington, Abraham Lincoln, and the Religious Editor." The item concluded, "It was a big day, and the religious editor's head—well you guess the rest."[73]

Unfortunately, the grand opening of the bridge was marred by the deaths of twelve people, including a fourteen-year-old girl named Margaret Sullivan, who were crushed to death when pickpockets panicked the crowd and caused a stampede. The *Gazette* led, with characteristic sensation, with the headline, "Death in the Air," adding in a subhead, "Twelve Corpses Dragged from the Closely Wedged and Trampled Mass of Humanity and Twenty Wounded Carried to the Hospitals."[74] The deaths took a page in that June 1883 issue. Fox's party consumed two. "The continuous popping of champagne corks sounded like picket firing in an enemy's front, but in this case it was friend firing upon friend."[75]

The new building was outfitted with a magnificent museum—another tourist attraction, and promotional vehicle, for Fox. The museum featured examples of the publication's awards, mostly presented by Fox, as well as large oil paintings of the leading figures of the day, from Buffalo Bill Cody to Fox. Sullivan's portrait also was allowed in the room.[76] The seven-story *Gazette* building, described in the magazine as a "veritable palace of journalism," was built by architect John Rogers of New York using Philadelphia-pressed brick with Belleville stone facings. It included a street-level windowed "apartment," running the length of the building, that housed ten presses, churning out the *Police Gazette* for passersby to see.

> These are constantly working in the sight of the public and it is a cold day indeed when our rubicund and jovial pressman isn't playing a star engagement in his department before a corwd of fifty or more specimens of every grade of society from highest to lowest, flattening their noses against the immese plate glass windows that led into this important department the floods of sunlight necessary to to aid the delicate task of printing an immense edition of our fine pictorial pages.[77]

Fox's offices were adorned with costly replicas of furniture and other articles from the Louvre.

> The adornments, the chandeliers, the dressing rooms, the book cases are all modelled after quaint patterns from the same noted palace and everything accompanying them is rich and costly yet restrained within the bounds of the most rigid good taste. There is nothing gaudy or flashy in the entire establishment. All is solid, substantial, rich, costly and planned to serve a purpose of utility without offending the eye educated in the forms of hues of refined taste or the mind subject to the canons of art.[78]

As impressive as these quarters were, visitors marveled most at the counting room and cashier's department, which were part of a $10,000 floor that included piles of bullion and bank notes, with half a dozen clerks and cashiers "counting, checking, bailing and stowing." Outfitted with plate glass windows, chandeliers, and rare glassworks, the walls and ceilings were finished in the finest woods. On the fourth and fifth floors were the stock and mail rooms of the *Gazette* as well as the books and other publications on sports, games, outlaws, and other matters that were making Fox's name world famous. Engravers, printers, and artists worked on the upper floors, accounting for many of the full workforce of about two hundred. All this, the *Gazette* reported, was much to the annoyance of Fox's enemies but to the delight of his friends as he proceeded with his plans to "revive sports in America."[79]

During this period Fox clearly enjoyed himself, as he published accounts of lighthearted contests, such as egg-eating, and of more serious matters, such as lynchings (under the column called "Noose Notes").[80] One "human pin cushion" promoted in the Gazette, Tony Alemi, said he would challenge any man in America to equal his feat of sticking 2,000 needles, twenty awls, and two knife blades in his body without drawing blood.[81] Fox's backing of all sorts of sports, and his awarding of trophies, attracted all sorts of cranks, much to his disdain. He told another newspaper that he was thinking of starting a crank's carnival.[82] One man wrote him from Chicago: "I propose to walk seven hundred (700) miles in one hundred and thirty-four (134) hours, covering this distance by walking around an ordinary flour barrel four thousand one hundred and ninety-eight (4,198) laps to a mile." All he asked for from Fox was to pay the rent for Madison Square Garden for a week, plus $50. Fox said he was inclined to agree with this offer if the man walked inside instead of outside the barrel.[83] For media sociologist David B. Welky, these contests had a purpose beyond the enrichment of Fox:

> These events seem silly today, and may have even then. It is also true that these novel contests, complete with championships, trophies and medals, were all ploys by Fox to garner attention and increase subscriptions. . . . But, crass motives aside, these events helped to address the working-class need for an escape from anonymity. The *Police Gazette* proved that anyone who had a modicum of talent in any so-called skill could be immortalized in print, and could even earn the immortal sobriquet of "champion." Were it not for the *Police Gazette*, T.F. Grant would have lived his life as a nameless cripple. Instead, in 1884, he became the *Police Gazette* champion one-legged clog dancer

of the world. Never mind that he was so far as known, "the only one-legged clog dancer in the world," he was a *champion*. We may consider Marquis Bibbero merely as a prime candidate for drowning, but after swimming ten miles in a river with his hands and feet tied, he became the *Police Gazette*'s champion scientific swimmer. Finally, we may not even know what to make of George Clegg of Cleveland, but after he established a new glass-eating record for Ohio in 1889, he too became a champion. In the first 16 years of operating the paper, Fox gave away 436 trophies, medals and other prizes. The overwhelming majority of these went to people who had no real claim to fame. But even so, the paper made them somebodies. For a short time, anyway, they escaped anonymity.[84]

One sport that tested a man's derring-do, which Fox claimed was increasing in popularity, was bridge-jumping. One famed jumper was Lawrence M. Donovan, a pressman for the *Gazette*, who, despite his sobriety, jumped from the Brooklyn Bridge in 1896 and was named *Gazette* champion "aerial jumper." He later successfully jumped off the suspension bridge at Niagara Falls and the London Bridge, but suffered a worse fate in August 1888 after jumping from London's Hungerford suspension bridge. Fox paid his funeral expenses.[85]

In 1885, the *Gazette* celebrated the jump of a man named King Callahan, who jumped from the Brooklyn Bridge with a pair of flotation devices (bull bladders) attached to his shoulders:

> "Look out!" he yelled, and then leaped out into space. As he flew through the air he assumed a perfectly straight position, with the small balloons fluttering above his shoulders. Then he seemed to lean backward and struck the water on his heels at an angle of about 30 degrees.
>
> The concussion could be heard on either side of the river. . . .
>
> "I have a pain here," he said, placing his hand over his heart. "Great Scott, but that was a jump!" Then he began expectorating blood.

The article noted that he was arrested, but was congratulated for his courage by policemen at the station house.[86]

The publicity reached all levels, from the newsboys Fox promoted in magazine biographies, to Theodore Roosevelt, who muttered that the *Gazette* could be found in the hands of every Western ruffian.[87] That might have been true. Fox often boasted of a barely legible note he received from Sempronius, Texas, dated December 20, 1879: "Please send me a copy of your paper (*The Police Gazette*), and greatly oblige—Jesse James."[88] Flushed with the success that fame provided, Fox published other scandal sheets, including *Fox's Illustrated Week's*

Doings in 1883, and *Illustrated Day's Doings and Sporting World*, in 1885, that included copy on lynchings, murders, arson, and other bizarre tales. These publications lasted only a year and five years, respectively, but they sent a signal that Fox was a publisher to be reckoned with, and his catalog would eventually include hundreds of pamphlets, tracts, and books.[89] This was partly because of Fox's instinct to aggressively expand his empire. In 1888 the *Gazette* announced it was being distributed in England; in 1893 it also published a Spanish-language edition, aimed at readers in Mexico, Cuba, Spain, and South and Central America. In September 1896, Fox announced that the *Gazette* was opening an office in London, at 149 Fleet Street, to publish issues concurrent with the American weekly.[90] The *Gazette*'s overseas circulation is difficult to gauge—Mott noted that in the days before audited circulations, "there is no more than a relative significance in the available figures."[91] But six months later Fox boasted, "How that London edition is booming! The presses over there can't go fast enough and can't print enough. Those Londoners know a good thing when they see it."[92] Fox claimed his was truly a global enterprise, and because of mail delivery, it probably could be classified as one of the first global media companies. He wrote the following in an 1893 editorial:

> It would not be an untruth to say that in every corner of the globe where the English language is spoken may be found a POLICE GAZETTE. In the wilds of Africa, in every known town of the Orient, and, in fact, in every land and upon the high seas, the POLICE GAZETTE is known, read and appreciated. There is no other paper in the world that has such a universal circulation.[93]

Even from Fox's earlier years the success was intoxicating. The first words in the editorial-page columns in the March 11, 1882, issue were: "POLICE GAZETEE circulation—350,000. Take a back seat all the rest of you."[94] During this period, the *Gazette* was so popular that its imitators multiplied, and Fox feared that he might lose readers. Under its standard sporting news column it ran a regular notice to readers, signed by Fox:

> Please be sure to ask your News Dealer for the POLICE GAZETTE of New York. There is only one POLICE GAZETTE, and it is published by Richard K. Fox, at the new POLICE GAZETTE publishing house, Franklin Square and Dover Street. Our immense and steadily increasing success has inspired imitation on the part of numerous feeble and unscrupulous publishing houses, and the public will do well to see that

they are not imposed on by any of these parasites who hope to live upon our reputation.[95]

The publisher did not hestitate to revel in his good fortune. In 1883 the *Gazette* ran a large, flattering portrait of him (figure 5.1), dressed in his finest, with top hat and cufflinks, sporting his thick, handlebar mustache, along with two smaller pictures of *Gazette* sports

RICHARD K. FOX,

EDITOR AND PROPRIETOR OF THE "POLICE GAZETTE," NEW YORK.

[From a Photograph by Napoleon Sarony.]

Figure 5.1

editor Harding and Billy O'Brien, Fox's "sporting representative." The story recounted the glories of Fox's enthusiasm for sport:

> The name of Richard K. Fox is inseparably associated with American athletic sport, and justly so, for to him that line of American sport owes the healthy and prosperous life it enjoys today. It is but a few years since he found it languishing in a barren field, unpopular, only practiced in a desultory way, without encouragement or efficient championship. He took it up and made its cause his own, and gave it the vitality it now has. . . .
> We write of the POLICE GAZETTE in a personal sense simply because it is a person. The POLICE GAZETTE is Richard K. Fox. The title of the paper is only another name for the man who, from a wreck drifting on the sea of journalism, has lifted it to an immense commercial property and a tremendous power in the newspaper world. The man and his work are inseparable.[96]

The story continued in the same vein, complimenting Fox for the medals and trophies he had awarded, allowing, "In all the history of sporting journalism, no man ventured so much money, without hope of a direct return, in the cause of sport, as Richard K. Fox."[97] Indeed this was true, but even the *Gazette*, by implication, acknowledged the depth of Fox's *indirect* returns. These were legion and they lasted for years, and the contestants came to him, eager for his power of publicity. By 1885, Fox boasted that the *Gazette* provided the nation with a binding identity, connecting San Franciscans to New Yorkers; he also claimed to be behind the nation's fitness and sporting boom.[98] By 1896, Fox was open to all kinds of stunts, including the backing of two Norwegian immigrants, George Harbo and Frank Samuelsen, desperate to make a name for themselves in an apparently foolish idea to row across the Atlantic Ocean. Fox went along with the idea; however, he shrewdly offered no money—only a *Police Gazette* medal if they completed the voyage—and he generously allowed them to call their rowboat the Fox.[99] In 1899, the *Gazette* ran a full-page list of the "manly" sports and the awards that Fox had sponsored in pugilism, pedestrianism, shooting, rowing, skating, bridge-jumping, bowling, bag-punching, yachting, baseball, and bodybuilding (highlights included contests between Sandow and strongman Louis Cyr, who at one point were matched for a $2,500 trophy in 1884[100]). Also congratulated were the banjoists, letter carriers, firemen, cakewalkers, policemen, barbers, bartenders, and dog trainers who had won prizes over the years. The story also mentioned the Atlantic Ocean rowing champions, noting that upon completion of their voyage Fox had given them "costly" gold medals at Huber's Museum in New York City.[101]

Realizing that he was viewed by some as a scandalmonger, and flush with power, Fox used his influence to go on the offensive against *Gazette* critics. He derided the "moralists of the morning papers"[102] and whenever he found a defender (as in an editorial in the Cincinnati *Sporting and Dramatic Journal* that congratulated Fox for his "manly" stance against weak-minded "frizzy old maids," preachers, and "temperance shouters"[103]), he published it with glee. In 1885, this diatribe served as a rebuke to those he viewed as ignorant and hypocritical:

> There are a good many very excellent people hanging on to existence by the eyebrows in the country, who profess to regard the POLICE GAZETTE as a horribly wicked and altogether abominable publication. If you press them to make a clear statement of the reason why they denounce the GAZETTE and rebuke Richard K. Fox, they treat you to a disappointment to begin with. For with one consent they declare that they never saw a copy of this fearful paper and couldn't be induced at any price to so much look into its villainous pages.
>
> Recovering from a very natural astonishment, one's next query is: "Well, if you haven't ever seen the POLICE GAZETTE, and if you don't know by personal experience and investigation what it contains, how the dickens can you pronounce it a wicked paper?"
>
> To which the worthy imbecile usually replies that he has heard the POLICE GAZETTE publishes sensational news, and above all patronizes and promotes the art and science of pugilism.[104]

To which the *Gazette* pleaded guilty—with an explanation. It maintained that it simply illustrated the sensational news already printed in other newspapers, naming the *Sun*, the *Herald*, the *Times*, the *Tribune*, the *World*, the Philadelphia *Times*, the Chicago *News*, and the Cincinnati *Gazette*. "If, then, our illustrations are wicked and criminal and altogether base, what language can be found sufficiently vigorous to condemn the big dailies?" Besides, said the *Gazette*, its promotion of boxing was picked up by other newspapers, noting that the *Sun*, "edited by Mr. Dana, who never hesitates to manfully attend all reputable boxing matches," had a few days earlier published a front-page interview with Sullivan. In addition, "every morning newspaper in New York has devoted at least a quarter of a column a day to a description of the practice and exercise" of Sullivan and Dominic

McCaffrey, his upcoming opponent. "If we are altogether infamous and damnable for doing this sort of thing once a week, how much viler and more despicable is the newspaper which offends in a like manner every day? Verily, consistency is a jewel—when you get hold of the real article."[105]

Despite Fox's boasts about all of the championships he had sponsored, it was clear that of all of the sporting feats, none held the public's attention like Sullivan's. And it was to Sullivan's train that Fox hitched the fortunes of the *Police Gazette*. In the fall of 1882, Madden, again acting as Sullivan's manager, engaged another tour, featuring singers, jugglers, wrestlers—and of course Sullivan, who received top billing. Sullivan and Madden sparred six nights a week, and Sullivan received the princely sum of $500 a night. A standing offer was allowed for anyone who wanted to take on Sullivan, for up to $5,000 a side.[106]

In an essay published on September 16, 1882, Sullivan gave *Gazette* readers a taste of personal, intimate, participatory journalism:

> During the first week I am passed through a course of physics by which the stomach is brought into a proper condition. During this time I get up every morning at 7 o'clock, walk a mile and breakfast at 8. My bill of fare throughout the training is a simple one. I avoid all greasy or heating food. My meats are cooked rare and I am prohibited from eating anything rich or sweet. The bread is either toasted or stale. In place of tea or coffee I am allowed ale or porter. After breakfast I take a cold shower bath, followed by a brisk rubbing of every part of the body with coarse towels. After resting an hour I walk twelve miles, six out and six back, coming in on the last half mile on a brisk run. This is followed by knocking with dumb bells for about an hour. They weigh a pound and a half and the exercise affects the muscles of the arm. . . . This is kept up every day until the day of the meeting. I will be relieved of about thirty pounds of superfluous flesh and ought to weigh 185 pounds when I step into the ring.[107]

In early 1883, followers of the *Gazette* were treated to yet another aspect of Fox's brand of journalism in the editor's public crusade to legitimize prizefighting, both legally and for the tastes of "polite society." In his attempt to find a challenger for Sullivan, Fox brought in another foreigner, a New Zealander named Herbert A. Slade, known as the Maori (or just Slade), to fight Englishman Jem Mace in a "sparring exhibition." Crowds followed the coppery-skinned, black-haired Slade everywhere, and he wore a buffalo-skin coat when he arrived at the *Gazette*'s offices for a publicity appearance. But the Mace-Slade

match hit a snag; a warrant was sworn out for the arrest of Fox as insti-
gator of a prizefight. The main contention of Fox and his lawyers was
that, while prizefighting was prohibited under an 1859 ordinance,
"exhibitions," in which contestants wore padded gloves, were legitimate. In the *Gazette*'s columns, opponents of fighting were portrayed
with utmost contempt. Activist Henry Bergh, the shiny-pated crusader against prizefighting, was said sarcastically in the *Gazette* to be
against the Mace-Slade fight because he could not get the men to box
for the benefit of the "Society for the Prevention of Cruelty to Bald-
Headed Men."[108]

Fox finally obtained a hearing, and in state court, his lawyers
argued that boxing was a legitimate form of entertainment and exercise. Judge Donohue (whose first name is nowhere in *Gazette*
accounts of the case) found that sparring was not necessarily an
unlawful act.[109] The *Gazette* could not resist a little crowing. The
headlines on February 17, 1883, said,

> ANOTHER VICTORY!/ The "Police Gazette" Triumphs Once More
> over Bigots and Sneaks./ Judge Donohue Decides Unreservedly in
> Favor of Richard K. Fox and His Champions, Mace and Slade./ The
> Sparring Match Not a Violation of the Law and the Interference of the
> Police Unwarranted.

In the body of the story, the text proclaimed that "the triumph of the
POLICE GAZETTE was signal and perfect."[110] But Fox was not
quite finished trumpeting his victory. In the next issue, under the
giant headline, "Richard K. Fox Wins," the *Gazette* proclaimed that
sportsmen—and newsmen—from throughout the country had
praised Fox for fighting for his principles. The *Gazette* published a
conversation between Fox and an unnamed reporter, in which the latter gave his publisher every chance to respond to critics and to con-
gratulate himself:

> "Suppose that another attempt is made to prevent the proposed
> exhibition?"
>
> "I do not desire any controversy or difficulty with Mr. Bergh or his
> friends but I am fully determined to resort to all lawful means for the
> purpose of protecting my rights."
>
> "You have been roundly abused by certain representatives of the
> anti-boxing element," said the reporter.
>
> "Yes, but abuse does not interfere with either my appetite or my sleep.
> It is a singular thing, yet some of the very men who have joined in the

hue and cry have frequently attended boxing exhibitions. I like to see men who have the courage of their convictions. If sparring is brutal and unlawful, as alleged, then our colleges and athletic organizations have turned out a great many brutes of high social standing. I remember the time when horse racing was as severely denounced as sparring now is, yet I have lived to see it one of the most popular sports of the day. The class of people who now attend races show what a deep hold it has on the public."

"It is charged by your enemies that you have endorsed ruffians."

"How? By bringing the most scientific boxers of the day before the public? Can a man like Mace, who has sparred before the Prince of Wales, the nobility of England and cultured American audiences, be justly termed a ruffian? Instead of hunting for ruffians I have sought the ablest and most reputable masters of the manly art."

"What will Mace and Slade do after they appear at Madison Square Garden?"

"They will, in company with the Police Gazette Athletic Combination, visit all the large cities of the country and exhibit their skill. I want the American people to see for themselves that Mace and the Maori are not ruffians but simply the most accomplished boxers of the present day."[111]

Mace and Slade did eventually spar in Manhattan, Baltimore, and other eastern cities, with Slade performing convincingly enough to win a chance against Sullivan on August 6, 1883, which he lost by knockout in three rounds.

As Fox made clear in his comments to his own reporter, the *Gazette* was not concerned solely with Sullivan. In its regular boxing column it featured all sorts of fights and all sorts of fighters, including Daisy Daly, the women's champion from California, and Harry Woodson, the "Black Diamond." (Throughout his life Sullivan refused to fight black fighters, but despite his publication's sometimes racist content about black criminals and others who were called "coons," Fox had no qualms about promoting black fighters in many bouts.[112]) Woodson, according to the *Gazette*, "was brought from Cincinnati recently by Richard K. Fox, to compete . . . for the POLICE GAZETTE medal representing the heavy-weight colored boxing championship of America."[113] The *Gazette* even brought up fighting in its traditional gender-bending contexts. On April 14, 1883, the front page of the *Gazette* carried its standard large wood-cut illustration showing a well-dressed woman standing over another, who was unconscious on the floor. The second woman was being fanned awake by a gentleman escort, and in the background stood an attendant, carrying drinks. The women were wearing boxing gloves. The caption read, "KNOCKED OUT IN ONE ROUND. The popular revival of the manly art reaches a Fifth Avenue palace and results in the introduction of a novel sport into the boudoir."[114]

The Sullivan fights remained the biggest draw for Fox, however. In April 1883 the Boston Strong Boy (a nickname supposedly given to him by an obscure lightweight boxer) drew 25,000 people to an exhibition in his hometown. Meanwhile, Madden had traveled to England with $5,000 of Fox's money in order to find a contender; Charley Mitchell emerged, and he was put up against Sullivan on May 14, 1883. Prior to the fight, the *Gazette* had announced that Sullivan had had health problems:

> Many supposed, when the wires flashed the news to the POLICE GAZETTE office that Sullivan had a severe hemorrhage, that the champion's fighting days were over, but we are pleased to learn that such is not the case. It was stated pretty generally, and believed by many that Sullivan's illness was the inevitable result of hard training. This is all nonsense. No athlete is in danger of injuring his constitution by a regular routine of training, but must derive benefit from such judicious exercise. [Famed Canadian sculler Edward] Hanlan, for instance, trains as fine as any man in the world, but after he rows a race he does not relax and build himself up on fine wines, as Sullivan and other famous athletes have been wont to do. The idea of pugilists dying from consumption is all bosh. If they do, it is not from training for fighting, but in consequence of a series of debauches.[115]

Sullivan won again, and at one point hammered Mitchell over the ropes. According to Fox and those associated with him, the Mitchell fight netted Fox about $20,000, although some historians believe this figure is too high.[116]

Like all sensational journalists before and after him Fox attempted to give his readers information about the personal side of his subjects—and the more scandalous the better. During the post-Civil War era the press was changing in response both to the shifts in society—immigration and industrialization—and to its own needs. Cultural changes demanded changes in coverage which in turn led to changes in the way journalism was practiced. The press evolved in the 1800s from simple opinion-featuring broadsheets manned by two-person print shops to newspapers containing complex reporting—from, as noted by historian Hazel Dicken-Garcia, "reprinting items as received to physically pursuing news across communities, nation, and world, to 'dressing up' information to entice readers, to 'manufacturing' news to retain them."[117] These changes not only led to charges of sensationalism or trivialization or invasions of privacy—all of which were criticisms of the *Gazette*—but they also led to standards and ethical practices governing journalistic conduct (although the first ethical codes for journalists would not be adopted until the twentieth century). Fox was not particularly restricted by the rise of new standards, but the *Gazette* highlighted its ability to secure "private information from our correspondents" to underscore its credibility.[118] He maintained that the *Gazette* maintained the highest ethical standards and journalistic integrity. He once railed about sensational treatment given by newspapers to an 1880 riot in Patterson, New Jersey, following a man's killing. Fox said it was the duty of the press to report all sides of the matter, not merely to try to stir up the rioters. "But this principle of journalism is ignored and the selfish principle rules. There was more money to be made by siding with the mob," he wrote.[119]

Of course, there was money to be made in the coverage of Sullivan as he gained fame, and Fox was not above chasing down stories circulating about the boxer and his wife, Annie Bates Bailey Sullivan. Upon their marriage on May 1, 1883, the rumors were that Sullivan beat his wife and that the two drank and engaged in quarrels.[120] Fox's pursuit of the story was another example of his intimate, celebrity-style journalism focusing on scandal; it prompted one twentieth-century historian to refer to his magazine as *The National Enquirer* of the nineteenth century.[121]

In June 1883, one of the most sensational stories emerged when Annie alleged to police that John L. had beaten her and destroyed some of their furniture, but no warrant was issued for his arrest. Later that month, reports out of Boston were that he had beaten not only his wife but also her sister. But when Fox sent a reporter, he got disappointing news. Both women denied the story, and Annie was quoted in the *Gazette* as saying that his "great misfortune is that he has a heart too big for his body, and is so lavish in entertaining his friends that he sometimes oversteps the bounds of prudence in his sociability and then is a little morose and surly."[122]

A little over a year after their first battle, Mitchell and Sullivan were scheduled for a rematch in the summer of 1884. Fox used all of his powers of journalism to promote the fight and thus, sales. The *Gazette* listed in fine print more than a column of names of those who were at ringside, including William K. Vanderbilt, reputed to be the richest man in the world; Rev. Henry Ward Beecher; Rev. De Witt

Talmadge; and a host of New York aldermen, assemblymen, and police. Also on hand were fighters Joe Goss and the up-and-comer Jake Kilrain.[123]

Madden, who was employed by Fox, introduced the master of ceremonies. After some preliminary bouts, there was a delay. Following some grumbling from the crowd, Sullivan finally walked into the arena—slowly. He mounted the ring with some difficulty and announced that he was sick and unable to fight. The *Gazette* suggested that the ongoing brewers' strike had not had any effect on the champion, who had gone beyond the beer-drinking stage. Most agreed that Sullivan might have been sick, but he was also "drunk as a Lord."[124]

Later that year, in 1884, Fox brought in yet another foreign contender in an attempt to create another attention-getting matchup for Sullivan. As an added publicity stunt, he unveiled the most impressive of his championship belts: The winner was to receive the *Police Gazette* Diamond Belt, fifty inches long, eight inches wide, and speckled with silver and gold. A ring in the center was encircled by diamonds, the top featuring a fox's head. The belt was valued at $2,500, and Fox was not accused of lacking promotional zeal.[125] In the early moments of the November 18 fight, Sullivan appeared to be handling the contender, Alf Greenfield of Birmingham, England, but the fight was most notable for what happened next: Superintendent George Washington Walling of the New York City Police Department ordered the men to stop fighting. Walling said the fight had gone beyond being a sparring match, and that the men were attempting to knock each other out.[126] Thus, eight days before Christmas in 1884, Sullivan and Greenfield were tried on the charge of prizefighting.[127]

As the trial unfolded, Fox's bankrolling of the defense began to pay off. Captain Williams, who was called for the prosecution, became a good witness for the defense. He testified that he had seen harder hitting, and more blood spilled, in bouts presented by the Police Athletic Association. Then Sullivan took the stand, much to the delight of the crowd. He testified that he and Greenfield were merely attempting to put on a show. Asked if he was angry during the exhibition, Sullivan replied, "No, sir. I have never been angry in any of the engagements I have been in."[128]

Judge Barrett, whose first name is not in *Gazette* accounts of the case, charged the jury with the instruction that "if it was a physical contention for supremacy, then the defendants are guilty under the statute." The jury filed out, taking the boxing gloves (which had been presented as exhibits) with them. They came back after eight minutes.

According to the *Gazette*'s account, "The defendants stood up, stared at the foreman, and the foreman stared at them. Then he sang out in a loud, clear voice: 'Not guilty.' "[129] In 1930, one historian wrote that the evidence showed that the money given by Fox, this time to help Sullivan, was well spent: "Fox, and the sport of pugilism, profited, of that there can be little question."[130]

His expenditures included the costly recruitment of foreign fighters. Fox's attempts to recruit abroad were so well known—and the reverence of Sullivan so strong—that boys could be heard chanting in the streets of America:

> The Fox may go to England
> And the Fox may go to France,
> But to beat John L., he can go to Hell,
> And then he won't have a chance.[131]

By 1885, Fox had begun to turn more often to American fighters in an attempt to find someone who could pose a legitimate challenge to Sullivan. In the following year, he became the backer of Jake Kilrain (born John Joseph Killion). In preparation for his fight with Sullivan, Kilrain, trained by Mitchell, went to England to fight the English champion, Jem Smith. After 106 rounds of bare-knuckle fighting in two-and-a-half hours, the fight was declared a draw. Many believed Kilrain had won it, though. That was enough for Fox, who called Kilrain his new "*Police Gazette* Champion." The *Gazette* headline screamed, "NIGHT OF BUTCHER."[132]

Sullivan unofficially lost his title when he failed to make a timely answer to Kilrain's challenge to fight. But that actually helped Sullivan: he became the "people's champion"[133] and instead of boxing, a "war of printers' ink"[134] occupied the sporting world for many months. Sullivan finally issued a challenge to Kilrain to fight for a total purse of $20,000, $10,000 to be put up by each side with the winner taking all. Fox immediately backed Kilrain with $10,000, and on July 8, 1889, the men battled for hours, in Richburg, Mississippi, in what is considered by boxing historians to be one of the greatest prizefights.[135]

The *Gazette*'s series of headlines printed on July 20, 1889, told the story:

John L. Wins!/ A Terrific Battle of 75 Rounds, Lasting 2 Hours and 16 Minutes./ At Richburg, Miss./ Thousands Gather at the Ring-side to Witness the Fight./ Jake Ill at the Start./ Notwithstanding this Fact, He Fights John L. to a Standstill./ No Strength to Follow it Up./ He Is Badly Used Up at the Finish, but Succumbs Gracefully./ John L. Not Unscathed./ He Has Two Black Eyes, a Split Ear and a Disfigured Face./ Was the Referee Impartial?/ Rumors that He was Not, and that He was Not Cognizant of the Rules./ The Pugilists Homeward Bound.[136]

Sullivan had beaten Fox again. But the *Gazette* had the last laugh. It spent several inches of column space chronicling Sullivan's mildly unfortunate adventures on the way home from the fight. Mississippi authorities had decided to arrest the fighters, but the accused escaped the state without incident. Sullivan later found himself detained at a train stop in Nashville, Tennessee, but he was released when the judge found that "under the law prize fighting was a misdemeanor in Mississippi and was not an extraditable offense."[137]

Sullivan, who continued his heavy drinking ways, would fall into the trap that has caught many aging champions—he did not know when to quit. After several years of retirement mixed with traveling exhibitions, he finally was defeated in 1892 by Jim Corbett. But for many, the true end of Sullivan was the Kilrain fight. Historian Mott wrote, "Thus ended the feud of Mr. Fox and Mr. Sullivan; and what Mr. Fox's many champions could not do, John Barleycorn accomplished in short order."[138] For his part, Kilrain won his share of fame in the *Gazette* pages. Fox commissioned a song, "Our Champion," written by M.H. Rosenfield to celebrate Kilrain's feats, and it published on November 10, 1888:

> No brawler in the fistic ring
> Our knight with courage stout
> Among the hosts he reigns a king;
> No whiskey knocks him out;
> The laurels on his honest brow,
> He won with might and main,
> Our hat we doff to him we bow
> Our champion Jake Kilrain.[139]

The story of the *Gazette*'s coverage of boxing and other sports does not end with Sullivan and Kilrain, of course. Jack Johnson, the first African-American world heavyweight champion, fought Jim Jeffries in 1910, and the *Gazette* covered the bout with relish. The match had not been without its controversies. For years after Jeffries won the championship in 1899, he refused to fight black fighters. He retired in 1905 only to see Jackson assume the title. When Jackson finally faced Jeffries (now dubbed the "Great White Hope") in 1910 at Reno, Nevada, the band played "All Coons Look Alike to Me." It was covered by hundreds of journalists, and American men looked to the contest with unparalleled interest; outside the *New York Times* offices, 30,000 men stood waiting for the results (Jackson battered the aging Jeffries and won in fifteen rounds, stunning the arena into silence).[140]

Were Fox and Sullivan truly rivals stemming from a snub at Harry Hill's? One doubts the particulars as well as the results. The *Gazette*'s coverage of Sullivan was largely objective, although it rarely resisted jabs at his drinking. In 1884 it even published a very positive biography of Sullivan, focusing on his fighting career, calling him "the scion of good old Irish stock."[141] Sullivan, for his part, felt confident enough in the *Gazette* to use it as a sounding board to argue against his coverage in New York dailies. In a letter on New Year's Eve of 1884, Sullivan wrote to Fox:

> I was surprised on arriving in New York to read in the morning papers that I had been made the hero of a series of brutal outrages in my native city. The reports state that I beat a waiter-girl in an oyster saloon, and that I had deserted my wife and child. There is no truth in the reports. I never insulted or inflicted injury to a woman in my life and I never will. In regard to leaving my wife and child, I stamp the report as a base and malicious fabrication circulated by enemies of mine to injure my reputation with the public. The report originated with the fact that while out sleighing, one of the runners became caught in the groove of the car track and I was thrown out and the horses dragged me for one hundred yards. I held on to the horses and received no damage, which proves I was not intoxicated. I joined Councilman Tom Denny, Dan Murphy and Colonel Tom Delay in Yeaton's saloon, and in a friendly way tapped the waiter-girl with the wet driving gloves. We sat down, had oysters and Bass' ale, and left the place on the best of terms. . . . Truth is always stronger than fiction.
>
> Yours Truly,
> John L. Sullivan[142]

The real story of the supposed Fox-Sullivan feud was that the fighter was the perfect hero (or antihero, depending on how much one believes in their supposed feud) for the editor. Sullivan was the giant of an era defined by defense of masculinities; Fox was there to chronicle those defenses. As Sullivan's biographer, Isenberg, wrote:

> The cult of masculinity celebrated the specialist in the applied use of
> force, because he provided a masculine model that resolved doubts and
> ambiguities; demonstrated all the old . . . sporting virtues—pluck, grit,
> competitive risk taking, the relentless urge to ultimate victory; and
> allowed spectators to partake painlessly in the theater of surrogate vio-
> lence. In an economic landscape where the road to the top was virtually
> impossible to negotiate and even the uphill climb tortuous and diffi-
> cult, the surrogate could provide a psychic outlet as well as a model of
> economic success. . . . The man who could defend himself, physically
> dominating others and forcing them to yield, was dealing in common
> and well-understood coin in the workshops, factories and saloons
> strewn across America.[143]

Sullivan was, literally, a figure of strength in a world of ambiguity.
Boxing historian Elliott J. Gorn wrote:

> Heroic strife broke through the sentimental clutter of lace and ruffles
> and curls. Sullivan rejected the routine world of work and family to live
> by his fists and his wits. If one may think of culture in terms of gender,
> then John L. Sullivan, the greatest American hero of the late nineteenth
> century, represented a remasculinization of America. . . . To turn of the
> century American men, Sullivan symbolized the growing desire to
> smash through the fluff of bourgeois gentility and the tangle of corpo-
> rate ensnarements to the throbbing heart of life.[144]

Of course, as has already been noted, Fox and his *Gazette* editors
had a few other ideas about the throbbings of their male readership.
And many would argue that the *Gazette*'s true demonstration of the
powers and contradictions of masculinities came not when it showed
the bare chests of fighters but the bare legs of showgirls.

6

THE GIRL ON THE *POLICE GAZETTE*

And my longing will increase
For the girl on the *Police Gazette*
For the pretty young brunette
On the pink *Police Gazette*.
—Irving Berlin, 1937

One may pick up any issue of the *Gazette* during the late nineteenth and early twentieth centuries and see women shown in athletic, violent, seductive, or celebrity-based endeavors. Though beauty sold (and sells) magazines, it was by no means the only criterion *Gazette* editors used to make decisions about editorial content regarding the activities of women. As has been noted, *Gazette* girls were not offered merely as sex objects; their activities—sometimes portrayed as deviant, sometimes not—ranged from smoking, drinking, and dancing to more mundane endeavors such as cycling, skating, bowling, or walking. Women also were shown fighting off unwanted suitors, taking revenge upon unfaithful lovers (or their lovers' outside female interests), fighting each other, or kissing for charity. The publication honored Annie Oakley for her marksmanship; it defended women against scoundrels and praised them for fighting back against abusive men. The portrayals were most obvious in *Gazette* woodcuts, and later, photographs, but they were by no means limited to illustrations. Often, the *Gazette* would run stories about women engaged in unusual or salacious activities, merely for the purpose of pointing out to readers that such things did, indeed, happen. In this sense it actually celebrated independent women.

It is clear that the great variety in the portrayals of women—indeed, the variety of all the portrayals of different sides of masculinities, threats to masculinities, and the responses to those threats, represented different ways to show the changing definitions of manhood during the industrial revolution. The changes—caused by modifications in work roles, demands for political and sexual liberation of women, immigration, and the development of a non-agrarian, post-frontier economy—were certainly not caused by the *Gazette*. But through its emphasis on sports and crime, the *Gazette* provided refuge and role models for men of the era. Through its emphasis on pictures of women, it provided entertainment and excitement of another sort.

A few examples of illustrations involving women, selected at random, are as follows:

1879: A daring beauty has herself lowered from a cliff to seek thrills.

1880: A showgirl, or "footlight favorite"; women smash bottles and clean out a saloon; a woman lets out a manly whistle to signal a street car.

1884: Two young women at the Brooklyn Academy of Music have a falling out and engage in a fistfight; women about to make the ultimate crossover into male territory by trying on pants (figure 6.1).

1889: A man attacks his wife and her lover as they embrace on a carriage—"A faithless wife's amour leads to a bloody tragedy near Salisbury, Maryland."

1894: A boy and his stepmother are caught in bed, and the boy is beaten to death by his father (figure 6.2); girls are shown playing a "boys' sport"—baseball (figure 6.3).

1895: A New York woman plants her heel in a policeman's eye and disables him; young ladies show off their legs in the new activity of lamp globe kicking (figure 6.4).

1902: Actress Hope Booth shows off a strapless dress and pearls, a "charming young woman who will shortly appear in a sensational dancing act."[1]

Examples such as these can be found in the *Gazette* over and over again. The portrayal of sexual or theatrical scenes were remarkably consistent over the years. Theatrical scenes were often the most overtly sexual of *Gazette* depictions; they gave the publication an opportunity to present costume-clad showgirls in glamorous poses as well as the excesses of the theater. In 1880 the *Gazette* averaged 2.25 pages of inside sexually suggestive[2] illustrations per issue; in 1900 the figure was 2.53 (see table 6.1). There were some fluctuations, but none that were statistically significant. Sexually provocative images (i.e., those that apparently were designed to be tantalizing to readers of the era) were also the most popular of *Gazette* covers over the years. Nearly 25 percent were glamor poses or scenes of actresses in theatrical settings, while another 20 percent featured other kinds of sexually provocative activity. But the covers also reflected the changing

THEY WEAR THE BREECHES.

HOW THE PHILADELPHIA LADIES ARE MAKING TRADE LIVELY FOR THE TAILORS AND ADDING TO THE VARIETY OF THEIR COSTUME.

Figure 6.1

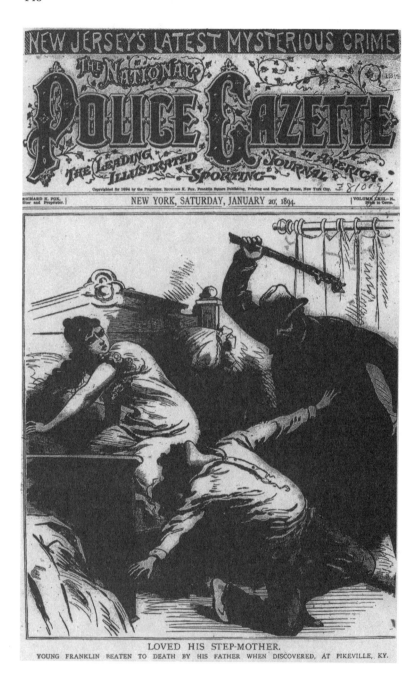

Figure 6.2

GIRLS PLAYED BASEBALL.
BUT THEY COULD NOT BAT THE BALL FAR FROM THE PLATE, IN WESTCHESTER COUNTY, N. Y.

Figure 6.3

FAIR GLOBE KICKERS.

NEW PASTIME INDULGED IN BY THE DAINTY AND AGILE YOUNG WOMEN OF ST. LOUIS, MO.

Figure 6.4

Table 6.1 Average number of inside pages per issue of portrayals of theater or sexually provocative poses at five-year intervals

Year	Theater	Sex	Total
1880	0.85	1.4	2.25
1885	1.5	0.13[a]	1.63
1890	0.5	0.9	1.4
1895	1.7[a]	1.2	2.9
1900	1.6[a]	0.9	2.5
1905	1.2	0.0[a]	1.2

Note: [a]Tukey HSD post hoc for analysis of variance shows significant differences at the .01 level in averages of inside illustrations comparing 1880 to these years.

roles of women: 15.7 percent showed drinking or carousing (almost always involving women); 7 percent showed fighting between women, and 6.1 percent pictured defense by women against men.

For comparison, only 4 percent of *Gazette* covers featured boxers, while another 3.5 percent showed murder (see table 5.1). Not surprisingly, nearly all of those shown on *Gazette* covers were white, and about 91 percent featured women in some activity.

In its coverage of women, the *Gazette* ran genuine news items of interest, most often in the "Masks and Faces" column that was one of the first genuine theater columns. For example, in 1894, an article appeared about chorus girls "tired of being unjustly fined, tired of being swindled by bogus managers, tired of being abused by rude stage managers," who decided to form a working guild. The article was overwhelmingly positive in support of working-class women,[3] but a year later appeared the more lurid, "Chorus Girls Are Anxious to Display Their Figures." In this article the up-and-coming were shown as eager in the art of skimpy dress, much to the dismay of old timers such as actress Lillian Russell, who remarked,

I never had but one sensation from the beginning to the end of my use of tights. That was of dislike and detestation. . . . I was obliged to make use of them for several years, however, but made up my mind that someday I should throw them off forever. A great many have unkindly said that I gave up tights because I was getting too stout, but my reason was because I hated to wear them. I don't think it is dignified for a woman. It detracts from her singing and acting, in my opinion. I don't like to see a woman in tights. I do not think she ought to exhibit her figure in that fashion; I don't believe in immodesty of dress.[4]

Fox certainly gave such comments their due, but just a short while later (and again and again) he managed to show immodesty of dress as well as excess violence. For example, he featured an article about "two Negroes and three Negresses" who were lynched after the murder of an Alabama man, Watts Murphy, who was the nephew of former Alabama Governor Thomas H. Watts (1863–65). The hanging women were shown most prominently in the picture of the lynching, their dresses dangling loosely off their shoulders, their knees and ankles showing. The lynchers, all "cool and brave," left the bodies hanging on limbs of trees on the side of the road so that they were "found hanging there in the morning by churchgoers." Like so many others of its kind, the illustration gave Fox an excuse to depict violence, but it also provided the opportunity to display female flesh.[5]

The variety of the depictions of women in the *Gazette* demands that they be considered in a variety of ways. As has been shown, one element in the selection of news content involves the deviance of the event, but interest is also an element; as sociologists Stanley Cohen and Jock Young pointed out, it may be unusual for a red-haired man to be arrested on drunken driving charges, but that event does not meet the level of interest to make it newsworthy. They name two models of news selection; one is the "Commercial Laissez-Faire" model in which news is seen as a body of events that occur and are pursued as news: In this model, "objectivity consists in reproducing the real world as faithfully as possible." Here, however, selection of news for publication demands that the portions of these real world events be reproduced only if they are interesting, tell a good story or give the public something that it wants. In the "Mass Manipulative" model, the selection is based more on ideological biases built in the news corporation's interests.[6]

There were elements of both models at work in the *Gazette*'s news selections; clearly Fox wanted to boost readership at all costs, so he was interested in what was marketable. At the same time, the pages were loaded with judgments—about the inferior qualities of other races or creeds (e.g., see the illustration of sinister-looking Chinese, figure 6.5), about health and lifestyle choices, about morality, about hypocrisy, about the need for justice to stamp out the causes of evil. With so many agendas at play, it was no wonder that the *Gazette* was loaded with stories that can be read as morality plays for an era.

As shown previously, the threats to masculinities and the reactions to those threats is one way to bind together these varying contents. But to assume an overarching ideology that speaks to specific concerns of readers in every case does a bit of a disservice to Fox and to

THE NATIONAL POLICE GAZETTE

THE LEADING ILLUSTRATED SPORTING JOURNAL IN AMERICA.

Copyrighted for 1884, by RICHARD K. FOX, Proprietor Police Gazette Publishing House, Franklin Square and Dover street, New York

RICHARD K. FOX, Editor and Proprietor.

NEW YORK, SATURDAY, AUGUST 23, 1884.

VOLUME XLIV.—No 36 Price Ten Cents.

MASHED ON A CHINESE BABY.

HOW A NEW YORK LAUNDRYMAN MANAGES TO INTEREST THE SOCIETY LADIES, AND GAINS THEIR WASHING BY APPEALING TO THEIR MOST TENDER INSTINCTS.

Figure 6.5

his readers. Above all, he was a businessman; one must never discount the pure entertainment factor in the pages of the *Gazette*. It was, indeed, a defender of the male faith in a confusing time—a vehicle for expressions of masculinity, for ridicule of deviance, for promotion of physical culture. But it was also, simply, a journal of spectacle and sensation that showed the world what it was in perhaps the most astonishing time in history—a contradictory, confusing, violent, happy, crazy, and ridiculous place.

As has been noted by many historians, the roles of women were changing dramatically from 1880 to 1920, as women sought suffrage, fought for temperance, became more active in sports, and developed into domestically dominant housekeepers and mothers. The rise of burlesque, vaudeville, and the theater gave women an outlet not just for expressing themselves, but for exposing themselves in a more joyful way. By the emergence of the flappers in the 1920s, wrote historian Mary P. Ryan, many women had evolved into a "solipsistic, hedonistic and privatized femininity, a gay abandonment of social housekeeping, women's organizations and dogged professionalism."[7]

Many of the flapper images were born in the likes of publications such as the *Gazette*, which presented weekly images of scantily clad belles in swimsuits, tights, or petticoats. In addition, the many kinds of women's poses in the *Gazette*—relaxed in parlors, participating in sports, fighting off "mashers," or showing bust or leg at the theater footlights—also were found in other publications. In 1897 the *Ladies Home Journal* began presenting the "American Woman" series, showing women in locales as varied as households, businesses, churches, schools, and the political arena. Articles and advertisements in the magazine covered the same ground.[8] Around this time publisher and illustrator Charles Dana Gibson began presenting the "Gibson Girl," an idealized version of American womanhood. The Gibson girl first appeared in *Life* but also showed up in the *Ladies Home Journal*, *Century*, *Scribner's*, *Good Housekeeping*, *McCall's*, and *McClure's*.[9]

The Gibson Girl, according to magazine historian Mark Gabor, represented the "first widely recognized female image to be appreciated for her own sake—not in the thematic context of theater, art or advertising." The Gibson Girl had class and was the "toast of the town and the belle of the ball." *Life* could in no context be called a "girlie magazine," but, like *Sports Illustrated* today, it owed jumps in circulation to its portrayals of desirable women such as the Gibson Girl.[10] Gabor calls the *Police Gazette* the earliest girlie magazine and one of the most influential publications of its day.

Though it had competitors, such as *Day's Doings, Stetson's Dime Illustrated, Last Sensation,* and later, magazines such as *Peterson Magazine, Nickell Magazine,* and *Metropolitan Magazine,* the *Gazette* was, to Gabor, a precursor to both *Playboy* and *The National Enquirer.* He wrote that it hated hypocrisy and lust, but published items about both with glee:

> Among popular magazines of the mid-nineteenth century, none stands out more for its impact on American and European society than the weekly *National Police Gazette* . . . [no other magazine] had quite the mystique and grisly allure of the *National Police Gazette.* . . . The magazine was based on the idea that sin existed and could be exploited in a morally ambivalent society. Its articles seem to say "Shame on you, you've done a despicable thing. Now let's look at all the gory details."[11]

Metropolitan Magazine was one of the most suggestive of the *Gazette*'s rival publications, frequently featuring leggy models in repose, sometimes in classical garb or while drinking alcoholic beverages.[12] But it was the *Gazette,* with its large displays and huge audience among boys and men and boys, that symbolized the ultimate in public presentation of naughty girls for a masculine audience.

In a nostalgic 1960 examination of the *Gazette* titled "Gems from the Gay Dog's Companion," *American Heritage* magazine presented a pink-paged layout of *Gazette* girls who had appeared in the *Gazette* magazine belly dancing (1894), playing lawn tennis (1881), pillow fighting (1878), driving a train (1883), mugging a "sucker" (1894), using a tape measure to compare their bust sizes to that of "Venus of Milo" (1881), and celebrating in luxury only to be later ruined by drink (1874). This last juxtaposition was no accident; "The pious moral was always introduced—after the editor forced himself to include every painful detail of the seduction, or crime, or hanging under discussion."[13]

Thus, these portrayals show that it is too simplistic to say that women of the era were presented by the *Gazette* as sex objects. Many were shown as independent, even as "pals" of men who were familiar with sports, cars, and the outdoors. Historian Donald Mrozek contended that such portrayals represented a reaction to sexual openness encouraged by Freudian psychology; another historian, T.J. Jackson Lears, speculated that they demonstrated the need for freedom from restrictive nineteenth-century clothing in a society placing more value on psychological and physical fitness as leisure time increased.[14]

Indeed, during this time women's health and fitness was an important part of editorial copy. An 1916 article in *Good Housekeeping* noted,

> It is as much a source of shame for . . . [a woman] to be sickly as it is for a man to be a weakling. Girls boast of their muscle and how they can play golf all day, dance or skate half the night, without turning a hair. The daughters of a house are quite as able-bodied as the sons, and a neurotic, hysterical young maiden lying about on a sofa, once a frequent and familiar sight, is now almost as uncommon a spectacle as a dodo.[15]

Meanwhile, Gabor noted that the *Gazette*

> used many of its "spicy" pictures to illustrate articles on subjects totally unrelated to girlie-type themes. These included crimes like murder, arson, religion, politics, business, war, current trends, adventure, human interest, and catastrophes. Whenever a woman could appear in a picture, even in the background, she was there—busty, low-necklined, well-corseted, and with a prominent rump.[16]

Even when sexual overtones were obvious in the illustrations, they were often not as simple as they seemed. Media scholars have long noted a "virgin-vamp" dichotomy in portrayals of women in the mass media. Women may be presented as either "bad" or "good" girls, with all of the accompanying meanings of masculine reinforcement or threats suggested by each of the portrayals. Although the *Gazette* often illustrated the plights of women in distress—of those "good girls" being preyed upon by bad men or the illicit ways of society— many of its illustrations took a decided tilt toward highlighting the playful wiles of more scandalous, coquettish, or athletic women. By the 1920s, the word "vamp" came to be applied to women who might have been fun but were not to be trusted. The term "vamp" came from the title of a Rudyard Kipling poem about a woman who drains everything out of a man through seduction and evil. The poem inspired a film starring Theda Bara in 1915, *A Fool There Was*, in which she played a vamp or vampire. As noted by image historian Carolyn Kitch, "The new 'playful woman' as imagined on the covers and inside pages of these magazines defined play as sin—whether in the form of alcohol or illicit sex, a temptation to men that seemed irresistible yet was ultimately destructive."[17]

These women, Kitch wrote, crossed class barriers in the sense that they might have had a dangerous appeal to upwardly mobile men while symbolizing the cheap amusements of the lower class. In the pages of the *Gazette* they amounted to guilty pleasures for thousands of men—many of them in the working class—who were all too aware of their temptations. Kitch puts media portrayals of these women into three types—the "party girl," the "vamp," and the "scheming beauty"—who were all shown as dangerous to men "in an era when social commentators worried publicly about men's virility and the survival of the white race."[18]

Many of the *Gazette*'s reports of these women amounted to entertainment-news items; the women frequently were shown as dancers or showgirls, and this was reflective of a general dance craze that was part feminist release and part athletic endeavor that was sweeping the nation. Dancing was a bit naughty and scandalous, making it all the more attractive, particularly for many middle- and lower-class men who were eager to escape the sameness of factory and city life by embracing diversions, whether they be athletic, alcoholic, or even scurrilous. New York City had more than 500 dance halls, along with thousands of dance studios and schools. Kitch noted,

> Dancing enabled a shedding of restraint, figuratively through the illusion of class mobility ("slumming") and literally through physical mobility. It also required a shedding of clothing and a transformation in dress styles. Women's fashions became less constraining, more revealing yet also more girlish.[19]

The power of such women was clearly of concern to men. In the early part of the twentieth century Charlie Chaplin's "little tramp" character was the stereotypical powerless male made all the more helpless by the shallow, vain, and beautiful women around him, Kitch wrote,

> All of these images were commentaries on the New Woman in a decade of Freudian psychology and women's suffrage. Their heavy-handed point was that if women gained control in the bedroom or at the ballot box, American manhood would suffer. But they articulated other concerns as well. Chaplin's little tramp struggled for potency not only with women but also in a society that was increasingly urban, corporate and bureaucratic. The little men of the era's media articulated what historians have called the "crisis of masculinity" . . . a dilemma having to do with societal changes that included but went beyond male-female relations.[20]

Tied to this crisis, of course, were threats to white male dominance from blacks and recent immigrants, leading to portrayals of the "strenuous life" and the rugged life as advocated in popular culture and by Theodore Roosevelt.

By the end of World War I, women were often no longer idealized as the buxom beauties who were seen in Fox's *Gazette*. The flappers were decidedly more thin and girlish—the term was from England and was a description of adolescent girls who "flapped" because their bodies had not reached maturity.[21] Some scholars see the celebration of a girlish figure as a backlash against suffrage, a slap at developed women by sensationalizing the thin, underdeveloped figure.[22]

Kitch argued that the representation of women was an ongoing process that developed during the latter part of the nineteenth and early twentieth centuries. The "New Woman," she wrote, became a concept in the late 1800s to be developed and commercialized in the subsequent decades. The representations of the New Woman in the mass media were a way to answer questions about womanhood and manhood—as well as what it meant to be an American—during this period.[23] She continued,

> Mass media exist not only to make money but also to make meaning. For a century, they have disseminated a particular group of visual stereotypes of womanhood and manhood (though mainly woman-hood) that stand for not just gender ideals but also issues of what it means to be "typically" American and what it takes to have status in American culture. Many of these ideals have such resonance with audiences that we talk about them as if they were real: the Gibson Girl was as real to many Americans in the year 1900 as Ally McBeal is in the year 2001. They have become cultural icons whose names symbolize the zeitgeist of particular eras and, in an ongoing sense, what it means to be "modern." Provocative and yet reassuringly familiar, they are our way of making sense of societal change. . . .
>
> The girl on the magazine cover is not a quaint historical phenomenon. She was the first mass-media stereotype, and in that role she has a long list of successors. She has now moved into other media as well, yet she remains recognizable. If the past informs the future, she will continue to tell us much about media and about American life in the twenty-first century.[24]

Thus, it is clear that magazines reflect changing fashions, values, and cultural norms. Nowhere was this more evident than in the *Gazette*'s portrayal of women as athletes often posed in revealing summer clothing. This trend was particularly reflected in swimwear, and the *Gazette* was one of the first to reflect it. By the beginning of the twentieth century, on beaches where heavily clad Victorian-era women had once been confined to carts that were then wheeled into the water, the skirt and full-body cover costumes were giving way to *swimsuits,* with all the form-fit the name suggested. Historian Michael Capuzzo wrote:

> Atlantic City—the glittering sea metropolis of four hundred hotels and fifty thousand guests . . . —was a seat of the rebellion, the *Philadelphia Evening Bulletin* reported. Under the headline "Startling Hosiery Fad Rules the Beach," the *Bulletin* noted that ladies wore bathing socks rolled down instead of up, *exposing the knee.* This moment was a turning point in American fashion; once that line was crossed, more flesh and less fabric became the style of the twentieth century.[25]

But style and athleticism aside, it is clear that many of the scantily clad women in large, splashy pictorials served a more basic instinct— that of the erotic. David Loth's historical survey of pornography noted that one should not be surprised that "the Golden Age of Prudery and the Golden Age of Pornography" coincided during the Victorian Age: by necessity one fed off the other.[26] Social historian Joseph W. Slade wrote that pornography and the debate it inflames are important because they "enshrine the sexual folklore of the species—the myths, legends, beliefs, customs, and mores that work both for and against establishing norms of behavior."[27] Slade cited *Fox's Illustrated Week's Doings* and his *Illustrated Day's Doings and Sporting World* as examples of magazines that offered "gravures of burlesque queens clad in tights and corsets, although editors avoided actual nudity in favor of drawings of topless but nippleless women." That would have to satisfy the voyeurs in the "buttoned-up" age, Slade wrote.[28] But the desexualization did not stop Fox's opponents, who would, as Slade suggested, feed and feed off the debate to help form the folklore of the sexual character of the Victorian age.

The original Society for the Suppression of Vice had been formed in England by 1802 with the goals of eliminating obscenity, fortune telling, blasphemy, and the profaning of the Lord's Day.[29] Nineteen years later Boston became the first American city to prosecute a book for lewdness (John Cleland's 1749 classic *Fanny Hill, or Memoirs of a Lady of Pleasure*), which was the beginning of the "banned in Boston" tradition. The first American obscenity statute was enacted by Vermont in 1821, followed closely by Connecticut and Massachusetts. In America, wrote Loth, the average citizen's distrust of literature, along with increased literacy, helped speed the discontent. By 1842, the U.S. federal government followed with an antiobscenity statute, aiming most of its ire at imported pictures. Paving the way for many censors to follow him was the Englishman Thomas Bowdler, whose name was made into a verb (to "bowdlerize," meaning to cleanse of impropriety or indecency) in honor of his most famous achievement, his edited, cleaned-up version of the Bard's works called *The Family Shakespeare*, which was a smashing success in 1818.[30] But the merchants of erotica came up with their own version of bowdlerization, noted Loth: "They took the already translated works of Boccaccio, Brantome, Casanova, etc., and cut out everything except the sexual adventures."[31] Thus, the warfare of class and taste was joined by the mid- to late 1800s, when illustrated magazines such as the *Gazette* had come to the attention of Americans growing more appalled and wide-eyed at what was being revealed. In 1866, New York's Young Men's Christian Association conducted a survey cataloguing influences on young men, naming saloons, brothels, billiard, and gambling halls, as well as the presence of "vile newspapers and . . . licentious books" ranging in price from thirty-five to sixty cents.[32] By 1868 the YMCA had successfully lobbied for a law suppressing obscene literature. One of the first to use it was an obscure dry goods store clerk who would have died in the same obscurity had he not become inspired to fight the published demons.

Anthony Comstock was born in 1844 in New Canaan, Connecticut. At eighteen he became enraged when a man tried to trade liquor for groceries, so he broke into the man's establishment and poured the offending liquid on the floor. He served in the Civil War without seeing battle action, held several jobs, and then moved to New York City. In his diary he once recorded that he had "spent part of the day foolishly" because he had read some of a novel, and he later blamed a book dealer for leading a friend to consume obscene materials, with the friend's subsequent death possibly caused by the era's "connection between masturbation, nervous disability, and susceptibility to illness."[33] He then had the dealer, Charles Conroy, sell him an erotic book and promptly had him arrested. His career thus begun, he launched the New York Committee (later the Society) for the Suppression of Vice in 1872.[34] One of its targets was Fox and the *National Police Gazette*; he and his society targeted the *Gazette* at least four times for the content of its racy advertising. The most serious fine leveled against Fox was for $500, and Comstock's campaign had little effect—the ads actually gained in explicitness over the years.

But Comstock also had a philosophical quarrel with the *Gazette* content. Historian Elliot J. Gorn noted, "Detailed and sensational news stories about wickedness, according to Comstock, glamourized the lives of libertines, harlots and criminals, and destroyed parents' best efforts" at protecting their children. He continued,

> Comstock's name evokes snickers today, but late 19th century America honored and respected him. His New York Society was supported and bank rolled by a powerful group of socially prominent men— J.P. Morgan (finance), William E. Dodge (copper), Samuel Colgate (soap, appropriately), Kilaen Van Rensselaer (of the old New York Dutch aristocracy), William C. Beecher (attorney and son of Henry Ward Beecher), and Morris Ketchum (merchant, banker, multimillion-aire). Such men were agents of America's transformation, for they built corporations that gave rise to mass immigration, unimagined concentrations of wealth, ever-finer specialization of labor, and bureaucracies employing a whole new class of white collar workers. But even as their efforts caused radical change, they lamented the lost world of their youth. Unruly and heterogeneous cities were quite unlike the small towns and farms of romanticized antebellum childhoods.
>
> The anti-vice campaign was an effort by reformers to patch up the cracks on the cultural edifice. Piety, hard work, sobriety, steady habits, frugality; a strict division of sexual roles into home, nurturance and moral elevation for women; productivity and patriarchal authority for men; above all, tight control of bodily desires and the checking of all forms of lust—these were the central virtues.[35]

Comstock indeed became the object of scorn, and much of it developed in his own lifetime. By the 1900s a word entered common usage and is found in today's dictionaries—"comstockery," meaning overzealous censorship that sometimes targets the arts and literature. But during Fox's heyday Comstock would seem unstoppable in his self-righteousness. In a January 1874 report, he reported the destruction of 134,000 pounds of books, 194,000 pictures, and 60,300 sundries such as "rubber articles," along with 5,500 indecent playing cards—all within two years.[36] The crusade continued for the rest of the century and into the next. Historian Walter Kendrick noted that Comstock's 1883 diatribe *Traps for the Young* contained an alarming

> portrait of American life that, if it had been accurate, would have revealed a country teetering on the brink of total moral and physical collapse. The landscape was so thickly littered with "traps" of all descriptions that only by miracle or the most improbable self-restraint could a child reach adulthood free from corruption. Newspapers, "half-dime" novels, advertisements, theatres, saloons, lotteries, pool halls, postcards, photographs, even painting and sculpture—wherever the poor child turned, in Comstock's nightmarish America, something lurked, ready to debauch him.[37]

In her study of sexual suppression in nineteenth-century America, Helen Lefkowitz Horowitz explored the conflicts and contrasts at work in key elements of society during the Gilded Age. Prohibitions and alarm greeted the gleeful openness of publications such as the *Gazette*, and the era was populated by such radically different figures as feminist Victoria Woodhull, who along with her sister became the first female brokers on the New York Stock Exchange and also ran for president, and Comstock. Horowitz drew a connection between the sporting weeklies and the growth of obscene literature, noting the arrival of the *Sunday Flash* in 1841 with its devotion to "Awful Developments, Dreadful Accidents and Unexpected Exposures; Doings About Town, Doings on the Road, in the Ring and on the Turf, the whole of which will be detailed with all the Horror, Satire, Sagacity, Humeur, Experience and Fun."[38] (One of its proprietors was future *Gazette* editor George Wilkes.) These papers shared a common guiding post for content—the leisurely activities of sporting men in the city and the countryside, and the attendant dangers and adventures that such a life entailed. They "carried news of fistic competitions, reviews and notices of theatrical productions, and ads for places of eating and drinking as well as patent medicines," Horowitz wrote.[39] From the beginning, she also noted, they featured celebrities and wrongdoers.

Horowitz described a war against the sporting press, beginning in 1841, that amounted to an attempt to pull in the reins of their salacious content. Sometimes the sporting publications, such as the *Sunday Flash*, would highlight sexual activities, including coverage of comings and goings at brothels, or make sexually suggestive remarks regarding individuals, which could lead to a libel charge against an editor. If circumstances warranted, a charge of obscene libel also might be filed.[40] The concept of obscene libel came from England, under Lord Campbell's Act of 1857, which allowed for prosecution for publication of material that depraved or corrupted those who were most susceptible to the influences of the obscene materials in question (i.e., women, the mentally challenged, sociopaths, or the young).[41]

In late October 1841, three proprietors of the *Sunday Flash*, including Wilkes, were charged with publishing an obscene paper. The jury was hung but later prosecutions brought more charges against the owners of the sporting journals the *Whip*, the *Rake*, and the *Flash*. George B. Wooldridge, an editor of the *Whip*, said the charges were probably the result of a picture that had run of a chambermaid and an older gentleman, who were shown locked in a lusty struggle with his legs straddling the handle of a warming pan that she had lit for him. In the illustration she is holding the handle, which in the picture is suggestive of an erect penis, and her grasp of the stick "can be seen as her masturbating him."[42] Editors claimed that such charges were usually the result of politics or personal vendettas, but some of the accused, including Wooldridge and Wilkes, were sent to New York's famed Tombs prison. James Gordon Bennett, the *Herald* editor, was angered by the hypocrisy and wrote an editorial with the overline, "The Tweedle-dum and Tweedle-dee in Morals."[43]

Following the *Flash* trial, Wilkes's case became problematic. He was given a suspended sentence and ordered not to work for another obscene publication. But then he appeared in court as a reporter for Mile Walsh's *Subterranean* while Walsh was being tried for libel. Wilkes's court appearance led prosecutors to conclude that he was still connected with obscene literature, and he was sent to the Tombs for thirty days. His jail diary became *The Mysteries of the Tombs*, a treatise on prison and the injustices of the libel and obscenity laws. He noted that published materials were prosecuted, but the acts they supposedly caused, adultery and fornication and assault, were not. "Is this not supremely absurd?" he argued.[44] As Horowitz noted, Wilkes would have later opportunities to reflect on libel laws as founder of the *Gazette*, and his arguments were used by others who fought obscenity laws. Wilkes also developed a sound strategy—by using court and police records, he was able to deflect libel suits, which had to prove falsity in the published material because of libel case law dating back to the 1735 trial of John Peter Zenger.[45] The crime reports were filled with abortions, rapes, seductions, prostitution, and such, but they were not invented. Thus, through the use of public records, he avoided prosecution.[46]

Obscenity laws outlawed materials believed to be "lewd," "indecent," "filthy," or "obscene," and, although the wording varied from state to state, they were all based on the notion that, wrote historian Marjorie Heins, "female sexuality . . . hardly existed—or certainly shouldn't in 'nice' girls."[47] The first American obscenity laws came in the early 1800s, with Vermont passing the first obscenity statue in 1820, followed by Connecticut, Massachusetts, New York, and others. All the laws concerned descriptions—and later, depictions—of lewd or indecent acts. The first federal law concerning obscenity was enacted a few months after Wilkes's trial, to limit the importation of French postcards and other similar materials.[48]

Wilkes ostensibly campaigned against obscene books, but he also pushed the law to its limits through his use of official records to get racy material in the *Gazette*. But the demand for the books remained;

Horowitz noted that one consequence of the 1842 Tariff Act, which attempted to cut back on the import of sexually suggestive foreign literature, caused the growth of an American adult-print industry.[49] The fact is that these licentious journals were published because they were popular. For example, George Thompson, who published *My Life* in 1854 and claimed his childhood home was near where Helen Jewett was murdered, later wrote for the *Gazette*. He was wildly popular and included sex acts of a great variety in his writings.[50]

During the late 1860s and early 1870s, George Matsell, the former police commissioner who was *Gazette* editor, began to emphasize crimes, often with a racial or sexual element. The *Gazette*'s competitors, including Frank Leslie's *Day's Doings*, also highlighted violence, sport, and theater. One of the purposes of these publications, including books, was to offer outsiders a glimpse of what was to many the most exciting place in the world, New York City.[51]

It was in this atmosphere that Comstock operated. Surprisingly, he was not treated with great disdain by Fox. He used ads in the *Gazette* to find booksellers, and in 1872 visited a variety of shops with a reporter from the New York *Tribune*, leading to arrests and a praise-filled editorial.[52] Horowitz noted of the *Gazette*,

> Unlike the sporting weeklies of the early 1840s, the *National Police Gazette* was no fly-by-night operation. Burgess, Stringer & Company served as its general subscription agent. This firm represented a fair sample of the mix of mid-nineteenth century literature: James Fenimore Cooper, Alexandre Dumas, and Eugene Sue.[53]

Wilkes was able to use the *Gazette*'s solid foundation to make it more successful than its counterparts; his crusade against Mme Restell lasted for years—one charge against her was that abortion encouraged adultery for married men by allowing women to have sex without worrying about children.[54]

In the end, Comstock was both a victim and a product of his times; he seemed to emerge famous from the old days only to be quickly dropped from the new. As Kendrick noted,

> Before he died, Comstock witnessed the advent of [the] telephone, wireless, motion pictures, automobiles, and airplanes—all of which contributed to a geometrical rise in the rate at which representations, even things themselves, could be disseminated. Until the end, Comstock resisted these developments; though he took full advantage of their power, his goal was always the damming up of the very channels he employed.[55]

Comstock's efforts, like many attempts at censorship, had the curious effect of promoting the very depictions he was trying to discourage. The same effect can be said of *Gazette* lamentations about crimes—or conduct—that it described with excruciating detail. Fox claimed he was an enemy of lust, but he did not hesitate to evoke lust among his male readership. His advertising, noted Gabor, was startlingly reminiscent of today's men's magazines, with their claims of virile enhancement. The ads, wrote Gabor,

> may also be seen as reflecting the libidinal concerns of the time and the concomitant naivete of the *Gazette*'s readers. One need only to flip through the back pages of today's girlie magazines to find that, while content and style may have changed, the gullibility level in many of the ads remains about the same.[56]

Fox may have condemned lustful urges, but that did not mean he could not profit from them. In his landmark work *Folk Devils and Moral Panics*, the sociologist Stanley Cohen called this dichotomy of effects and intents "amplification"—media reports tend to amplify the very behavior they are trying to condemn. Cohen found this process at work in his study of a 1964 Easter Sunday skirmish between groups called Mods and Rockers on the East Coast of England, determining that the media history of events of the "riot" included exaggeration and distortion, prediction, and symbolization.[57] According to Cohen, the descriptions of deviance serve the amplification process in the following ways:

1. the deviation was assigned, allowing "further stereotyping, myth making and labelling";
2. media created the expectation that this sort of deviant behavior almost certainly would happen again;
3. a "wholly negative" stereotyping of Mods and Rockers had been created;
4. the elements were clear enough "to allow for full-scale demonology and hagiology to develop: the information had been made available for placing the Mods and Rockers in the gallery of contemporary folk devils."[58]

The *Gazette*'s treatment and portrayals of women can certainly be seen as amplifications of deviance—the pictures of women stretching, posing, drinking, and smoking were of interest precisely because these were women behaving outside the norms of "nice" society. But by no means were the stereotypes wholly negative. The issue of July 25, 1895, provides a perfect example. On the cover was a picture of "globe kickers," women who kicked lamp globes as a "new pastime indulged in by the dainty and agile young women of St. Louis, Mo." The picture gave the publisher a good excuse to show the women with legs raised high, in a rather suggestive parlor game. On the next page, in the long-running column "Masks and Faces," which told the details of stage life for young women, an article served as a warning: "Cigarettes and Champagne Robbed Lizzie Rietz of Her Voice./ She was Once a Gaiety Girl."[59] The cover picture was admiring enough, but the inside column, accompanied by a woman in short shorts drinking champagne and smoking, served as a morality warning. Eventually, having lost her talents, she "went crazy." She was confined for a while in an asylum at Westport, Connecticut, but her mother could not afford the charges, so she was brought to Bellevue Hospital, where she was sent to Ward's Island. "It is said," the article concluded, "the actual cause of her trouble was the deadly cigarette."[60]

So while the *Gazette* loved cheesecake and gay girls, it often warned against the consequences of the high life. Thus, the *Gazette*, through the efforts of Comstock and others, was a target of those who invoked moral panics, but it as often as not warned against the same lapses of morality as they did. The big difference was that as a general-interest publication, it also carried salacious content that in effect promoted (for the times) aberrant morals. This is not surprising; a newspaper may appeal to a variety of interests or perspectives at the same time. As Kenneth Thompson noted in *Moral Panics*, a newspaper's "ideological reproduction" of news is not due to a conspiracy, and it is not mechanical or automatic:

> It is subject to the *transformation* which the media perform on the "raw materials," even if this is confined within certain ideological limits. Each newspaper may differently appropriate the criteria of selectivity, particularly in view of their sense of their own audience. They will also vary in their transformation of the material in keeping with the particular personality of the newspaper and its version of the language of the public to whom it is addressed. The newspapers' translation of the statements of the primary definers into a public idiom not only makes them more available to the uninitiated; it also invests them with popular force and resonances, naturalizing them within the horizon of understandings of the various publics.[61]

In addition, as noted by sociologists Erich Goode and Nachman Ben-Yehuda, the notion of *who the audience is* is important in the consideration of how moral panics strike. "We would be naive to assume that panics somehow suffuse the society as a whole to the extent that all members of a given society are obsessed about the issue, and that they are obsessed about it all the time," they wrote.[62] Comstock and his followers may have been panicked by alcoholism, dime novels, dirty pictures, and the showgirls and crimes depicted in the *Gazette*. Richard K. Fox may have occasionally worried about the effects of too much champagne on the character of young girls. But he probably thought that panic was too strong a reaction for any of these conditions, and it certainly was not widespread throughout society. Fox saw his job as accurately reporting the human condition; he never saw himself as promoting bad morals, he was simply reporting what people did. His was simply a framing of structured action, and it followed his publication's ideological sphere in the age in which it thrived.[63]

This framing of structured action is a product and process of the social and historical occurrences of the era. The period between 1880 and 1930, which happens to include the peak years of the *National Police Gazette*, were the primary years of America's bachelor subculture, as historian Howard P. Chudacoff contended. One way to understand this trend, he maintained, is to examine bachelors in the context of societal stigma, deviance, and identity. He suggested that bachelorhood may be understood as a stigmatizing element, yet that bachelors formed a specific social group that acted to their advantage as a whole (through common interests, including scandalous magazines). In this manner bachelorhood "constructed a functional existence for itself in society" that amounted to a form of an oppositional masculinity that was powerful in its presence in gangs, pool halls, saloons, and clubs. Chudacoff contended that this form of masculine assertion helped "reorient the blossoming American consumer culture of the late nineteenth century and early twentieth in the direction of youth and the individual, rather than toward the family."[64]

As Chudacoff noted and has been discussed previously, one of the most important trends involving the bachelor subculture was the emergence of the sporting culture in the early and mid-nineteenth century. This culture of sports and games, including gambling, prizefighting, horse racing, and cockfighting, was "coincident" with the bachelor subculture.[65] Historian Timothy Gilfoyle wrote that the sporting culture, including its concomitant attraction to prostitution and gambling, was caused by the increased transience of the immigrant population, which changed the forms of social surveillance. In addition, economic uncertainties caused by changing labor forces made many men unsure of their ability to marry and start a family; sexual relationships and courtship became liberalized; and increasing outspokenness and power of women made some men uncertain of their desire to marry.[66] The men of sports were particularly apt to cling to bachelorhood and to celebrate it. British essayist Donald Mitchell, noted Gilfoyle, wrote a diatribe against marriage in 1850 called *Reveries of a Bachelor*. Civil War-era songs and poems also lamented the end of bachelorhood, and these lyrics fed vaudeville acts that would follow.[67]

In 1890, the U.S. Census counted more than 40 percent of males over 15 as single, the highest percentage in U.S. history until the sexual revolution of the 1960s and 1970s.[68] Why did this happen? Chudacoff explored several possibilities, including demographics (not enough available females), and economics (many men could not afford marriage), but concluded that cultural shifts probably accounted for much of the reason. That is, the offering of new diversions—entertainment from dance halls, pool halls, taverns, and mass media—led men to believe they had few better things to do in their youth than to immediately settle down and get married. "Such diversions helped create a new heterosocial culture, one that brought together young, unattached men and women in social and sometimes sexual relationships that minimized personal commitment,"[69] he wrote. A key component of this new social accessibility, of course, was the city.

The tramp, criminal, and scoundrel Jack Black published his autobiography *You Can't Win* in 1927, but he had long-since reformed from his ways by then. The book focused on his drifting youth that reached an apex of sorts in Kansas City in the 1890s, when he began to understand the bachelor subculture: "I found lots of papers lying around—some cheap novels, *Police Gazettes*, etc.—and I read them all, everything I could get hold of."[70] Black also recounted how one of his heroes, Jesse James, had been built up by the papers such as the *Gazette*—and he followed the story for weeks. When that story was over,

> I turned to other crime stories and read nothing else in the papers. Burglaries, robberies, murders—I devoured them all, always in sympathy with the adventurous and chance-taking criminals. I reconstructed their crimes in my boyish mind and often pictured myself taking part in them. I neglected my studies and prayers to rove about in fancy with such heroes as Jimmy Hope, Max Shinburn, and "Piano Charlie," famous "gopher men" who tunneled under banks like gophers and carried away their plunder after months of dangerous endeavor.

Looking back now I can plainly see the influence the James boys and similar characters had in turning my thoughts to adventure and later to crime.[71]

For Chudacoff, Black was an example of how the mass media (and its twin brother, the rapidly growing consumer culture) responded to and helped create the bachelor subculture. The "availability of newspapers and male-oriented publications such as the *National Police Gazette* reinforced the sense of a masculine outpost" in saloons, cigar stores, or barbershops, signaling to young men and boys the attractions of an exciting lifestyle. And Chudacoff noted that there could be no mistake what was the target audience for such male-oriented advertisements in the *Gazette* as camphorated oil tonic and rosemary hair tonic to prevent hair loss.[72] The *National Police Gazette*, he argued, "for half a century served not only as one of the nation's most popular and unique journals published exclusively for men but also functioned as the unofficial scripture of the bachelor subculture."[73]

Satirically adding to this script was George Ade, a fabulist and humorist born in Kentland, Indiana, just after the Civil War ended, who wrote at least 2,500 published pieces, including books, plays, and fables.[74] His zinging indictments of society and musings on bachelor life included this note on culture of media and consumer goods in 1922:

> Newspapers, magazines, picture plays, novels, current anecdotes—all have fallen into the easy habit of making it appear that the bachelor is a devil of a fellow; that the spirit of youth abides with him after it has deserted the stoop-shouldered [married] slave commonly depicted as mowing lawns and feeding furnaces. The bachelor, as an individual, may sell very low in his immediate precinct; but the bachelor, as a type, has become fictionalized into a fascinating combination of Romeo and Mephistopheles. You never saw a bachelor apartment on the stage that was not luxurious and inviting. Always there is a man servant: It is midnight in Gerald Heachcote's princely lodgings. Gerald returns from the club. Evening clothes? Absolutely![75]

Chudacoff contended that the *Gazette* was able to attract such a wide readership, nearly all of whom were men, because it "catered to all the idiosyncrasies of working-class and middle-class male culture and made special overtures to the bachelor subculture"[76] by exploiting women and crime.

> *The National Police Gazette* offered a particular sort of vulgarity, an illicitness that matched the bachelor's position at the edge of

acceptability but not quite beyond the pale and not too iniquitous. In addition to the gory and distressing tales of murder and revenge, the low life described in *Police Gazette* pages challenged Victorian propriety and represented a reality that existed below—but not too far below— prevailing standards of respectability. Fox and his staff seemed to take pleasure in leading their readers slightly off the primrose path into a dusky world where brutal, manly pursuits, such as dogfights, cockfights, and demonstrations of human strength or unusual skills in water drinking and haircutting masqueraded as sport. The denizens of this world, titillating characters such as Beefsteak Mike, the champion opium smoker of Colorado, and Minerva, the San Antonio, Texas, strongwoman who could catch balls fired from a cannon, graced every issue. And the lingo of this world, common slang terms such as "dizzy blond," "racket" (swindle), "fancy" (boxing aficionado), and "fly" (sporting gentry), entered bachelor vernacular nationwide through the pages of *The National Police Gazette* and its imitators.[77]

Chudacoff did not argue that the *Gazette* was read by bachelors only—many married men took a peek at it—but he contended that its unique position in the marketplace, including its advertising, text, and illustrations, "situated it squarely within bachelor society and reflected the influence that unmarried men wielded on popular consumer culture" during the peak of their demographic influence.[78] He added:

> Richard K. Fox and his writers manifested a peculiar combination of attitudes and values: intensely narrow and bigoted on the one hand, openly permissive and tolerant on the other. Sometimes falsely moralistic, at other times genuinely humanitarian, *The National Police Gazette* promulgated virtues that blended the modern with the antimodern, while at the same time serving up tasty morsels to satisfy bachelor male hunger for vicarious entertainment.[79]

As has been discussed, the illustrations served to "enhance the prurience of the prose," as Chudacoff contended; he cited one example from 1878 involving a feral cat that invaded a St. Louis bathhouse as an excuse by *Gazette* editors to "present a half-page illustration that featured bare-breasted young women cowering from the feline threat to their ablutions."[80] In 1880, after having introduced his sporting department and established his crime reporting, Fox began the "Footlight Favorites," featuring portraits of vain young female coquettes (the word came from French, literally meaning "little cocks"). These women were frequently called soubrettes (meaning flirtatious females, who were often involved in intrigue and were sometimes actresses).[81]

By 1883, Fox was boasting to advertisers, who were charged up to
$2.50 a line, that his publication had a million readers a week. Although
subscriptions were only a sixth of that, with its availability in bachelor
hangouts, that may have not been too much of an exaggeration.[82]

But a strange thing happened during this period. Through the
1880s,

> Fox also cultivated a fascination, perhaps even a fetishistic fascination,
> for reporting about females who behaved in unwomanly ways, such as
> a woman who created her own militia company, a female pastor who
> conducted baptisms, a lady bicyclist who raced against horses, and an
> occasional column of news tidbits titled "Woman's Pranks: Latest
> Eccentricities and Peccadilloes of the Fast and Loose of the Fair Sex."
> More intriguingly, the *Police Gazette* often . . . featured news stories
> about women who engaged in fistic battles with each other or who
> wreaked revenge on a man or men through physical violence that
> ranged from spankings to beatings to murder.[83]

Why did this happen? Chudacoff contended the depictions of
women in "manly" activities "probably represents irony and eclecti-
cism more than it does contradiction or some feminist tendency."[84] If
so, the irony here was important—these portrayals could be said to
have served as a type of "oppositional masculinity" that was sometimes regarded seriously, other times humorously. Chudacoff also
hinted that there was some sort of sacrifice of "manhood" to domi-
nating women in these portrayals.[85] In some cases that may be true;
more likely, at least on a subconscious level, the device was probably
presented as deviance to further define sex roles.

Robert C. Allen, in a study of burlesque and its impact on American
mores and traditions, called attention to the way that having fun with
sex roles was empowering to women. Alan Trachtentenberg wrote in
the foreword to Allen's book, "Initially dominated by women writers
and producers as well as performers, burlesque took wicked fun in
reversing roles, shattering polite expectations, brazenly challenging
notions of the approved ways women might display their bodies and
speak in public."[86]

Allen wrote that Fox took advantage of the burlesque culture:
"sensuality, alcohol and the lure of the city juxtaposed with the paper's
celebration of burlesque's feminine sexuality."[87] The *Gazette*'s
"Footlight Favorites" feature began a twenty-year run in late 1878,
giving a certain legitimacy to women of entertainment; these women
were "freed from the moral restraints of bourgeois culture, both

onstage and elsewhere."[88] In these depictions, women were more like men—they drank beer, smoked, and played poker, and often, they dressed as men as well.

Allen pointed out that the women of this era began to become like men in another important way—they became sexual predators, most notably in the form of gold diggers. The term gold digger first appeared in popular culture during this time. In an 1899 *Police Gazette* short story cited by Allen, called the "Dolly of the Casino," a young woman learns how to use her wiles. She overhears a chorus girl remarking, "The fellow with the blond mustache in the box last night blew me off to six bottles. . . . I'm getting a friend to find out what business he's in, and if he's got any coin. I'm an expensive piece of furniture, I am." When Dolly is surprised the woman can afford a $200-a-month apartment on $15 a week, "The girl looked at her a minute and then burst out laughing." She learns the game quickly, then refuses an offer of marriage despite gifts of diamonds and a brougham because she realizes that men lose interest in women after marrying them.[89] Allen noted that the stereotypical home-wrecking femme fatal was another type of the era. A theatrical publication, the *New York Clipper*, a *Gazette* competitor, spoke of them this way:

> By nature women are plastic, more governed by impulse and passion than reason, generally of an emotional, nervous temperament, with strong affinities and repulsions, but capable, when guile or vice have destroyed the natural disposition, of degenerating into cold, calculating, cunning beings, making all things subservient to one pet object or ambition.[90]

Not surprisingly, these notions amounted to contradictions, serving as both warnings and attractions to men. Women's predatory nature was shown as seductive; a man would do well to be wary.

Allen pointed out that burlesque eventually gave way to the striptease, another news development covered by the *Gazette*. This was overt provocativeness; in 1896, the *Gazette* described the act of Lona Barrison as "remarkable for its suggestiveness." Tellingly, she began in a man's suit and then undressed to the point that "she gets down to what a mining man would call 'hard pan' or what I would call the limit. Then she stands quivering and trembling for a moment before the audience, and in an instant she is out of sight." She had thus acquired a "wide reputation for wickedness." Allen noted dryly, "As with most of the PG's commentary on burlesque, it is impossible to tell here whether this wickedness is being advertised or castigated."[91]

The answer, of course, was both in keeping with the multiple takes on masculinities and its responses.

The *Gazette* was not above promoting "marriage agencies," which offered chances for men to meet unmarried women. But at the same time, said Chudacoff, it "expressed an explicitly antimarriage slant." Stories and illustrations "often lampooned the henpecked husband and extolled the benefits of an independent, unmarried existence." More simply and perhaps more tellingly, noted Chudacoff, the *Gazette* de-emphasized marriage by ignoring it. Very few of the athletes or stuntsmen featured by Fox in more than four decades ever mentioned the person's wife or family. In fact, the opposite was implied—that they were not married.[92]

As has been shown, these conflicting portrayals of women were not surprising, in the context of defending and isolating masculinities. Historian Kevin White wrote,

> Victorians were hypocrites. . . . If Victorians accepted that men should be gentlemen, this was because they also understood men as primitives. If Victorians believed in purity, they also recognized what they called male "sexual necessity" and a double standard of morality: men could relieve their primitive desires and urges by having sex before and even after marriage with lower-class prostitutes.[93]

In some cases men were turning away from the old styles of drab clothing and rigid behavior to a more vigorous approach emphasizing fitness and youth. And the mass media exhibited a manipulation of their desires, through representations that horrified, enraged, and enraptured.[94] One man may have simply wanted to look at racy pictures; another may have admired the new athleticism of women and seen it as a challenge or stimulant to his physical fitness to which he should respond; and a third may have shaken his head (titillated, nevertheless) at girls who smoked and drank. As *American Heritage* noted in 1960:

> In the late nineteenth century, it has often been remarked, a lady's name appeared in print only three times—at birth, at marriage, and at death. However, there were other women, just as there was—and always is—another history than that which appears in the textbooks, a kind of tabloid obbligato to more important events. . . . If soiled doves and brazen society hussies alike shocked the Victorian godly, they titillated the sporty male and allowed the plebeian the ineffable pleasure of scoffing at the sins and follies of what purported to be the upper classes. Any resemblance, of course, between real life and that reported in the gossip columns was as purely coincidental as it is today.[95]

All of these reactions, within the horizons of the readership of the *Gazette*, involved understandable reactions in the context of historical interpretations of masculinities in fin de siecle America. But no reader should ever fail to acknowledge the romanticism and raw sexual power of presenting women in sexual ways. This became so ingrained in the minds of young men and boys during the Fox era that many looked back on the years with an undisputed sentimentality. Consider Irving Berlin's tribute to the Fox *Gazette*, which he wrote for a 1937 musical, *On the Avenue*, starring Dick Powell, Madeleine Carroll, and Alice Faye, about a 1920s era romance:

> Some fellows see the girl that they love in a dream
> Some fellows see their love in a rippling stream
> I saw the girl that I can't forget
> On the cover of a *Police Gazette*.
> If I could find her life would be peaches and cream.
>
> Oh my search will never cease
> For the girl on the *Police Gazette*
> For the pretty young brunette
> On the pink *Police Gazette*.
>
> And above my mantelpiece
> There's a page of the *Police Gazette*
> With a pretty young brunette
> On the pink *Police Gazette*.
>
> I love to stop—la la la la—
> At my favorite barbershop—la la la la—
> Just to take another look at
> The girl that I haven't met, yet—
> And my longing will increase
> For the girl on the *Police Gazette*
> For the pretty young brunette—young brunette—
> On the pink *Police Gazette*—la la la la.
> Where's that pretty young brunette
> On the pink *Police Gazette*?
> And above the mantelpiece
> There's a page of the *Police Gazette*.
> Where's that pretty young brunette
> On the pink *Police Gazette*?
>
> I love to stop—love to stop, love to stop—
> At my favorite barbershop—barbershop, barbershop—

Just to take another look at
The girl that I haven't met, yet.
There's that pretty young brunette
On the pink *Police Gazette*.

And above my mantelpiece
There's a page of the *Police Gazette*
With a pretty young brunette
On the pink *Police Gazette*.

"Gosh, you're beautiful."
"Oh, it's so sweet of you to say that."
"Could I—have a picture of you?"
"Surely."
"Thanks. Thanks. Gee, you ain't got one in tights, have you?"

And my longing will increase
For the girl on the *Police Gazette*
For the pretty young brunette
On the pink *Police Gazette*.[96]

The song is romantic enough until the spoken dialogue near the end. The male seems genuinely grateful for her photo, but the last line, "you ain't got one in tights, have you?"—is spoken breathlessly, with a hint of the prurience it intends, and the song moves from a rather innocent yearning into a squinty-eyed leering. This was the overall effect of reading the *Gazette*—it had dualistic natures of bawdiness and morality, of shocked innocence and newly born cynicism, of outrage amid the winks and nods. This may explain why the *Gazette* became an object of nostalgia not long after it appeared. It was recounting its readers' innocence while simultaneously stimulating their excitements. In this sense it was truly a product of a contradictory, quickly changing age. Barely two decades after the end of the Fox heyday, Edward Van Every, in the foreword to his *Sins of New York* that excerpted some of the more sensational highlights of the Fox *Gazette* era, called the publication a "cherished though bawdy souvenir of the bygone."[97] That describes the publication's treatment of women rather well, as does the book's introduction by Franklin P. Adams:

I remember a feeling of disappointment when the picture of a pugilist appeared on the front page; for the pugilistic world was not my interest, even as it bores me now. But Women and Crime—that magic front-page partnership, dear to the heart of every circulation manager past, present, and future—interested and thrilled me. That is, pictorially, for I never read anything but the description of the picture—and I would gaze at the picture a long time.

Usually it was the picture of a woman, or of many women. Sometimes they were pursuers, sometimes pursued. Occasionally somebody had a revolver, later known to headline writers as a gun or gat. But it was ankles and legs that really got me. Those were the days when a woman's shoe-top was considered, as you might say, uptown. And these pictures showed women's skirts—thousands of skirts—in abandoned disarray. Women were running, and were ostentatiously careless whether they displayed their legs almost to the knee. Yes, I used to stare at those pictures, and so did all the boys that I knew. Some of those boys have attained distinction in one field or another; but none has yet served a jail sentence or a term in the poorhouse. And while this proves nothing, I submit, to the censors who talk of Harm to Youth, that all these things—the amorous movies, the pornographic tabloids, the so-called obscene books—do no harm whatever. I am not controversial enough to prove that they do good. For either Wisdom or Age—or the mixture—tells me that nothing does youth much harm. Or good.[98]

As the twentieth century arrived, the *Gazette* had to some extent become a curiosity that belonged to another age. Other publications covered, with more timeliness, the sports and crime that had become *Gazette* signatures. And its reliance on sexual titillation had become ho hum and even, in retrospect, a bit coy. Still, for a moment in history, it had changed a generation. As Gabor noted, "The discovery of ankles, calves, and thighs albeit covered by tights, had a potent effect on a fairly naive and puritanical population."[99] Yet it was not long before the *Gazette* amounted to little more than an object of longing and nostalgia.

7

Patron of Sport: Richard Kyle Fox (1846–1922)

It was to become a historical irony that Richard K. Fox fought for more open-mindedness in the way that people viewed the contents of his treasured publication. He clearly did not consider the *Police Gazette* to be indecent or salacious; in an open July 1887 letter to a Florida editor who had criticized the immorality of *Gazette* illustrations, Fox challenged the man, in print, to name a single picture that was "immodest" or "lustful":

> You surely must have had some such picture in your mind when you wrote your article. If you had not, naturally and logically you must be a poor sneaking sort of liar trying to cover up your own naughtiness and bestiality by calling attention to defects which do not really exist in others. . . .
>
> If you can mention a single illustration or a single line of letter press that will, under the most vigorous distortion, even seem to support you with a microscopic proof of your rash, hypocritical and lying charge, let us have it. Stand on no ceremony and waste no time.
>
> For a long period I have stood with silent contempt for this sort of innuendo at the hands of Pecksniffs like you. Now, I demand that you shall make good what you say.
>
> I fear that I expect too much of you when I call upon you to prove the truth of the inky utterances under which, like a cuttle fish, you hide your own devious morality. You will, in all probability, shirk away from the challenge like a noisy and senseless cur that has been whipped into quiet.
>
> But I do not intend to let you earn the Pharisaic congratulations of your kind so easily. You shall either prove that you had evidence to justify you in squeaking of the "immodesty," "immorality," "lustfulness" and "licentiousness" of the POLICE GAZETTE or you shall be pilloried from Singapore to Hudson Bay as a cheap and paltry sneak who not only lied but who knew that he was lying when he lied. Yours always,
>
> Richard K. Fox, 1887

Three months later, in a blistering editorial, Fox spent an entire column railing against a typical "pharisaical fraud" who, Fox said, was ever too eager to gain publicity for his cause by criticizing the *Gazette*. He noted pending legislation in Nebraska to restrict the sale of the journal, but remarked that it would not be enforceable because of federal protections for freedom of the press. The "same old gang of frauds and hypocrites" would fail, Fox wrote, because anyone who claimed the *Gazette* was "immoral," "obscene," or "indecent" is "a willful and deliberate liar."[1]

Perhaps what rankled Fox most was how sensationalists such as Joseph Pulitzer and William Randolph Hearst could be considered "respectable" newsmen while he was viewed as little more than a smut peddler. But—and this was the irony—his battles for freedom of expression and liberalized sexual portrayals probably helped speed the demise of the *Gazette*. He helped create a media climate of sensationalism, crime, and sex that soon made the *Gazette* look like a purveyor of old news and quaint raciness. As noted by magazine historian Mark Gabor, after the turn of the century,

> Daily newspapers were covering crime and sports with more accuracy and immediacy than the *Gazette*. . . . This forced it to rely more heavily on its sex-and-sensation features. Sadly for the magazine, the moral climate . . . [became] more relaxed; the subject of sex was less taboo, more open, and certainly freer of the strictures of the "naughty nineties." The *Gazette* was never able to shed its stigma of sin and crime, and so it slid steadily downhill toward eventual bankruptcy in 1932.[2]

Did Fox really believe the *Gazette* to be respectable and modest? Perhaps he would not have used those terms, but above all he considered his a publication that reflected the truth—and it was a truth that resonated across the land as well as overseas. It would not have been unreasonable for him to conclude that those who criticized the Gazette were simply jealous of his success.

In the 1890s, Fox began offering, through the mail, what amounted to girlie pictures. One advertisement for the dime "cabinet" photographs listed the names of more than 150 "actresses . . . showing bust," nearly 100 "actresses . . . in tights," and 100 or so more other "actresses . . . in costume." For example, an ad on the back of Fox's book *Rube Burrows' Raids. Historic Highwaymen. Night Riders of Ozark; Or, the Bald Knobbers of Missouri*,[3] said one of the actresses "showing bust" was the actress Lillian Russell. In addition, as requests for reprints, photographs, and fighting colors poured in, he realized that he had a perfect hub for distribution of other products. By the 1890s Fox had established a sort of sporting *amazon.com* of the nineteenth century, a "supply and purchasing department" that featured sporting balls, games, books, hammocks, foils, fencing masks, ice skates, cards, jerseys, tights, and "trunks, leotards, body dresses . . . English Perculine Running Pants, Improved Jock Straps, Running Shoes, . . . Imported Sheffield Spikes, Seamless Shoes, Boxing Gloves and Foot Balls."[4]

Fox's ability to branch out into sales of sporting goods may be considered an early form of branding, which economist Stewart Pearson defined as adding value to a product through marketing, association, and differentiation.[5] Fox's products met this definition, as he had the vehicle (a publishing house) to market his sporting goods, associate them with his expertise, and provide them with a differentiation that set them apart from other like products (that difference being the *Gazette* and Fox himself). This tying of products to corporate emblems grew rapidly during this period; scholar M.M. Manring wrote that between 1870 and 1906, mass production and marketing led the number of trademarks in America to grow from a hundredfold to more than 10,000. One of the most successful early brands was promoted by flour king R.T. Davis, who bought the Aunt Jemima trademark in 1890. He then created a fictional life story for her in which she rescued a Confederate Louisiana colonel from certain death by distracting threatening Union soldiers with the most delicious pancakes in the world. She demanded to be paid in gold rather than currency.[6]

Though Fox had no use for such obvious mythmaking in his sporting goods enterprise, he used the *Gazette*'s creation of outlaw heroes to good advantage in marketing literature that also carried his brand surname. The Richard K. Fox publishing house carried titles that sometimes credited Fox with authorship of books on boxing and other sport and games, but often these books would simply acknowledge they were "published" by Fox, with no credited author.[7]

The valuable and apparently profitable publishing house, which flourished during the prime years of Fox's career, from the 1880s to the 1910s, was famous for its ten- to twenty-five-cent paperbacks on topics ranging from prizefighting to cockfighting. Titles included books that told tales of heroes as well as villains, which were important *Gazette* symbols and part of Fox's brand-making that helped sell his books. In their 2001 book *The Hero and the Outlaw*, authors Margaret Mark and Carol S. Pearson discussed the ways that marketers trade on myths and archetypal symbols to sell products. They note that advertisers have always used these collections of mythical imagery to sell products, from the Jolly Green Giant—the "archetype of the Green Man, a figure associated with fertility and abundance"— to the winged goddess Nike, who symbolized victory. The authors wrote that meaning is an asset to a brand, and that advertising is a method for the management of meaning.[8]

Fox used the heroes and criminals of his books—many of whom had appeared in the *Gazette*—in a similar way. Many of his publishing house's volumes were fiction disguised as "authentic," but they used truth in the sense that today's tabloid tattlers use it—they divulged escapades to illustrate, aggravate, and satiate the contemporary cultural passion for drama, lust, gossip, and excitement. In other words, they told the deeper realities about society through the use of legend and symbols rather than facts. Of course, some books were factual, particularly those on card games, New York slang, detective work or, for example, the Johnstown flood. In these cases, if the books did not closely adhere to the truth, their authors at least made a fairly serious attempt to be factual. For Fox, the "non-fiction" element of his business was important. In an 1884 editorial-page item dubbed "Dangers of Fiction," Fox or one of his assistants told the tale of a writer who had attempted suicide by jumping out of a fourth-story window only to somehow survive to be arrested and brought to Tombs Police Court:

> Upon investigation, it appeared that he had been writing tales for the newspapers and had lived so long in the realms of fancy that fancy had turned his brain. When questioned by the judge whether he was engaged in writing a new story, he answered that he was, that it was real and that he had just been to Jersey City, where he had killed a beautiful young lady who rejected his love. Surely, this is a terrible example. "Mad as a hatter" is a trite adage, but if this sort of thing continues, it will have to be changed to "cracked as a story writer."[9]

In another item in the same year, a *Gazette* writer told the tale of a "youth who has been ruined by dime novels." The young man, William Willet, of Chipocee Falls, Massachusetts, was held on charges of killing a Kingston, New York, saloon-keeper, Edwin Keiland, after plotting a crime that read "like a chapter from one of the dime novel detective stories of the day." The article concluded that Willet appeared to have been wholly corrupted by dime novels.

According to the *Gazette*, Willet, after finding employment on a Hudson Valley farm as an errand boy and berry picker, began pestering the farm owner, Patrick Barry, on his errands into town, to buy him "blood and thunder novels." Then Willet would lie awake for hours in the barn, where he should have been sleeping, reading the stories. One day he got drunk and was discharged but ended up on another farm owned by Eli Harcourt. He reported to the *Gazette* "that on the main he was a steady boy, but he had a mania for reading flash literature. In four weeks' time he purchased and read fifteen five-cent novels. His whole frame would be in a tremor of excitement, and his eyes would glisten while holding one of the Jesse James series in his hand." It was in the tradition of James, reported the *Gazette*, that Willet planned his bold robbery that resulted in the saloon-keeper's murder.[10]

Although many of his published offerings were considered at least as flashy as the flash fiction, Fox apparently saw no irony in condemning blue literature while spitting out the material himself. For Fox, one supposes, the real danger was in fiction, not in fact. So, he became a millionaire, a dime at a time, and he branched out into other investments. He became a major landlord, buying a row of tenements in New York's Chinatown in the 1890s. He renovated the housing with marble staircases, steam heat, gas, and bathrooms, and erected several bronze statues in public areas, including one of Libby Ross, the champion female boxer of the world. But Fox allowed the low-income renters to remain and kept rent at $10–$15 a month. That may have been a mistake: the inhabitants of the "Fox Flats" sold the bronze statues and plumbing for beer and rent money.[11]

Up to and even past the turn of the century were clearly some of Fox's most prosperous days; on the back of one of the books he published was a proudly displayed, finely detailed woodcut of the impressive *Police Gazette* building at Franklin Square. It had an American flag and a *Police Gazette* flag atop it, and a *Police Gazette* delivery wagon was parked out front, winning the admiration of passersby.

In the early 1900s, he bought a country home in Red Bank, New Jersey, and also bought a ranch at Arcadia, California, in Los Angeles County. On his many trips to England, he spent considerable time with the gentlemen's sporting class, particularly those interested in the turf and ring, and counted Hugh Lowther, the Fifth Earl of Lonsdale, among his many friends. Lonsdale, who was the first president of England's National Sporting Club, helped develop boxing all over the world. His association with Fox is remembered largely because he solicited Fox's help in his great race against the Earl of Shrewsbury in 1891. The race arose after Shrewsbury and Lonsdale got into a brandy-fed argument over whether a trotter could beat a galloper in a long race, and it evolved into an elaborate wager involving four legs and twenty miles. The contest captured the imagination of England, and it made headlines for weeks.

In one leg of the race, Lonsdale was to drive a light carriage pulled by a horse, but after searching all of England, he could not find a suitable buggy. He called upon Fox, who had a special lightweight buggy sent across the Atlantic. The idea of the race caught the fancy of the British public, and the press and gamblers followed its developments for months. Just before the race, Shrewsbury cabled that he was snowbound, and he won from the referee a one-day postponement. Lonsdale, however, would have none of it. In Shrewsbury's absence, using Fox's buggy during a portion of the event, he raced against the clock and covered twenty miles in a remarkable fifty-four minutes and fifteen seconds.[12]

Fox's financial and journalistic fortunes peaked in the 1890s. But as the United States entered the American Century, there were signs, when viewed in retrospect, that spelled doom for the *Gazette*. At the center of American journalism was not Fox; rather, this period of journalism history would be dominated by another contemporary immigrant—Pulitzer—and his rival, the Californian Hearst. These giants played major roles in transforming journalism, and they borrowed many of Fox's tactics, from emphasizing sports to sponsoring stunts and promotions. Like him, they were geniuses at public relations, sometimes garnering national attention. It was the fight between Pulitzer and Hearst that became this era's key journalism history in the popular imagination—and it was the competition between Hearst's New York *Journal* and Pulitzer's *World* that gave yellow journalism to history.[13]

One may call Fox's unique product pink journalism—the *Gazette* was the attention-getter that died when it could no longer attract attention. Soon after the turn of the century, wrote Gabor, "its circulation declined sharply, probably due to a new generation of magazines appealing to younger readers. . . . The *Gazette* was dying of old age."[14] This was happening long before Fox's death in 1922, but it became worse in the 1920s; in 1930, writer Franklin P. Adams noted, "what with the daily newspapers printing pictures that make even the old *Gazette* seem conservative, and tabloids out-sensationalizing the *P.G.* at its pinkest period, the once popular weekly is in what the boys call a Tough Spot." The "zippiest picture" Adams found in the June 7, 1930, issue was a costumed pose featuring Clara Bow, "a further cry from the nude" that could been seen then in movies.[15]

By this time, even the pink *Gazette* was no longer the vilified, sometimes frightening carrier of lust and mayhem that had alarmed the Victorians. Instead, it was remembered fondly as a companion to the rites of boyhood passage. Adams wrote of his and his friends' days in late-nineteenth-century Chicago,

> To most of us the *Police Gazette* was something that we saw in barber-shops of the Eighties and Nineties. One of the first jokes I ever heard (at Sam T. Jack's Madison Street Opera House, Chicago) was "Seen the *Police Gazette?*" "No, I shave myself." Of course, the names *Puck* and *Judge* sometimes were substituted, but that wasn't funny to me, because we used to have *Puck* and *Judge* every week at home. But I never saw a copy of the *Police Gazette* outside of Frank's barber-shop, which was on the south side of 35th Street, between Indiana and Michigan Avenues.[16]

The novelist Tom Wolfe also was brought to nostalgic heights when he was asked to produce the Foreword to the 1972 compilation of *Gazette* articles by Gene Smith and Jayne Barry Smith. And he tipped his hat to its references to manhood:

> It would be mere posturing to claim any literary distinction for the *Police Gazette*. Yet its writers did provide a look at a side of American life that more serious and fastidious writers, including the major novelists of the period, approached. I am talking about a style of living that was not so much the opposite of High Victorian Gentility as its underside: namely, the world of the Sport, or the Sporting Man . . . who led The Sporting Life . . . the uncultivated *macho* dandy whose love of sport had nothing to do with the High Victorian ideal of "athletics" and everything to do with, simply . . . the eternal gamble against Fate . . . who would bet on anything and was therefore willing to turn loose all the minor vices (gambling, lechery, gluttony, profanity and blood sports) that were kept leashed in the social sphere above him.[17]

One gets the sense that the era was passing even as it flourished. Gene Smith wrote,

> The women peeped at Kilrain's muscles and John L.'s massive (naked!) chest. The men read the Bible of the Barbershop in an atmosphere of cigars and bay rum. They lived in towns where the street paving ended where the trolley made its turnaround. Their wrists were thick and their nails were not clean. They drank, being largely of the lower orders (as was 95 percent of the populace) and therefore pretty much immune to the genteel Women's Christian Temperance Union ideas of the middle

classes. Their surroundings were grimy and dreary. Coal dust covered them in winter and mud in spring, and they always smelled of horse manure. . . .

We have to read awfully far to find our past. But something of it is here in the *Police Gazette* to say that once upon a time these our own breathed, yelled, fought, made love, had great and terrible passions—that they lived.[18]

Smith believed that the *Gazette* was in decline for twenty years before Fox's death in 1922: "Hearst and Pulitzer and [Robert] McCormick long afterward admitted their debt to him. . . . Their time began when his ended with the rise of the tabloids."[19] Though he was editor for more than forty years, the best of his "run" was less than twenty-five. "Then at the turn of the century the dailies, copying him, out-sensationalized and out-yellow-journalized him. And they had photographs too,"[20] Smith wrote. Fox tried pandering to barbershops and saloons exclusively, "but the life and spirit were gone. The dailies had sports sections and theatrical gossip columns too. By the time he died, his rag was as dull and lifeless as it had been when he began."[21]

In a similar vein, historian Howard P. Chudacoff remarked, "Times change . . . and popularity is fleeting."[22] To put it simply, the *Gazette* became a victim of its own success:

Seizing an opportunity to satisfy an ever more curious public, enterprising publishers began printing daily tabloids and confession magazines that exceeded *The National Police Gazette* in disseminating news of sin, scandal, and sensation. Capitalizing on new frankness in the discussion of sexual matters, Sunday newspaper magazines also began to print similar sensational stories. As well, legitimate metropolitan daily newspapers, such as those in the Hearst and Pulitzer empires, began to include separate sports sections that surpassed Fox's ability to offer full coverage, especially because he had invested his major commitments to boxing, to the neglect of most other sports.[23]

By the turn of the century, said journalism historian Frank Luther Mott, the *Gazette* was a producer of secondhand news.[24] As Chudacoff noted, the Sunday magazine sections had supplanted its crime reporting; in addition, some of its sports columns focused on histories of sport rather than current events.[25] By the time of the Spanish-American war in 1898—a great booster for his newspaper rivals—Fox's circulation had dropped to 60,000. Mott, using prizefighting terms, said the Eighteenth Amendment creating prohibition delivered a "solar plexus" blow to the *Gazette* by cutting off its bar-room circulation. He added, "Richard K. Fox died in 1922, and that very year came another shattering blow: women began to bob their hair." The new fashion opened barbershops to women, and many barbers decided they did not want to have "naughty pictures" around with women in their shops. "Dame Fashion, transformed into one of the female pugilists whom the *Gazette* used to feature, had delivered a right uppercut to the chin of the old pink paper," Mott wrote.[26]

Fox's son Charles assumed the editorship after Fox's death, and the *Gazette* enjoyed some prosperous times with the championship of Jack Dempsey, but the success did not last long. It was sold as bankrupt in 1932 for $545. A few publishers attempted revivals; in 1935 Harold H. Roswell became editor, made the *Gazette* into a slick paper monthly, and pushed its circulation to more than 300,000 by using the old-style *Gazette* ingredients. But its circulation gains were temporary, and it was eventually sold to a concern in Montreal, Canada. It ceased circulation by 1975.[27]

Fox was seventy-six years old when he died on November 14, 1922, at his home on Branch Avenue in Red Bank, where he had bought a house in 1904. The cause of his death was "hardening of the arteries," according to his death notice in the Red Bank *Register*.[28] The *New York Times* of November 15, 1922, said in his obituary, "His name was known years ago wherever sport was a subject of conversation, although his intimate friends said that he knew nothing of any sport, except boxing." The obituary said he gave away more than $1 million in prizes, with the diamond-, emerald-, ruby-, and sapphire-studded championship boxing belt, worth $4,000—which Sullivan had scorned after his battle with Kilrain in Richburg, Mississippi—the best known. "He also gave medals for sculling, football, shooting, running, wrestling and every other branch of sport," the obituary said.[29] Services were held on November 20 in the Funeral Church, at Sixty-Sixth and Broadway, with the Rev. Nathan A. Seagle of St. Stephen's Protestant Episcopal Church presiding. Pending the erection of the mausoleum, Fox's body was placed in a vault. "More than a hundred persons attended the services, including many figures of the sporting world," said the notice.[30]

A month later the *Times* ran a two-paragraph item saying that Fox left a $3 million estate. His personal property in New York was worth $500,000, which he left to his wife Emma (whom he married in 1913; his first wife died in New York in 1890), as well as $150,000, his Red Bank residence and its contents, plus a third of the residuary estate. His sister received $150 a month; two business partners received

$5,000 each; and his children—Mary Kyle, Charles J., Frederick G., and Richard Kyle Jr.—shared two-thirds of the residuary estate. Fox also set aside $50,000 for a mausoleum and plot.[31] Six months later the *Times* reported that Fox's estate had been finally appraised at $1,796,169; he owned several real estate properties outright but refused to increase rents at a time when others were doing so, thus reducing their appraised value. At the time of his death, Fox had debts of only $11,439 but had an outstanding judgment against him for $200,000. William Rafter, then a sporting editor for a Brooklyn newspaper, had sued Fox for $600,000 for breach of contract. A former managing editor of the *Police Gazette*, he claimed Fox had agreed to pay him $25,000 a year for life but had fired him soon afterward. He won a $200,000 verdict that was appealed.[32]

The estate owned Empire City Job Print, worth $72,210, at 338–344 Pearl Street in Manhattan, which was valued at $150,000, and several other parcels of Manhattan realty. Fox also owned at least four properties in Brooklyn worth more than $100,000, and he held $92,298 in cash, $16,125 in gold and currency, *Gazette* stock worth $160,305, and $141,036 in Liberty bonds.[33]

The *Times* accounting also revealed that the *Gazette*, despite all of its troubles, remained profitable until his death. Its average annual profit from 1918 (when it sustained a loss of $6,237) to 1922 was more than $50,000.[34]

Fox was remembered fondly in death. He was genial and amiable, supported local baseball clubs, and was a full-time resident of Red Bank since 1913, according to the Red Bank *Register*.[35] George Jean Nathan and H.L. Mencken wrote an admiring obituary for Fox in the *Smart Set*, interestingly sandwiching it between antifeminist screeds (one item decried the disrespectful habit of married women addressing their husbands by their first names rather than by "Mr. Smith" or "Mr. Jones"; the other repeated the old joke that "For the normal man there is but one use and value in marriage; it protects him, at least temporarily, from another marriage"). Nathan and Mencken said Fox was consistently underestimated in his life and was perhaps responsible for influencing the "practical side" of American journalism more than anyone except Charles Dana and Hearst. They gave Fox credit for inventing sports coverage that forced imitation from James Gordon Bennett, Pulitzer, and Hearst; he was also credited with inventing "condensed journalism" by telling his reporters, "Tell your story in three paragraphs at most. . . . If you can't tell it in three, tell it in two. And if you can't tell it in two, get the hell out of here!" Even the upscale *Smart Set* imitated Fox, the authors noted, printing on pink paper for a while but abandoning the practice after it became too expensive. Fox went to pink paper shortly after he took over the journal in the 1870s, and Nathan and Mencken remarked that other publishers had later imitated Fox's use of tinted stock, including Bennett in the New York *Telegram*, Hearst in the *Journal*, and Pulitzer in the *Evening World*, along with publications in London, Paris, Rome, Berlin, and Venice. Nathan and Mencken also gave Fox credit for being the first to hold sporting and other events directly under the auspices of a publication. He was scorned and ridiculed in America, said Nathan and Mencken, but he was a world traveler (often to England) and a sophisticated collector of rugs and antiques who counted among his friends four U.S. presidents: Ulysses S. Grant, James Garfield, Grover Cleveland, and, they claimed, Lincoln, who died nine years before Fox came to America.[36]

> Looked on with social disfavor at home, he was the pet of the British aristocracy. Looked on as the editor of a mere low barbershop paper in America, he was regarded on the Continent as the most enterprising, the most audacious and the most thoroughly honest of the American editors of his day. Richard K. Fox, two humble editorial followers salute your genius and your memory! May God rest your noble bones.[37]

In a similar laudatory tone, an editorial in the *Herald* said that Fox "capitalized the arms and legs of celebrities. He knew the weaknesses of his public. Men of that day wanted to gaze on the terrific biceps of Paddy Ryan and on the classic curves of Lydia Thompson."

Gazing back at the *Gazette* even twenty years before, the New York *Herald* noted "the horror with which it was regarded is to understand the great changes that the years have brought." But, in 1922,

> compared with the pictures of female swimming champions, Winter Garden heroines and interpretative Greek dancers, how modest look the ladies that Mr. Fox pictured! If somebody had brought to the *Police Gazette* office in the early '80s a photograph of a Long Beach bathing group of 1922 we can fancy Mr. Fox giving him a lecture."[38]

The editorial continued, "As in pictorial representation, so in text. The *Police Gazette* in its reports of scandals went as far in its revelations as it thought the average man would care to have it go." If some of the books published "since the war" had been brought to Fox's attention, the editorial said, "he would have turned the novels down as too utterly vile." The writer added, "If James Joyce's 'Ulysses' had been printed in the *Police Gazette*the patrons of that publication would have torn up their copies lest they be contaminated."[39]

This dubious praise, of course, probably would not have suited Fox. Although he did not consider the *Gazette* to be indecent, at every turn he championed the right of free expression. One supposes that not only would he have welcomed the publication of *Ulysses*, he would have been pleased to find that the *Gazette* was mentioned in it. The *Gazette* was uncharacteristically subdued upon Fox's death. In a short, albeit laudatory obituary, it remarked, "By reason of his numerous costly gifts to sports in the way of belts and medals to champions in many lines, he achieved a universal reputation as a large-hearted patron of athletic endeavor."[40]

As has been noted, men such as Pulitzer and Hearst made sure that Fox's brand of journalism lived on after his death. Even the *Times* was not immune. In 1926, it used the same point size headline for the Tunney-Dempsey prizefight as it had used for the Armistice ending World War I. A dozen years later, it was running a full sports section, pictures on nearly every page, headline digests, theater and entertainment columns, and even poetry.[41] Some believe Fox's influence contributed to the tabloid mentality that survives among media even today.[42] This is true in the sense that he had a similar talent at building circulation. Fox was a master of marketplace and promotion: he gave the people (in this case, mostly men) what they wanted, both by creating as well as covering events. His real contribution was in recognizing the characteristics of his era—an idealization of physical fitness, a thirst for competition, a yearning for robust living, and a fascination with the bizarre world then unfolding—and accordingly producing his pages to raise the eyebrows and quicken the pulse. Not surprisingly, the *Gazette* was anchored on a leering sensibility toward women who were as apt to ignore it as pounce on it, to tease it as to dispel it, to encourage it as to defy it by acting or dressing as men. "It lessens a woman's opinion of a man when she learns that his admiration is so pointedly and generously distributed," wrote Theodore Dreiser in 1900's *Sister Carrie*. "She sees but one object of supreme compliment in this world, and that is herself."[43]

Media scholar Michael Parenti said that framing is the selection of images, vocabulary, and labels that work by "bending the truth rather than breaking it."[44] He was writing primarily about political symbols, but the description works for Fox because of his ability to frame the movements of society—its structured actions in a time of masculinities running scared and running amok—and his ability to bend, stretch, laugh at, abhor, and enjoy the truth. Fox showed the truth but showed it in a way that was not always factual. Yet these fictionalized accounts of shootings, trysts, killings, and other physical recreations, so lovably drawn in the *Gazette* woodcuts, were truer to his readers than the events themselves. Author Wendy Lesser, in her *Pictures at an Execution*, wrote that "Fictional murder seems more credible because more can be known about it."[45] So it was with those woodcuts—imagined by the artists, they gave people an ability to see and, as Lesser maintains about murder,[46] identify with the strange and deviant acts they saw. That was Fox's legacy: creating images of men and masculinities that repelled, attracted, and influenced all at once.

Sociologist Michael Kimmel wrote in 1996 that men are still burdened with the expectations of "masculinity," and he believed that men should try to free themselves from attempts to prove themselves because "the battle to prove manhood is a battle that can never be won."[47] But that concept had not been discussed much in the Gay Nineties; it was in this battle that Fox found his great fortune, as he helped create lasting images of the American man.

The *Gazette* is remembered today because of its outrageousness and, some would say, tawdriness. But, as in so many things, the most remembered is not always the first. Historian Simon Bessie gave credit to the *Daily Graphic* for being the first true tabloid; it began in 1873, three years before Fox engineered his takeover of the *Gazette*. A glance at a typical *Graphic* cover, with large, sensational illustrations, shows its similarities to the *Gazette*. But it died in 1879, leaving the tabloid legacy to Fox and his golden years. Eventually, though, Bessie concluded (as did others) that the tabloids beat the *Gazette* "at its own game."[48] When it lost its ability to shock, it lost its shocking circulation numbers.

What is the legacy of Fox's *Gazette*? The question has many answers. As has been shown, the *Gazette*'s portrayals of sex, crime, and sports vividly illustrated that it was indeed a powerful framer of masculine culture during a time of economic, political, and social changes that affected men and their relationships to women, other men, and themselves. Particularly during the Fox era, the *Gazette* gave its audience of men and boys glimpses into worlds that played off their hopes, dreams, desires, and fears. As has been illustrated, in these pages were stories of crime, daring, sexual adventure, and sporting heroics, all vividly drawn and pressed into the minds of generations of new, and relatively inexperienced, consumers of mass media. No study on masculinities and its framing by the news media during this period can be complete without a review of the *Gazette*, for it helped create some of the most powerful images and ideas associated with manliness in all their qualities, from grace to greed, from strengths to helpless-ness, from the depths of brutal ugliness to the loftier search for beauty. This study has quantified many of these representations, and it has dis-cussed qualitatively what they meant to America in the late nineteenth and early twentieth centuries.

Yet there is another legacy of the *Gazette* that cannot be ignored—its place in the history of journalism. For the *Gazette* offered working- and middle-class men something that they needed in Victorian America—entertainment. At once lurid and fantastical, personal and universal, full of gossip and jokes and crime and lust, it was the con-summate entertainment magazine—what today we would call a tabloid. "Historians," wrote Elliott J. Gorn, "ignore the *National Police Gazette* at their peril." Why? Because Fox encouraged his read-ers to have fun, and his publication was the most wildly successful early tabloid entertainment rag that proved big money could be made from gossip, sports and celebrity news, sex, crime—and pictures. Moral crusader Anthony Comstock, Gorn believed, gave the *Gazette* too much credit for contaminating American morals. He continued,

> Still, Comstock had a point. The moral universe he and his friends grew up in was beginning to fall apart. In the dawning age of gratification, of spectacles, of image production, Richard Kyle Fox and his spiritual heirs helped set the cultural tone for the nation, shape its values, and amass fortunes along the way. If Comstock's Victorianism was a survival of an earlier era of entrepreneurial capitalism, Fox represented the new age of consumption . . . Fox and his publication were at the vanguard, and the sensibility they represented, for better or worse, became a significant part of American life.[49]

That sensibility, of reliance on spectacle, fantasy and illustrations, lives even today. One must not forget that tabloidism, and its empha-sis on personalization, dramatization, and sensationalism, is the father of other qualities in today's media environment—including reality tel-evision and the hyping of sex and violence as commodities. Of course, one cannot say that the *Gazette* caused public fascination with these topics—they are there because people want to watch—but its place in the history of tabloid journalism should not be ignored.

The earliest definitions of tabloids referred to their physical characteristics; a tabloid was folded in a half-page size as compared to the standard broadsheet. But historian Mott added a couple of other characteristics to the definition—the devotion of a big proportion of the paper's space, including its front page, to pictures; and a "terse, condensed," lively presentation style. Mott also considered tabloids to be daily newspapers, not magazines such as the *Gazette*.[50] Still, even under Mott's characterization, the *Gazette* partially fits the bill. Its writing, while not always terse, was certainly lively, and its reliance on pictures was well known.

But this definition leaves out what other historians consider to be a tabloid's key ingredients; media scholar Colin Sparks wrote that the typical tabloid

> devotes relatively little attention to politics, economics, and society and relatively much to diversions like sports, scandal and popular entertainment; it devotes relatively much attention to the personal and private lives of people, both celebrities and ordinary people, and relatively little to political processes, economic developments, and social changes.[51]

The tabloid also feeds on scandal, giving it a hysterical quality.[52] This certainly describes the *Gazette*, and places it among less serious publications that follow tabloid methods. But the *Gazette* was not the cause or originator of tabloid journalism. As has been discussed, the *Daily Graphic* of New York is considered a pioneer in the American version of tabloidism. But sensationalism in the news began long before America was ever founded. Historian Erika J. Pribanic-Smith wrote that the Sumerians, in 2000 B.C., printed sensational items of war and gossip. Sir Alfred Harmsworth (Lord Northcliffe) began the form in Great Britain in the late nineteenth century with the *London Daily Mirror*.[53] But in America the *Gazette* helped spread tabloid sensibilities or what Jostein Gripsrud called the "melodramatic" understanding of society.[54]

There has long been a fear that journalism, as journalist David J. Krajicek wrote, would "transform itself into a hybridized combination of *Police Gazette* and *Confidential Magazine*."[55] Sparks concluded that today there is a "moral panic" over tabloid media because of their threat to serious journalism.[56] The very existence of tabloid media, and their popularity, demand responses from mainstream press that change their approach to news. That, in turn, threatens the credibility of reporting. In addition, sensationalism is seen by some to debase society and erode moral structures. Indeed, on these grounds Comstock instigated a moral panic against the *Gazette* and like publications.[57] But there is a powerful incentive toward sensationalism. It gets readers' (and viewers') attention. Media barons, in responding to the pressure for more readers and better ratings, have often tried to focus on the most intimate tastes of readers—that is, whatever sells. In some cases, that means that news "is whatever the competition is covering," Krajicek wrote.[58]

But this type of myopic reporting has (and had, in Fox's day) real consequences. One of those is the distortion of reality. Media critic Barry Glassner warned in 1999 that irresponsible journalism focusing on crime and "baseless scares" created a society afraid of the wrong things.[59] If viewed in that light, the *Gazette* was an early purveyor of Glassner's "culture of fear"—its endless stories about depravities, immoralities, hypocrisies, foul acts, and criminal deeds served to create the impression that the world was a more dangerous and corrupt place than it really was.

And, despite his protestations, Fox was no stranger to fear-mongering. Pick up virtually any *Gazette* during the era and one will find violence, immorality and/or alarm at such conduct. For example, on January 20, 1894, the *Gazette*'s front page carried a large illustration of a young man being beaten to death by his father—because the youth had been in bed with his stepmother, who was shown in night-gown watching in horror at the assault.[60] Inside the publication were stories on morphine addiction, an exciting elopement, and a murder of a jealous lover. Did such things happen very often? No, but no reader of the *Gazette* could be blamed for thinking they did. This does not mean the *Gazette* should be blamed for the ills of modern journalism, or for the depravities it depicted. For Fox and his *Gazette* were merely doing what tabloids do—creating entertainment and meaning for readers.

Sparks argued that tabloids should not be casually dismissed as vulgarly inferior; they carry content that has significance and worth. By featuring articles on events or people exciting to their readers, tabloids do address issues of social concern and social structure. They are interested in class as well as social conflict, and the tales they feature are important to their readers partly for that reason, Sparks wrote. In addition, their focus on personalities and personalization means

> that they are quicker to identify significant new social trends or public issues. At their very best, they can transcend the patronizing limitations of the journalistic adoption of a popular conversational style and actually give voice, and thus public legitimacy, to groups.[61]

Perhaps most important, Sparks wrote, "Tabloid journalism facilitates private enjoyment and pleasure."[62]

For Gripsrud, the tabloids' focus on melodrama suggests a public fascination not merely with pap or pulp, but with active opposition to traditional channels of information. One way of looking at the popularity of tabloids is empowerment of its readers—that is, ordinary people.[63] It is only natural for the newspapers to respond to these demands, and in this role the *Gazette* was suited perfectly.

The *Gazette* has been discussed as a purveyor of masculinities, as a companion to pornography, as a vehicle fighting and sensationalizing crime, and as a promoter of sporting events and popular culture. But it was also an outlet of expression—and thus, an organ of enjoyment and therefore empowerment—for working- and middle-class men. Its tabloid characteristics may have alarmed Comstock, but they were welcomed by the loyal readers who demanded entertainment and a sort of "privileged" information for unprivileged lives. In this sense Fox's *Gazette* is perhaps best remembered as a loud, early example of the "popular press," with all the faults, frailties, vices, shortcomings— and the pep, potency, vigor, and lustiness—that the term implies. It may not have been the voice of a generation, but it was, as much as any of the better known examples of the press of the period, typical of the era's searching, contradictory, and mutating characteristics.

Tabloidism, with its half-truths, raised eyebrows, and gleeful shocks, was the perfect vehicle for the *Gazette* to convey the sort of outrages and hypocrisies it both condemned and embraced. Its illustrations told bawdy and brave stories to boys and men (including immigrants struggling with English) who may not have been so eager to pour over columns of words. Its pictures became signposts of the harrowing possibilities of life for men and boys who were part of a confounding time.

It is important not to overstate the matter; the *Gazette*, after all, was just one publication in a world offering myriad alternative amusements, printed or not, that allowed men to temporarily escape from their sometimes dreary, working-class lives. But in reading the reminiscences of those who grew up with or stepped out to read the *Gazette*, one finds a very profound thing. These remembrances, in all their sentimentality and nostalgia, reveal a simple truth: The *Gazette* had *meaning* for these men. It was a meaning that touched their lives in personal and exciting ways, and it taught them lessons about the things that mattered the most to them—sex, love, violence, and strength. The *Gazette* was populist not just because it exposed the hypocrisies of the wealthy and the clergy, and not just because it favored workers over capitalists. It was populist because it was popular, because it told the amazing tales of beauties, beasts, and brutes who inhabited the dreams and nightmares of the men and boys of New York, America, and many parts of the world. It could not have had that impact if it had been exactly like other publications that competed against it. It had to use mythology—in journalism what is called tabloidization—to tell the great, simple truths of people's lives.

It is clear that while a tabloid may not always have the best information, its appeal to ordinary people always serves as a vivid reminder of the power of press freedom. That freedom may make one cry, cringe, or chuckle, but it is undeniably there. In the end, that may have been one of the most compelling messages left by Fox for modern readers: Because of the power of the First Amendment, the *Gazette* could thrive in and even change a society that, at least in upper-crust circles, ostensibly valued restraint.

A famous story told by Mott recounted one of the many serendipitous ties linking the *Gazette* to free expression. In a recollection concerning his chapter chronicling the history of the *Gazette*, Mott wrote that he struggled to find a publisher for his voluminous *A History of American Magazines*. It was finally rescued by the Harvard University Press and its estimable publisher, Dumas Malone. To help sales, Malone decided to place a racy cover illustration from the *Gazette* (taken from Mott's chapter) in the Press's catalog announcing its coming attractions. Predictably, there were some protests. In Volume V of his history, Mott quotes the St. Louis *Post Dispatch's* rather amused recounting of the controversy:

> [Harvard University Press] publications are sizable tomes on such things as prehistoric remains, Indo-Iranian languages, early Greek elegists, boundary conflicts in South America, Chinese historiography, time budgets of human behavior, the physiocratic doctrine of judicial control, and the old Frisian Skeltana-Riucht.
>
> And yet the first illustration in the current catalog to fall beneath our eye was of deepest saffron. Two buxom dames of the hourglass school of feminine charms are presented as entertaining two heavily-mustached, silk-hatted gentlemen in a lavish chamber. The blonde is reclining on a royal couch, while the brunette perches on the knee of the other guest, an endearing arm about his neck. Champagne bottles are in evidence and tell-tale goblets in air. The caption: "A masher mashed—How a Chicago youth of the 'too awfully sweet for anything' variety, while essaying the role of a lady killer, was taken in and done for, like the veriest countryman, by a brace of sharp damsels and their male accomplice. See page 7." . . .
>
> Let the editor and his cohorts defend their illustration on the score of historical scholarship if they will. Just wait until they hear the teacups that tinkle cross the blue Charles [River] in prim and proper Back Bay![64]

Mott reported that some letter-writers had noted that the "reprehensible illustration from the naughty Seventies" had been published on the verso of a reproduction of Oliver Wendell Holmes. That portrait was the frontispiece of Felix Frankfurter's *Mr. Justice Holmes and the Supreme Court*, which also was being promoted in the catalog for publication that fall. The editor of the catalog answered, "To pained protesters against the indignity to the revered Justice, the reply has been made that he himself would undoubtedly be tickled to find the *Police Gazette* on his august back."[65] That is probably so. Fox, too, surely would have been so honored. Holmes wrote in 1859, "The very aim and end of our institutions is just this: that we may think what we like and say what we think."[66] Fox, through forty-four years of trumpeting the exploits of men, put Holmes's words into action like few others. What better way to remember the daring and ribald Fox *Gazette* than having one of its cover illustrations placed squarely on the back of a man who recognized that the reason for America was freedom of speech?

EPILOGUE

In *The Rise of Modern America: 1865–1951*, historian Arthur Meier Schlesinger described nearly a century's worth of forces that helped shape America as it became a world power. These included westward expansion, Progressivism, the expanding gender spheres, the invention of the automobile that allowed a symbolic (but temporary) reclaiming of nature, the rise of sports and media, the march of imperialism, the manly Rooseveltian culture, the Jim Crow laws creating exclusion and separation, and finally, grand economic development, military might, and the creation of tycoons.[1]

Many of these same forces became directly linked to the creation of the modern American man. In fact, it can be argued that during the earlier years of this period, from about 1879 to 1906, when the *National Police Gazette* was entertaining, reflecting, and scandalizing society at its heyday, American manhood was born into a body that still preens and genuflects over America's culture and politics. The *Gazette*, as a successful marketer of tabloidism, sensational reporting, health products for men, sporting fare, and girlie pictures, was as much the *Maxim* or *Men's Health* of its day as it was the *National Enquirer*. And its character reveals almost as much about who (white) American men are today as it does about who they were then.

This link to *white* sensibilities on the part of the *Gazette* cannot be denied. Its male audience was primarily white, and lower- to middle-class. And, as has been noted, many discussions of the rise of masculinity during this period have a racial component to them, largely because the white men of the nineteenth century were being challenged in so many different ways—through economic, political, and gendered forces. But the increase of freed blacks into northern cities posed another, perhaps more imminent, threat—a threat that was answered in overt discrimination and, in the South as well as in the North, "the literal emasculation of despicably gendered torture." Men sought to return to an earlier time, and that meant an end to the "rising tide of color," as noted in historian Michael Kimmel's *Manhood in America*. This tide of color, seen as coming from blacks as well as immigrants, hindered the white man's chances at self-made manhood (or so the common man believed). The efforts to combat the competition went so far as to employ pseudo science to "prove" the superiority of the white male, and Social Darwinism "proved" that the supposed superiority was justified.[2]

So it's not hard to imagine that many of the white men of today also feel a sense that their superiority is being threatened. Not all of the men in these classes are the same, of course, just as they weren't in the *Gazette*'s day. But there is a certain percentage of them who identify with the hegemonic white masculinity of twenty-first-century America. They vote for what they perceive as toughness and independence. They are against gay marriage, and they resent the inroads into their traditionally dominant spheres. Their culture includes football, NASCAR, and girls. They resent the underclass, who they often resemble most closely, and they support policies that help the wealthy at their own expense. They, like their brethren of the nineteenth century, do have a few outsiders to look down upon—the African-Americans, the Hispanics, the liberals, the intellectuals, the gays. And they, like *Gazette* readers, might muster either a chuckle or outrage at the cultural landscape depicted before them. Today's white male might consider himself a partial heir to what E. Anthony Rotundo described the "self-made" men who emerged as the model for men in America in the nineteenth century. Among these men, as the market economy grew and the middle class prospered, it was work, not birth or as the head of household, that became key components of their identities.

But as the nineteenth century developed, and men tried to fulfill themselves through achievements in their professions and businesses, their competitive passions naturally grew. Gone was the country gentility of earlier middle- and upper-class generations. "Ambition, rivalry, and aggression drove the new system of individual interests," Rotundo wrote.[3] Thus, a natural follow-up to self-made manhood was born—the "passionate manhood" of the late nineteenth century. "In the closing years of the century, ambition and combativeness became virtues for men; competitiveness and aggression were exalted as ends in themselves. Toughness was now admired, while tenderness was a cause for scorn." Even sexual freedom became valued, and the body became a key part of the expression of manhood: strength and appearance became more important than in the early parts of American history.[4]

These characteristics, of the passionate man and the self-made man, are found in some of the dominant masculinities—and indeed, in society as a whole—embodying America today. Anyone who watches presidential campaigns cannot escape the conclusion that the qualities of manhood seem to drive their messages. Rotundo wrote,

> These notions of manliness have left their imprint . . . on political language, with its profusion of sports metaphors and its preoccupation with toughness. They have framed our definition of the male homosexual as a man bereft of manhood. And they have nurtured our cultural romance with competition as a solution to all problems, from economic productivity to a fair divorce settlement.[5]

Indeed, one may say that America's market economy is by definition a competition, and Rotundo argued that modern institutions, with their emphasis on debate, competition, and winners and losers, are based on these early concepts of manhood.[6] Modernity's new emphasis on toughness even affected religious views. For example, the doctrine of "Muscular Christianity" emerged, emphasizing a tougher, warrior-like Christ, with "rippling muscles" who was an "enforcer"— an image that survives even today in some fundamentalists' justification for war. Along with that notion came a general scramble for wealth that, while it was only just maturing, was decried in the nineteenth century as robbing men of their independence. Kimmel noted sociologist Max Weber's denunciation of the pursuit of money as a replacement for the pursuit of happiness, giving it the character of sport and competition. "Or, in the words of a bumper sticker from the Reagan era: He who has the most toys when he dies, wins,"[7] Kimmel wrote.

As we have seen in the *Gazette*, the same competitive attitudes permeated the sporting life. Rotundo wrote that before the Civil War, sports were seen primarily as a way to refresh the body and soul. In the postbellum era, though, the main object of the game was to win—and winning at any cost became a mantra for the twentieth century.[8]

Thus, during this critical period of the birth of the modern American man, men continued in their roles as breadwinners and providers, to be sure, but they also strove to develop separate spheres[9] in which to prove themselves. This emphasis on seeking out new identities and passions has taken hold in modern manhood, as well, in the "spiritual warrior" movement, popularized by Robert Bly, which encourages men to get in touch with their premodern selves.[10] Kimmel wrote,

> The search for the deep masculine is historically anachronistic, echoing late nineteenth-century masculinist complaints against the forces of

feminization. But it is also developmentally atavistic, a search for lost boyhood, an effort to turn back the clock to the moment before work and family responsibilities yanked men away from their buddies. . . . Weekend warriors seem to believe themselves to be entitled to the power that is men's privilege. But they do not feel it yet.[11]

This masculine mystique has even found its way into America's foreign policy. The "War on Terror" is just the latest example of a connection between "war and the cult of toughness." For American politicians and presidents, wrote historian Marc Fasteau, "being tough, or at least looking tough, has been a primary goal in and of itself." Fasteau found in the policymakers who drove America's Vietnam War and Bay of Pigs policies an obsession with trying to prove themselves formidable and worthy. In Secretary of Defense Robert McNamara, Fasteau noted a "distrust of feeling, of intuition, of nuance," echoing denials of nuance voiced by President Bush's description of his own thought processes. In addition, Fasteau saw in President Johnson an obsessive insecurity about his own masculinity and whether he was manly enough for the presidency.[12]

This theme can be found repeatedly in American history. Consider the role of the cowboy persona in American presidential politics. From Andrew Jackson to Teddy Roosevelt to Ronald Reagan and George W. Bush, presidents have loved to evoke the image of the bad, independent, outdoorsy, and lonely hero who backed countrified, common-sense political policies—even if the world be damned. This is a nod to common man's admiration of the Western adventurer (or outlaw) so celebrated in the *Gazette* and in other American literature. Kimmel noted of the cowboy, "He moves in a world of men, in which daring, bravery, and skill are his constant companions. He lives by physical strength and rational calculation; his compassion is social and generalized, but he forms no lasting emotional bonds with any single person."[13] Under Reagan, wrote Kimmel, "In a replay of the frontier cowboy myth, America was once again sitting tall in the saddle, willing to take on all comers, asserting its dominance in world affairs."[14] Under Bush, the nation became governed by a man who used cowboy language ("smoke them out of their holes") in the fight on terrorists, and who spent much of his vacation time on his Crawford Ranch, which was purchased only just before his first run for the presidency. Even the first President Bush was a part of this phenomenon, albeit on the wrong end of the stick—he was a victim of the "Great American Wimp Hunt," a term coined by Kimmel to describe the attacks on wimps in American life,[15] when he was the subject of a glaring

Newsweek magazine headline, "Fighting the Wimp Factor." Bush's successor, Bill Clinton, did little to deflect the trend, Kimmel wrote, and made the current "crop of right-wing Republican leaders appear leaner and meaner than ever." The result, he contended, is that today's American male is confused—with some media urging on his sensitivity even as others implore him to jump back into the old fray of competition against outsiders such as gays, blacks, the poor, and women.[16]

Kimmel explores these meanings in the context of today's politics and popular culture, quoting from a Guns N' Roses song that lamented the coming of "immigrants and faggots." He argues that these attitudes are found in the politics and leanings of today's white, male working-class culture, attitudes that shape electoral outcomes through "the politics of resentment and retaliation."[17] Kimmel argues that America can move past these attitudes through a "Democratic manhood" of inclusion.[18]

Yet, a glance at a couple of nineteenth-century copies of the *Gazette* shows the enduring nature of definitions of masculinities even today. As has been noted, classified advertisements in the *Gazette* in the 1880s and 1890s included the imploring headlines "Weak Men Made Strong," "Manhood Restored," and "Certain Parts of the Body Enlarged." In the same issues are the usual tales of pugilisitic triumphs and disasters, stage gossip, baseball news, winks at affairs with pretty girls, and of a serial assaulter called "Jack the Kisser." One cover depicts white women beating up a "meddlesome colored woman"; the other shows a philandering woman who "Preferred the Gay Young Lothario" even after being confronted by her husband.[19] That these images aren't so different from today's attitudes about sex, race, crime, and sports may tell a great deal about how unlikely change is to come soon. Given today's cultural, political, and international environment, Richard K. Fox and his *Gazette* may have foretold more about modern American manhood than we would care to admit.

Did the old *National Police Gazette* portend today's American man? Not by itself, of course. But it can be said that it was one of a variety of cultural influences that anticipated the kinds of identities that men sought in the late nineteenth and early twentieth centuries. By doing so, it predicted an aspect of culture that still defines much of America's economic, social, and political life.

Richard K. Fox and his beloved *Gazette* got it right: They served the male readers who identified with the tough guy, the loner, the no-nonsense talker, the romancer, the fighter, the hero. In short, their masculinities are our masculinities. Many historians have speculated about what really caused the demise of the *Gazette*. Was it its quaintness, the new women's hairstyles, Prohibition, the mass-marketing of improved tabloid journalism, the death of the woodcut? The answer is, it was all of these, and none of them. For as a reflection of the modern American man, the *Gazette* still lives, and it may be a very long time before it ever really dies.

Notes

Introduction

Epigraph. Franklin P. Adams, introduction to *Sins of New York as "Exposed" by the Police Gazette*, by Edward Van Every (New York: Frederick A. Stokes Co., 1930), vi.

1. "Our Illustrations," *National Police Gazette*, July 2, 1881, 6; *National Police Gazette*, July 2, 1881, 1.
2. Elliott J. Gorn, "The Wicked World: *The National Police Gazette* and Gilded-Age America," *Media Studies Journal* 6 (Winter 1992): 6.
3. Adams, *Sins of New York*, vi.
4. Anthony Comstock, *Traps for the Young* (New York: Funk & Wagnalls, 1883), 20.
5. James Joyce, *Ulysses* (New York: Random House, 1934), 317. Although Joyce never named the Homeric episodes of his *Ulysses*, scholars later did so, and the episode mentioning the *Police Gazette* is commonly labeled "Cyclops" in modern scholarship. It fits; the one-eyed gaze may be particularly fixed, and in the case of the *Gazette* reference, Joyce conveys several meanings in the line "—Give us a squint at her, says I" (e.g., a "squint" is a leer, and the "I" is an "eye"). For more elaboration on this point, see Joseph Valente, "The novel and the Police (Gazette)," *Novel* 29, no. 1 (Fall 1995): 8–25.
6. Turner, a thirty-one-year-old instructor at the University of Wisconsin, noted the closing of the Western frontier in his then widely ignored lecture, "The Significance of the Frontier in American History," delivered at a meeting of the American Historical Association held in conjunction with the Chicago Columbian Exposition in 1893. See Thomas L. Hartshorne, *The Distorted Image: Changing Conceptions of the American Character Since Turner* (Cleveland: Case Western Reserve University Press, 1968).
7. David Montgomery, *Citizen Worker: The Experience of Workers in the United States with Democracy and the Free Market During the Nineteenth Century* (New York: Cambridge University Press, 1994), 50.
8. Jeffrey P. Hantover, "The Boy Scouts and the Validation of Masculinity," in *The American Man*, ed. Elizabeth H. Pleck and Joseph H. Pleck (Englewood Cliffs, NJ: Prentice Hall, 1980), 289–92.
9. John Higham, "The Reorientation of American Culture in the 1890s," in *Writing American History*, ed. Higham (Bloomington: Indiana University Press, 1970), 79.

10. Elizabeth H. Pleck and Joseph H. Pleck, introduction to *The American Man*, ed. Elizabeth H. Pleck and Joseph H. Pleck (Englewood Cliffs, NJ: Prentice Hall, 1980), 6. Today's era is likely the beginning of a "new epoch in the history of gender relations," they wrote.

11. See John Beynon, *Masculinities and Culture* (Philadelphia: Open University Press, 2002), for a summary of the ideas of the nineteenth and early twentieth centuries as an important time in the development of ideas about masculinities.

12. Margaret Marsh, "Suburban Men and Masculine Domesticity, 1870–1915," in *Meanings for Manhood: Constructions of Masculinity in Victorian America*, ed. Mark C. Carnes and Clyde Griffin (Chicago: University of Chicago Press, 1990), 111–27.

13. *National Police Gazette*, February 18, 1882, 1; "$32,000 Worth of Revenge," *National Police Gazette*, February 18, 1882, 6.

14. Kevin White, *The First Sexual Revolution: The Emergence of Male Heterosexuality in Modern America* (New York: New York University Press, 1993), 9.

15. *National Police Gazette*, June 25, 1881, 1.

16. Pleck and Pleck, *The American Man*, 23.

17. Mitchell Stephens, *A History of News: From the Drum to the Satellite* (New York: Viking, 1988), 204; ibid., 201.

18. Cited in Robert W. Desmond, *The Information Process: World News Reporting to the Twentieth Century* (Iowa City: University of Iowa Press, 1978), 6.

19. Stephens, *A History of News*, 201.

20. Beynon, *Masculinities and Culture*, 46.

21. George L. Mosse, *The Image of Man: The Creation of Modern Masculinity* (New York: Oxford University Press, 1996), 56–57.

22. As will be discussed, the depictions of women in the *Gazette* were so varied it is impossible to view them in only one way.

23. *National Police Gazette*, February 4, 1882, 1; February 24, 1894, 1; February 10, 1900, 1.

24. *National Police Gazette*, September 27, 1879, 1; January 25, 1902, 1.

25. Daniel Riffe, Stephen Lacy, and Frederick G. Fico, *Analyzing Media Messages: Using Quantitative Content Analysis in Research* (Mahwah, NJ: Lawrence Erlbaum, 1998), 99.

26. Under the category of crimes, subheadings included murder, robbery, sexual assault, nonsexual assault, rioting, and lynching. The category of sports/physical recreation included boxing, rowing, baseball, football, horse racing, weight lifting, and bodybuilding. In order to look at *Gazette* promotional activities, the sporting category also included under separate headings *Gazette* promotions for such activities as "physical culture" (bodybuilding) or bartending. The category for sexually provocative illustrations included those featuring skimpy attire, adultery, carousing, prostitution, or provocative poses featuring showgirls or other women.

27. Stephens, *A History of News*, 209.

28. "Richard K. Fox," *National Police Gazette*, May 23, 1885, 2.

1   LIVES OF THE FELONS

Epigraph. The item served as a description of its editorial content. See the *National Police Gazette*, November 8, 1845.

1. Tweed would be released by January 1875, only to be sued for $6 million by those he victimized. Unable to come up with the $3 million in bail, he was jailed again, but then escaped on a home furlough to Florida, and then Cuba, only to be arrested by Spanish authorities and delivered on an American warship back to New York for another stint in the Ludlow Street Jail. He died in prison in 1878. See Seymour J. Mandelbaum, *Boss Tweed's New York* (New York: J. Wiley, 1965).

2. Edwin G. Burrows and Mike Wallace, *Gotham: A History of New York City to 1898* (New York: Oxford University Press, 1999), 1005–8.

3. Walter Davenport, "The Nickel Shocker," *Collier's*, March 10, 1928, 26.

4. Burrows and Wallace, *Gotham*, 977–78.

5. Susan Douglas, *Inventing American Broadcasting, 1899–1922* (Baltimore: Johns Hopkins University Press, 1987), 3.

6. For example, see Gail Bederman, *Manliness and Civilization: A Cultural History of Gender and Race in the United States, 1880–1917* (Chicago: University of Chicago Press, 1995), 10–11.

7. Ibid., 192.

8. The Harkaway stories became so popular that stories abounded of news agents fighting with each other in the street outside the publisher's office in order to be first to get copies of a new Harkaway. See Jean-Marc Lofficier, *French Science Fiction, Fantasy, Horror and Pulp Fiction: A Guide to Cinema, Television, Radio, Animation, Comic Books and Literature from the Middle Ages to the Present* (Jefferson, NC: McFarland, 2000).

9. David E. Nye, *American Technological Sublime* (Cambridge: MIT Press, 1994), 33.

10. Ibid., 43.

11. "The New York Herald as Science Prophet," *Manufacturer and Builder*, July 1874, 158.

12. Ibid., 158–59.

13. Douglas, *Inventing American Broadcasting*, 9.

14. Hy B. Turner, *When Giants Ruled: The story of Park Row, New York's Great Newspaper Street* (New York: Fordham University Press, 1999), 3–5.

15. *The Sun*, June 30, 1835, 2.

16. Turner, *When Giants Ruled*, 7.

17. Andie Tucher, *Froth and Scum: Truth, Beauty, Goodness, and the Ax Murder in America's First Mass Medium* (Chapel Hill: University of North Carolina Press, 1994), 51.

18. New York *Herald*, September 5, 1835, 2.

19. Andie Tucher, "In Search of Jenkins: Taste, Style, and Credibility in Gilded-Age Journalism," *Journalism History* 27, no. 2 (Summer 2001): 50–55.

20. See Tucher, *Froth and Scum*, for a discussion of humbuggery in journalism. Although some of this kind of reporting is remembered with a certain fondness today, it did carry its dangers. As Tucher noted, in 1836 Day published an account of "Awful Disclosures" that involved a nun by the name of Maria Monk. As Tucher put it, she maintained that the sisters of her former convent "were brutish and corrupt harpies who fornicated with monks and murdered their own bastards." The tensions between Catholics and Protestants were not improved by such accusations, even devoid of truth as they were.

21. Dan Schiller, *Objectivity and the News: The Public and the Rise of Commercial Journalism* (Philadelphia: University of Pennsylvania Press, 1981), 77.

22. Ibid., 95. The notion of objectivity as an organizing device that has shaped the way the news business is practiced can also be discerned in Pamela J. Shoemaker and Stephen D. Reese, *Mediating the Message: Theories of Influences on Mass Media Content*, 2nd ed. (New York: Longman, 1996).

23. Schiller, *Objectivity and the News*, 97.

24. Just three weeks before the Moon Hoax series, another fantastic moon voyage was published in the *Southern Literary Messenger* called "Hans Pfall." The author, Edgar Allen Poe, read the articles by Locke and then destroyed the rest of his own story, believing that fiction could not offer much more to the sensational accounts of Herschel.

25. "Atrocious Murder," *New York Herald*, April 11, 1836, 1.

26. Mitchell Stephens, *A History of News: From the Drum to the Satellite* (New York: Viking, 1988), 242–48.

27. Oliver Carlson, *The Man Who Made News: James Gordon Bennett* (New York: Duell, Sloan and Pearce, 1942), 237.

28. John D. Stevens, *Sensationalism and the New York Press* (New York: Columbia University Press, 1991), 42.

29. Schiller, *Objectivity and the News*, 57.

30. Ibid., 68–69.

31. Turner, *When Giants Ruled*, 28–29.

32. Stephens, *History of News*, 191.

33. Turner, *When Giants Ruled*, 34.

34. Lloyd Morris, *Incredible New York: High Life and Low Life of the Last Hundred Years* (New York: Random House, 1951), 74–83.

35. Ibid., 82.

36. Ibid.

37. Ibid.

38. Colin Wilson and Donald Seaman, *Scandal!: An Encyclopedia* (London: Weidenfeld and Nicolson, 1986), 9.

39. Emile Durkheim, *The Rules of the Sociological Method*, ed. Steven Lukes, trans. W.D. Halls (New York: Free Press, 1982), 50–59.

40. Stephens, *A History of News*, 114.

41. Turner, *When Giants Ruled*, 47.

42. Alexander Saxton, "George Wilkes: The Disintegration of a Radical Ideology" (paper presented to the Conference on Labor History, Walter Reuther Library of Labor and Urban Affairs and History Department, Wayne State University, Detroit, October 1979).

43. Edward Van Every, *Sins of New York as "Exposed" by the Police Gazette* (New York: Frederick A. Stokes, 1930), 10–11.

44. Newcastle, as he was called, was derided by some historians as being indecisive, effeminate, and unable to serve as an effective leader. But he served as prime minister twice. He added the name "Holles" in 1711 as required by the will of his uncle John Holles, who left him the bulk of his estates. Newcastle owned vast property in eleven counties, which some speculate might have fueled his interest in lower-class crime, and the holdings enabled him to influence elections in multiple constituencies. See Reed Browning, *The Duke of Newcastle* (New Haven: Yale University Press, 1975).

45. Schiller, *Objectivity and the News*, 96.

46. Ibid., 97–98.

47. Simon Michael Bessie, *Jazz Journalism* (New York: E.P. Dutton, 1938), 64–65.

48. Schiller, *Objectivity and the News*, 102.

49. Davenport, "The Nickel Shocker," 26.

50. *National Police Gazette*, October 25, 1845, 1.

51. Thomas C. Leonard, *The Power of the Press: The Birth of American Political Reporting* (New York: Oxford University Press, 1986), 142–43.

52. *National Police Gazette*, November 8, 1845.

53. Davenport, "The Nickel Shocker," 28.

54. Ibid.

55. Schiller, *Objectivity and the News*, 103–04.

56. Ibid., 105.

57. Ibid., 108.

58. Ibid., 109.

59. *National Police Gazette*, October 31, 1846.

60. Schiller, *Objectivity and the News*, 110.

61. Ibid., 131.

62. Ibid., 140.

63. Ibid., 142.

64. Ibid., 145.

65. Ibid., 163.

66. Ibid., 153–65.

67. Schiller, *Objectivity and the News*, 178.
68. Elizabeth H. Pleck and Joseph H. Pleck, eds., *The American Man* (Englewood Cliffs, NJ: Prentice Hall, 1980), 26.
69. Peter N. Stearns, *Be a Man! Males in Modern Society* (New York: Holmes & Meier, 1979), 40.
70. E.M. Jellinek, "Recent Trends in Alcoholism and Alcohol Consumption," *Quarterly Journal of Studies on Alcohol* 8 (June 1947): 2.
71. Jon M. Kingsdale, "The 'Poor Man's Club': Social Functions of the Urban Working-Class Saloon," in *The American Man*, ed. Elizabeth H. Pleck and Joseph H. Pleck (Englewood Cliffs, NJ: Prentice Hall), 262, 255–83.
72. Stearns, *Be a Man!*, 43.
73. Ibid., 57.
74. Ibid.
75. *National Police Gazette*, January 28, 1846, 2.
76. Van Every, *Sins of New York*, 58.
77. Cited in Van Every, *Sins of New York*, 58–59.
78. Cited in Davenport, "The Nickel Shocker," 38.
79. Cited in Van Every, *Sins of New York*, 60.
80. Davenport, "The Nickel Shocker," 38.
81. "Restell, the Female Abortionist," *National Police Gazette*, February 21, 1846, 6.
82. Van Every, *Sins of New York*, 91.
83. Ibid., 97. Van Every, who noted that Edgar Allen Poe published *The Raven* in 1845, the year the *Gazette* was founded, said that it "was in the *Gazette* tradition" that Poe wrote for the *Gazette* as a staff member sometime between 1846 and 1849, the year of his death. See Edgar A. Poe, *The Raven and other Poems* (New York: Wiley and Putnam, 1845). Poe did serve as an editor for the *Broadway Journal*, another weekly, and he was a poor struggling writer for most of his life, so he may have willingly worked for the *Gazette* simply to earn a paycheck. But if he did, he never signed his name to any *Gazette* article.
84. "Almost a Mob," *National Police Gazette*, February 28, 1846, 2.
85. Van Every, *Sins of New York*, 104.
86. Davenport, "The Nickel Shocker," 38.
87. Ibid.
88. The panic began with the failure of the New York branch of the Ohio Life Insurance and Trust Company and was exacerbated by the loss of a shipment of gold from California. See James L. Huston, *Panic of 1857 and the Coming of the Civil War* (Baton Rouge: Louisiana State University Press, 1987). The loss affected banks, businesses, and investments, and left Wilkes in debt. According to Davenport, "The Nickel Shocker," 40, Wilkes continued publishing for a time, exposing the famed Dead Rabbit Riots as "politically inspired to divert the public's attention" from frauds involving the municipal government. But he was forced to give up the *Gazette* to Matsell because of his debts.

2 AN ILLUSTRATED JOURNAL OF SPORTING AND SENSATIONAL EVENTS

Epigraph. *Christian Herald*, October 24, 1878, 5.

1. See the *National Police Gazette*, December 5, 1874, 2–3.
2. "To Our Readers—Something New," *National Police Gazette*, December 5, 1874, 2.
3. For example, see John A. Garraty and Mark C. Carnes, eds., *American National Biography*, vol. 8 (Oxford: Oxford University Press, 1999), 344–45.
4. For a history of the Orangemen to modern times, see Andrew Boyd, "The Orange Order, 1795–1995," *History Today*, September 1, 1995, 17. The members call their movement the Loyal Orange Institution, a name taken from the family name of King William III of England, who defeated King James II in the Battle of the Boyne in 1690. The July 12 anniversary of this event is celebrated throughout the world, with members wearing organge-colored flowers and sashes, often in parades.
5. Walter Davenport, "The Dirt Disher," *Collier's*, March 24, 1928, 26.
6. Garraty and Carnes, *American National Biography*, vol. 8, 344.
7. Ibid. Many biographies of Fox say he worked first at the *Wall Street Journal*, but the *Journal* was not founded (by Charles Dow) until 1889. The *Bulletin* may be said to be a precursor to the *Journal*.
8. Sam G. Riley, "Richard Kyle Fox," in *Dictionary of Literary Biography*, vol. 79, *American Magazine Journalists, 1850–1900*, ed. Sam G. Riley (Detroit: Bruccoli Clark Layman, 1989), 143–48; Garraty and Carnes, *American National Biography*, vol. 8, 344–45; Allen Johnson and Dumas Malone, eds., *Dictionary of American Biography*, vol. 6 (New York: Charles Scribner's Sons, 1931), 571–72.
9. Davenport, "The Dirt Disher," 30.
10. Ibid. Mackeever died in 1880 in Florida, where he had tried without success to ease his "consumption," at the age of thirty-two. A native of Philadelphia, he had been an active balloonist and was jovial and well-liked, according to his obituary in the *Police Gazette*, April 3, 1880, 2. The *Gazette* notice said he was "familiar with the sumptuousness of Fifth Avenue and the Squalor of Five Points, with the boudoir of the great actress and the cell of the condemned man."
11. *National Police Gazette*, September 28, 1878, 2.
12. Ibid., 15.
13. *National Police Gazette*, October 5, 1878, 1.
14. Berlin wrote the song for the 1937 musical *On the Avenue*, a comedy about the romantic misadventures of a showman and the daughter of a rich family. A soundtrack is available at www.disconforme.com.
15. *National Police Gazette*, October 5, 1878, 2.
16. For example, *National Police Gazette*, January 14, 1882, 2.
17. W. Joseph Campbell, *Yellow Journalism: Puncturing the Myths, Defining the Legacies* (Westport, CT: Praeger, 2001), 4.

18. Frank Luther Mott, *American Journalism: A History: 1690–1960*, 3rd ed. (New York: Macmillan, 1962), 539.

19. Ibid.

20. Campbell, *Yellow Journalism*, 7–8.

21. See Campbell, *Yellow Journalism*, 25–41, for a discussion of the diffusion of the term.

22. Frank Luther Mott, *A History of American Magazines*, 5 vols. (1938; reprint, Cambridge: Harvard University Press, 1957). Mott's decision to include a portrait of the *Gazette* in vol. 2 of this work indicates his belief that it was properly classified as a magazine.

23. See Elliott J. Gorn, "The Wicked World: *The National Police Gazette* and Gilded-Age America," *Media Studies Journal* 6 (Winter 1992): 1–15.

24. Riley, *Dictionary of Literary Biography*, vol. 79, 144.

25. George Juergens, *Joseph Pulitzer and the New York World* (Princeton, NJ: Princeton University Press, 1966), 47.

26. Mott, *American Journalism*, 411.

27. New York *World*, June 3, 1872, 1.

28. Mott, *American Journalism*, 417.

29. Ibid., 417.

30. Mott, *American Journalism*, 418, recounts one story in which a drunken Bennett ordered the writing of an editorial attacking the Catholic Church. The editorial never ran, however, because a prudent secretary put a stop to it. This is a bit ironic; Bennett was lampooned in a famous Thomas Nast cartoon after Bennett wrote an editorial calling for the appointment of an American cardinal; Nast envisioned Bennett as the self-annointed cardinal.

31. Mott, *American Journalism*, 418.

32. Ibid., 419.

33. Ibid.

34. See Mott, *American Journalism*, 420–21, for a discussion of circulation figures.

35. Sidney Kobre, *The Yellow Press and Gilded Age Journalism* (Tallahassee: Florida State University Press, 1964), 27.

36. Robert W. Jones, *Journalism in the United States* (New York: E.P. Dutton, 1947), 376.

37. Hy B. Turner, *When Giants Ruled: The story of Park Row, News York's Great Newspaper Street* (New York: Fordham University Press, 1999), 85–91.

38. Simon Michael Bessie, *Jazz Journalism: The Story of the Tabloid Newspapers* (New York: E.P. Dutton, 1938), 67.

39. Mott, *A History of American Magazines*, vol. 3, 5.

40. Ibid.

41. Ibid., 6–7.

42. John Vivian, *The Media of Mass Communication*, 6th ed. (Boston: Allyn & Bacon, 1991), 52.

43. Ibid., 6.

44. *Christian Herald*, October 24, 1878, 5. Mott noted that the YMCA was founded to help wayward young men who found themselves tempted on the streets of New York City.

45. Mott, *A History of American Magazines*, vol. 3, 28.

46. Walter D. Kamphoefner, Wolfgang Helbich, and Ulrike Sommer, eds., *News from the Land of Freedom: German Emigrants Write Home* (Ithaca: Cornell University Press, 1991), 23.

47. Scott M. Cutlip, *Public Relations History from the Seventeenth to the Twentieth Century* (Hillsdale, NJ: Lawrence Erlbaum Associates, 1995), 170–76.

48. Ibid., 171.

49. The woman, Joice Heth, was supposedly a slave owned by Washington's father and alleged to be 160 years old as "proved" by a bogus bill of sale executed in 1727.

50. Thomas C. Leonard, *News for All: America's Coming-of-Age with the Press* (New York: Oxford University Press, 1995).

51. Ibid., 221.

52. Edwin Emery and Michael Emery, *The Press and America: An Interpretive History of the Mass Media* (Englewood Cliffs, NJ: Prentice Hall, 1984).

53. Stuart Ewen, *PR! A Social History of Spin* (New York: Harper Collins, 1996), 45. Ewen mentioned the idea of public relations overtaking the promise of utopianism in his discussion of an 1888 novel by Edward Bellamy. A reporter for the *Springfield Union* in Massachusetts, Bellamy wrote *Looking Backward: 2000–1887*, in which he predicted that "the people" would by the end of the twentieth century take "control of their own business." The novel, which featured a nineteenth-century New Englander, Julian West, who slept in suspended animation for a hundred years, predicted that the nineteenth-century's abominable suffering, poverty, and squalor would be replaced by an energized, efficient, utopian system of progressive industry and informed consumers. See Edward Bellamy, *Looking Backward: 2000–1887* (1888; reprint, Boston: Magnum Books, 1968), 54.

54. Brooke Kroeger, *Nellie Bly: Daredevil, Reporter, Feminist* (New York: Random House, 1994), 143.

55. Ibid., 150.

56. Ibid., 162–71.

57. Mott, *A History of American Magazines*, vol. 4, 373–74.

58. John Dinan, *Sports in the Pulp Magazines* (London: McFarland & Co., 1998), 4.

59. Ibid., 5.

60. Rex Lardner, *The Legendary Champions* (New York: American Heritage Press, 1972), 47.

61. Mott, *A History of American Magazines*, vol. 2, 334.

62. See Gorn, "The Wicked World," 15.

63. For example, see the *National Police Gazette*, October 23, 1880, 1.

64. Paul Messaris and Linus Abraham, "The Role of Images in Framing News Stories," in *Framing Public Life: Perspectives on Media and Our Understanding of the Social World*, ed. Stephen D. Reese, Oscar H. Gandy Jr., and August E. Grant (Mahwah, NJ: Lawrence Erlbaum, 2001), 217.

65. 1879 marked the first full year that the *Gazette* came out in its sixteen-page format; by 1906 its circulation had declined and it no longer ran many woodcut illustrations. Only a few copies of the *Gazette* can be found outside of these years, and the preservation of the copies even in these years is not complete. Thus, in some years fewer than twelve copies were quantified. Coder reliability ranged from 100 percent in nominal categories such as date of issue to no agreement in categories that rarely arose, such as water sports. These categories were eliminated from the analysis. Overall reliability was 89 percent, with agreement judged according to the percentage of agreement of page estimate for each illustration. For example, if one coder said an illustration was .6 of a page and another said it was .5, their agreement was calculated at $5/6 = .833$ or 83 percent. If all categories are collapsed into only crime, sex, or sports, agreement is at 94.2 percent.

66. Daniel Riffe, Stephen Lacy, and Frederick G. Fico, *Analyzing Media Messages: Using Quantitative Content Analysis in Research* (Mahwah, NJ: Lawrence Erlbaum Associates), 99.

3 This Wicked World

Epigraph. From the Civil War-era movie *Gangs of New York*, this is from a scene in which gang leader William Cutting (Daniel Day-Lewis), admired the publicity given in the *Gazette* to the gang exploits of an associate, Amsterdam (Leonardo DiCaprio). The *Gazette* headline that amused Cutting was "Ghoul Gang Slaughters\Then Sells to Medical Science."

1. "The Assassin's Story," *National Police Gazette*, December 17, 1881, 11.

2. *National Police Gazette*, December 17, 1881, 2.

3. *National Police Gazette*, May 28, 1892, 2.

4. "Whitechapel's Fiend," *National Police Gazette*, August 17, 1889, 3.

5. See Richard Gordon, *Jack the Ripper* (New York: Athenaeum, 1980).

6. Gerald Gross, *Masterpieces of Murder* (New York: Bonanza Books, 1961), 4.

7. Elliot J. Gorn, "The Wicked World: The *National Police Gazette* and Gilded-Age America," *Media Studies Journal* 6 (Winter 1992): 6–7. See also issues of the *Gazette* during this period. One of the first, if not the first, mentions of the phrase "wicked world" in the *Gazette* was on July 17, 1880, when a headline contained a quotation from a country man alarmed at the sight of the goings-on in a city brothel. "Maria, This is a Wicked World," he said to his wife. See *National Police Gazette*, July 17, 1880, 6.

8. "This Wicked World," *National Police Gazette*, July 9, 1887, 3. The same column rather matter of factly said that the head of Charles J. Guiteau, preserved in alcohol in a glass jar, was soon to be displayed at Coney Island.

9. *National Police Gazette*, April 1, 1882, 2, 10.

10. Gene Smith and Jayne Barry Smith, eds., *The Police Gazette* (New York: Simon & Schuster, 1972), 14.

11. "A Barbarous Lynching," *National Police Gazette*, February 18, 1893, 2.

12. See the illustration captioned, "Defenseless Negroes," *National Police Gazette*, July 9, 1887, 5; "A Reign of Terror," *National Police Gazette*, January 12, 1895, 6.

13. "Do We?" *National Police Gazette*, June 20, 1885, 2.

14. "A Naughty, Naughty Parson!" *National Police Gazette*, January 14, 1882, 6.

15. "Editorial notes," *National Police Gazette*, March 23, 1889, 2.

16. An analysis of variance determined that there were significant differences in the means for crime coverage over several of the years analyzed. The post hoc Tukey HSD test identified most of those differences as occurring between the years at the beginning of the analysis (in the early 1880s) and the years near and after the turn of the century. Spearman's rho for the crime illustrations is $-.684$. This indicates a negative correlation, significant at the .01 level, between the number of pages of crime illustrations and the increase in the year. In other words, as the years went by, crime illustrations were fewer in number at a statistically significant level. For sports, the correlation was positive—.723—meaning that as the years went by, sporting illustrations increased at a statistically significant level. The correlation for sexually provocative portrayals was .105, not statistically significant. In order to facilitate understanding of the analysis, for the most part, future discussion will be confined to average numbers of illustrations per issue.

17. W.A. Swanberg, *Pulitzer* (New York: Charles Scribner's Sons, 1967), 265.

18. James W. Messerschmidt, *Nine lives: Adolescent Masculinities, the Body, and Violence* (Boulder, CO: Westview Press, 2000), 6.

19. Jeff Ferrell and Neil Websdale, eds., *Making Trouble: Cultural Constructions of Crime, Deviance, and Control* (New York: Walter de Gruyter, Inc., 1999).

20. Ibid., 11.

21. Ibid.

22. Mitchell Stephens, *A History of News: From the Drum to the Satellite*, revised edition (Fort Worth: Harcourt Brace & Co., 1997), 99.

23. Craig LaMay and E. Dennis, eds., *The Culture of Crime* (New Brunswick, NJ: Transaction, 1995), 3.

24. David Pritchard and Karen D. Hughes, "Patterns of Deviance in Crime News" *Journal of Communication* 47, no. 3 (September 1997): 49–67.

25. For a discussion of this dichotomy see Marian Meyers, *News Coverage of Violence Against Women: Engendering Blame* (London: Sage, 1997). For a discussion of hypermasculinity, see Joseph H. Pleck, *The Myth of Masculinity* (Cambridge: MIT Press, 1981), 95–115.

26. Stephens, *A History of News*, 98–99.

27. This book is hard to find today. The Texas State Library holds an incomplete copy. Belle Starr biographer Glenn Shirley quotes extensively from the volume in his book *Belle Starr and Her Times: The Literature, the Facts, and the Legends* (Norman: University of Oklahoma Press, 1982).

28. Sam G. Riley, "Richard Kyle Fox," in *Dictionary of Literary Biography*, vol. 79, *American Magazine Journalists, 1850–1900*, ed. Sam G. Riley (Detroit: Bruccoli Clark Layman, 1989), 143–44.

29. Allen Johnson and Dumas Malone, eds., *Dictionary of American Biography*, vol. 6 (New York: Charles Scribner's Sons, 1931), 572.

30. Gail Bederman, *Manliness and Civilization: A Cultural History of Gender and Race in the United States, 1880–1917* (Chicago: University of Chicago Press, 1995), 170.

31. Matthew Basso, Laura McCall, and Dee Garceau, *Across the Great Divide: Cultures of Manhood in the American West* (New York: Routledge, 2001), 2.

32. Ibid., 5. See also John Higham, "The Reorientation of American Culture in the 1890s," in *Writing American History: Essays in Modern Scholarship*, ed. John Higham (Bloomington: Indiana University Press, 1970), 79.

33. Peter Lyon, *The Wild, Wild West* (New York: Funk and Wagnalls, 1969), 35.

34. Ibid., 35–36.

35. Frank Richard Prassel, *The Great American Outlaw: A Legacy of Faction and Fiction* (Norman: University of Oklahoma Press, 1993), 227.

36. *National Police Gazette*, February 23, 1889, 12.

37. "A Desperate Woman Killed," *New York Times*, February 6, 1889, 1.

38. Shirley, *Belle Starr and Her Times*, 3.

39. Ibid., 5.

40. Richard K. Fox, *Bella Starr, The Bandit Queen, or The Female Jesse James. A Full and Authentic History of the Dashing Female Highwayman, with Copious Extracts from Her Journal. Handsomely and Profusely Illustrated* (New York: Richard K. Fox, 1889), 5.

41. The bony arches on either side of the face just below the eye.

42. Gina Lombroso Ferrero, "The Criminal Man," in *Criminological Theory: Past to Present*, ed. Francis T. Cullen and Robert Agnew (Los Angeles: Roxbury Publishing, 1999), 8. Gina Lombroso Ferrero, who was Lombroso's daughter, published a summary of *The Criminal Man* in 1911 (New York: G.P. Putnam's Sons, 1911) in which she recounted the remarks of her father—then a young doctor—upon his postmortem examination of a man named Vilella, an "Italian Jack the Ripper" who had murdered viciously in the province of Lombardy. She noted his comments: "At the sight of that skull," says my father, "I seemed to see all at

once, standing out clearly illumined as in a vast plain under a flaming sky, the problem of the nature of the criminal, who reproduces in civilised times characteristics, not only of primitive savages, but of still lower types as far back as the canivora." Lombroso described the people who had not evolved from this state as "atavistic."

43. "Nigger Sam's Brain," *National Police Gazette*, May 4, 1878, 4.

44. See Shirley, *Belle Starr and Her Times*, for a full discussion of the Fox-Lombroso connection.

45. Here Lombroso refers not to the fictional character in Charles Dickens's *A Tale of Two Cities* (New York: Dodd, Mead, & Co., 1942), who knitted at the guillotine, but to the famed Frenchwoman accused of poisoning her husband.

46. Caesar Lombroso and William Ferrero, *The Female Offender* (New York: Philosophical Library, 1958), 174.

47. Lombroso and Ferrero, *The Female Offender*, 187–89.

48. Prassel, *The Great American Outlaw*, 228–29. Belle Starr's famous refusal to identify her husband is reversed in the film, with Sam refusing to identify her body.

49. Richard K. Fox, *Bella Starr*, 20.

50. Ibid., 23.

51. "The Dalton Gang Killed," *National Police Gazette*, October 22, 1892, 6.

52. Ibid.

53. "The Bandit's Boast," *National Police Gazette*, April 1, 1882, 10.

54. Ibid.

55. Ibid.

56. T.J. Stiles, *Jesse James: Last Rebel of the Civil War* (New York: Alfred A. Knopf, 2002), 222.

57. Ibid., 223.

58. Ibid.

59. *Kansas City Times*, September 25, 1872.

60. *Kansas City Times*, September 28, 1872.

61. Stiles, *Jesse James*, 225.

62. Ibid., 226.

63. Welche Gordon, *Jesse James and His Band of Notorious Outlaws* (Chicago: Laird and Lee, 1891), 9.

64. Paul Kooistra, *Criminals As Heroes: Structure, Power & Identity* (Bowling Green, OH: Bowling Green State University Press, 1989), 25.

65. Ibid., 26.

66. Claude Levi-Strauss, *Structural Anthropology*, vol. 1 (New York: Basic Books, 1963), 38–39.

67. Lyon, *Wild, Wild West*, 146.

68. "For Heaven's Sake, Stop," *National Police Gazette*, July 17, 1880, 2.

69. For an account of the Beecher-Tilton scandal, see Richard Wightman Fox, *Trials of Intimacy: Love and Loss in the Beecher-Tilton Scandal* (Chicago: University of Chicago Press, 1999).

70. "The Scandal Duet," *National Police Gazette*, April 27, 1878, 2.

71. *National Police Gazette*, April 27, 1878, 4.
72. George Bernard Shaw, "My Memories of Oscar Wilde," in Frank Harris, *Oscar Wilde, including My Memories of Oscar Wilde, by George Bernard Shaw* (East Lansing: Michigan State University Press, 1959), 330.
73. Robert Keith Miller, *Oscar Wilde* (New York: Frederick Ungar Publishing Co., 1982), 1–2.
74. Ibid., 15.
75. Ibid., 16.
76. Gary Schmidgall, *The Stranger Wilde: Interpreting Oscar* (New York: Dutton, 1994), 171. Although many may have had trouble saying the word, others had fun with visual puns. On his famous lecture tour of America in the early 1880s, one Chicago men's clothier welcomed the aestheticist with an advertisement featuring the "tail of a coat," with "pants down again." Oscar himself was referred to as an "ass-thete."
77. See Richard Ellmann, *Oscar Wilde* (New York: Alfred A. Knopf, 1987).
78. "The Fall of Oscar Wilde," *National Police Gazette*, May 4, 1895, 6.
79. "Wilde on the Treadmill," *National Police Gazette*, June 15, 1895, 6.
80. Ibid.
81. Ibid.
82. See "Billy the Kid's Dash for Liberty," *National Police Gazette*, October 26, 1901, 6, for a tale of Billy the Kid showing his bravado through a daring jail escape.
83. Charles E. Rosenberg, *The Trial of the Assassin Guiteau: Psychiatry and Law in the Gilded Age* (Chicago: University of Chicago Press, 1968), xi–xii.
84. "The Assassin's Story," *National Police Gazette*, December 17, 1881, 11.
85. Ibid.
86. *National Police Gazette*, December 17, 1881, 2.
87. Rosenberg, *The Trial of the Assassin Guiteau*, 237.
88. "Outraged by a Farm Hand," *National Police Gazette*, December 17, 1881, 11.

4   MASCULINITIES AND THE MANLY ARTS

Epigraph. "Paddy Ryan," *National Police Gazette*, July 2, 1881, 4.
1. Elliott J. Gorn, *The Manly Art: Bare-Knuckle Prize Fighting in America* (Ithaca, NY: Cornell University Press, 1986), 136–37. Michael Kimmel, *Manhood in America: A Cultural History* (New York: The Free Press, 1996), 3.
2. Peter N. Stearns, *Be a Man! Males in Modern Society* (New York: Holmes & Meier, 1979), 76.
3. Gail Bederman, *Manliness and Civilization: A Cultural History of Gender and Race in the United States, 1880–1917* (Chicago: University of Chicago Press, 1995), 15.
4. Steven A. Riess, *City Games: The Evolution of American Urban Society and the Rise of Sports* (Urbana: University of Illinois Press, 1989), 13.

5. Ibid., 73.

6. Ibid., 109.

7. John Beynon, *Masculinities and Culture* (Philadelphia: Open University Press, 2002), 46.

8. Ibid., 45.

9. Elizabeth H. Pleck and Joseph H. Pleck, eds., *The American Man* (Englewood Cliffs, NJ: Prentice Hall, 1980), 24.

10. These are broadly defined as recreational activities; these illustrations averaged only about half a page per issue in 1880, and not quite a page in 1883. But by 1886 sporting illustrations—usually boxing or bodybuilding—averaged two pages per issue.

11. The arrival of photographs made illustrations of actual crimes rare in other publications as well; however, noted historian Simon Michael Bessie, some newspapers used creative approaches to get unavailable images into their pages. In the 1930s, the *New York Evening Graphic* began using the composograph—a staged picture that was retouched to resemble an actual event—with great circulation success. In a 1936 case, a rich playboy sued his wife for divorce on the grounds that she had deceived him about the fact that she was partly Negro. She stripped to the court to prove that he should have known all along that she had "Negroid characteristics," but the judge banned photographers from taking picutres of her nude body. The *Graphic* simply recreated the scene with an actress and actors, then retouched the final product and ran it in the newspaper. The *Graphic* carried a tiny disclaimer that the image was faked, but circulation jumped. See Simon Michael Bessie, *Jazz Journalism: The Story of the Tabloid Newspapers* (New York: Russell & Russell, 1938), 197.

12. A calculation of Spearman's rho shows a significant correlation between year and sporting illustrations, with sporting pictures increasing over the years.

13. Pamela J. Shoemaker and Stephen D. Reese, *Mediating the Message: Theories of Influences on Mass Media Content*, 2nd ed. (New York: Longman, 1996), x.

14. The model is illustrated throughout the volume by Shoemaker and Reese, *Mediating the Message*, 64.

15. Raymond Williams, *Marxism and Literature* (New York: Oxford University Press, 1977), 109.

16. Definitions of the influences on media content are in Chapters 5–9 of Shoemaker and Reese, *Mediating the Message*.

17. Shoemaker and Reese, *Mediating the Message*, 225.

18. Ibid.

19. Ibid., 226.

20. James W. Messerschmidt, *Nine Lives: Adolescent masculinities, the body, and violence* (Boulder, CO: Westview Press, 2000), 6.

21. Ibid., 7–9.

22. James W. Messerschmidt, *Nine Lives: Adolescent masculinities, the body, and violence* (Boulder, CO: Westview Press, 2000), 8.

23. R.W. Connell, *Masculinities* (Berkeley: University of California Press, 1995), 77.

24. Ibid., 79.

25. Ibid., 37.

26. Ibid., 79–80.

27. Messerschmidt, *Nine Lives*, 9.

28. Ibid., 10.

29. Ibid., 13–14.

30. "A Valuable Gift," *National Police Gazette*, November 27, 1880, 2.

31. Ibid., 2.

32. "The Bartender's Medal," *National Police Gazette*, November 16, 1901, 6. Use a mixing glass, fine ice, half a lemon, a dessert spoonful of fine sugar, a jigger of rye whiskey, half a jigger of port wine, and the white of one egg. Shake well, strain in a small fizz glass; fill with fizz and garnish with slice of pineapple.

33. Ibid.

34. Michael T. Isenberg, *John L. Sullivan and His America* (Chicago: University of Illinois Press, 1988), 48.

35. Based on comments like this, it is apparent that many of the woodcuts in the *Gazette* were fanciful—creations of the artists' imaginations. They were usually purported to be based on fact and served an editorial purpose; that is, to illustrate a larger point. But it is clear from the context that not all of the woodcuts depicted actual events.

36. "Our Fallacious Excise Laws," *National Police Gazette*, March 5, 1881, 2.

37. Gene Smith and Jayne Barry Smith, eds., *The Police Gazette* (New York: Simon & Schuster, 1972), 14; Elliott J. Gorn, "The Wicked World: *The National Police Gazette* and Gilded-Age America," *Media Studies Journal* 6 (Winter 1992): 10–11.

38. Ibid.

39. "The Reason Why," *National Police Gazette*, November 27, 1880, 2.

40. Jon M. Kingsdale, "The 'Poor Man's Club': Social Functions of the Urban Working-Class Saloon," in *The American Man*, ed. Elizabeth H. Pleck and Joseph H. Pleck (Englewood Cliffs, NJ: Prentice Hall, 1980), 255–84.

41. See the *National Police Gazette*, July 2, 1881.

5 FOX AND SULLIVAN: THE BRAWL THAT STARTED IT ALL?

Epigraph. Edward Van Every, *Sins of New York as "Exposed" by the Police Gazette* (New York: Frederick A. Stokes, 1930), 261.

1. Michael T. Isenberg, *John L. Sullivan and His America* (Chicago: University of Illinois Press, 1988), 4.

2. Rex Lardner, *The Legendary Champions* (New York: American Heritage Press, 1972), 47.
3. Van Every, *Sins of New York*, 261.
4. Isenberg, *John L. Sullivan and His America*, 6.
5. R.F. Dribble, *John L. Sullivan: An Intimate Narrative* (Boston: Little, Brown, 1925), 8.
6. Ibid., 10.
7. Richard Hoffer, "John L. Sullivan & Jake Kilrain in the Outlaw Brawl that Started it All," *Sports Illustrated*, May 6, 2002, 64.
8. Van Every, *Sins of New York*, 261.
9. Hoffer, "John L. Sullivan," 68.
10. David B. Welky, "Culture, Media and Sport: The *National Police Gazette* and the Creation of an American Working-Class World," *Culture, Sport, Society* 1, no. 1 (May 1998): 78–97.
11. John F. Kasson, *Houdini, Tarzan, and the Perfect Man: The White Male Body and the Challenge of Modernity in America* (New York: Hill and Wang, 2001), 19.
12. Ibid., 112.
13. Ibid., 19.
14. Ibid., 29.
15. Ibid., 29–30.
16. Ibid., 41.
17. Ibid., 47–48.
18. Ibid., 48.
19. Ibid., 50.
20. Ibid., 56–57.
21. *Mirror*, March 7, 1835, 4.
22. Isenberg, *John L. Sullivan and His America*, 60.
23. Frank Luther Mott, *A History of American Magazines*, vol. 2 (1938; reprint, Cambridge: Harvard University Press, 1957), 11.
24. "Midnight Pictures," *National Police Gazette*, November 22, 1879, 15–16. Five years after this portrait ran, Fox was soliciting *Gazette* readers to give to a fund for Hill, who had lost a fortune on "unfortunate speculations" and who was then disabled and living in poverty at Maspeth, Long Island. See "The Harry Hill Benefit," *National Police Gazette*, April 28, 1884, 10.
25. Some writers disagree as to the particulars of the meeting. In his book *John L. Sullivan and His America*, Isenberg says that boxing manager and trainer Billy Madden, a friend of Sullivan's, told the boxing writer Nat Fleischer that Sullivan actually first met Fox in his office and that Sullivan did not show much respect for Fox. Madden said Fox, who was used to fighters praising him and bowing down to him in order to win mention in the *Police Gazette*, was offended by Sullivan's attitude. But the story about the saloon meeting is in many accounts of Sullivan's life and is also featured on the International Boxing Hall of Fame's web site at http://www.ibhof.com. In either case, nearly all historians agree that

Fox held Sullivan in low esteem, and that—along with the money and publicity that Fox gained from promoting boxing—was a factor in his attempts to teach the Boston brawler a lesson. Since Fox was such an integral part of the boxing scene, and Harry Hill's was known as a gathering place where fighters associated with businessmen, publishers, lawyers, and others, it does not seem unlikely that Fox and Sullivan could have crossed paths there.

26. See www.ibhof.com

27. Cover headlines ran in about 70 percent of *Gazette* issues during the period studied, with most of them occurring after the early 1880s.

28. Mott, *A History of American Magazines*, vol. 4, 373–74.

29. John Rickards Betts, "The Technological Revolution and the Rise of Sport, 1850–1900," in *The American Sporting Experience: A Historical Anthology of Sport in America*, ed. Steven A. Riess (New York: Leisure Press, 1984), 141.

30. Madison Square Garden had electric lights as early as 1882, three years after Thomas Edison developed the incandescent bulb. See Betts, "The Technological Revolution and the Rise of Sport, 1850–1900," 150.

31. Betts, "The Technological Revolution and the Rise of Sport, 1850–1900," 151.

32. Ibid., 146, 149; Mott, *A History of American Magazines*, vol. 2, 479.

33. Betts, "The Technological Revolution and the Rise of Sport, 1850–1900," 148, 150.

34. Mott, *A History of American Magazines*, vol. 2, 479–80.

35. John Rickards Betts, "Sporting Journalism in Nineteenth-Century America," *American Quarterly* 5 (Spring 1953): 50.

36. Alan Nourie and Barbara Nourie, *American Mass-Market Magazines* (New York: Greenwood Press, 1990), 287.

37. Michael Oriard, *Reading Football: How the Popular Press Created an American Spectacle* (Chapel Hill: University of North Carolina Press, 1993), 218.

38. Ibid., 219.

39. Ibid.

40. Steven A. Riess, *City Games: The Evolution of American Urban Society and the Rise of Sports* (Urbanna, IL: Univeristy of Illinois Press, 1989), 20.

41. Cited in G. Edward White, *The Eastern Establishment and the Western Experience: The West of Frederic Remington, Theodore Roosevelt, and Owen Wister* (New Haven: Yale University Press, 1968), 155. Roosevelt became a hero by leading his horseless Rough Riders at San Juan. The Spanish, vastly outnumbered, put up a good fight, but the result was not victory but rather the promotion of Roosevelt from "a colonelcy to the presidency." See Samuel Eliot Morison, *The Oxford History of the American People* (New York: Oxford University Press, 1965), 804.

42. Oriard, *Reading Football*, 141.

43. Ibid., 216.

44. Ibid., 218; *National Police Gazette*, December 20, 1884, 11.

45. Oriard, *Reading Football*, 223–24.
46. Ibid., 226.
47. Ibid., 224.
48. Ibid., 224–26.
49. Ibid., 226.
50. Michael Kimmel, *Manhood in America: A Cultural History* (New York: Free Press, 1996), 137.
51. Ibid., 170.
52. Ibid., 169.
53. Kimmel, *Manhood in America*, 121.
54. Jeffrey P. Hantover, "The Boy Scouts and the Validation of Masculinity," in *The American Man*, ed. Elizabeth H. Pleck and Joseph H. Pleck (Englewood Cliffs, NJ: Prentice Hall, 1980), 285–99.
55. Kimmel, *Manhood in America*, 169.
56. R.W. Connell, *Masculinities* (Berkeley: University of California Press, 1995), 225–43.
57. "A New Departure," *National Police Gazette*, March 20, 1880, 2.
58. Insenberg, *John L. Sullivan and His America*, 94. Isenberg said the volume was error-filled.
59. Van Every, *Sins of New York*, 262.
60. Dribble, *John L. Sullivan*, 11–12.
61. Ibid., 68–81.
62. Van Every, *Sins of New York*, 265.
63. "Sullivan wins!" *National Police Gazette*, February 18, 1882, 2.
64. Van Every, *Sins of New York*, 265.
65. "Sullivan wins!" *National Police Gazette*, February 18, 1882, 2.
66. Fox rather theatrically pulled out of his backing of the 1885 bout, claiming that he was being held up as a scapegoat by other editors who said he was sponsoring illegal prize fights. "The morning newspapers will continue to publish accounts of sanguinary fights under club protection in New York—but hereafter other patrons than myself must be held responsible," Fox wrote in the page 2 editorial of May 2, 1885. He printed a copy of a letter addressed to "Friend John"—Sullivan—explaining his decision. But his effort to remain on the sidelines did not last until the end of the column; "At the same time," he wrote, "I shall continue to serve in the future with money, energy and influence, the good and wholesome cause of manly sport in America."
67. *National Police Gazette*, February 18, 1882, 2.
68. Van Every, *Sins of New York*, 265.
69. Ibid., 122.
70. Ibid., 266.
71. *National Police Gazette*, June 2, 1883, 8. The issue carries a reproduction of the dining card presented at the gala; the menu included boned salmon, pickled mussels, lobster salad, boned turkey (in jelly), and as it was stated, "Barbecue Lamb. Barbecue Ox. Barbecue Pig." In addition to various desserts, the menu also listed wines, champagne, sherry, claret, cognac, whiskey, and "Milwaukee beer."

72. David McCullough, *The Great Bridge: The Epic Story of the Building of the Brooklyn Bridge* (New York: Touchstone Books, 1982), 527.
73. "The Religious Editor," *National Police Gazette*, June 16, 1883, 7.
74. *National Police Gazette*, June 16, 1883, 6.
75. "Our Celebration," *National Police Gazette*, June 16, 1883, 7.
76. Van Every, *Sins of New York*, 169–70.
77. "The 'Police Gazette'," *National Police Gazette*, March 10, 1883, 7.
78. Ibid.
79. Ibid.
80. Mott, *A History of American Magazines*, vol. 2, 330–31.
81. Isenberg, *John L. Sullivan and His America*, 96. The sports championed by the *Gazette* ranged from what are now considered modern standards, such as cycling and rowing, to what would seem strange to today's fans. In the February 3, 1883, issue of the *National Police Gazette* is a feature on a "purring" match—a shin-kicking contest. In a large woodcut illustration, which is almost painful to look at, two men are showing kicking at each other's bleeding shins, with a group of top- and derby-hatted men behind them, waving money. The article begins, "A shin-kicking match was the novelty that stirred the blood of the sports at Camden, N.J., on the happy New Year." Five hundred dollars was at stake, and the men, wearing knee breeches and bare-legged from knee to ankle, had argued over whether to conduct the contest in regulation shoes. On the objection of one man that regular shoes might leave him crippled, the contest was conducted in "purring" shoes—No. 7 Brogans. The winner was Dave McWilliams, of Plymouth, Pennsylvania, who left his opponent's legs "raw as beefsteak."
82. Van Every, *Sins of New York*, 165.
83. Ibid., 166.
84. Welky, "Culture, Media and Sport," 84. The "escape from anonymity" for modern record seekers was later offered by the *Guinness Book of Records*, which was established in the mid-twentieth century after England's Sir Hugh Beaver and his hunting companions decided they needed a general reference book when they argued over what was Europe's fastest game bird.
85. *National Police Gazette*, August 25, 1888.
86. "Another Bridge Jumper," *National Police Gazette*, August 10, 1885, 6.
87. Theodore Roosevelt, *Ranch Life and the Hunting-Trail* (New York: Century Co., 1888), 126.
88. Isenberg, *John L. Sullivan and His America*, 96.
89. Mott, *A History of American Magazines*, vol. 3, 42. In June 1883 Fox was claiming that his *Illustrated Week's Doings*, a nickel weekly published on Sundays as the only illustrated Sunday newspaper in America, had 100,000 readers a week. But the claim seems inflated—or the readers fickle—given the short life of the journal.

90. *National Police Gazette*, August 4, 1888, 2; "A New Departure," *National Police Gazette*, January 26, 1893, 2; *National Police Gazette*, September 5, 1896, 2.
91. Mott, *A History of American Magazines*, vol. 3, 6.
92. *National Police Gazette*, February 13, 1897, 2.
93. "Known the World Over," *National Police Gazette*, January 28, 1893, 2. The same item quoted a letter from a reader, A. De Vos, who was living in a settlement on the Malay Peninsula, who said residents had eagerly followed *Gazette* accounts of sporting events, particularly the prizefight involving John L. Sullivan and Jim Corbett. De Vos said he was able to collect his wager against Sullivan after the *Gazette* arrived via Singapore announcing Corbett's victory.
94. *National Police Gazette*, March 11, 1882, 2. Historians' estimates of *Gazette* circulations are based on its published claims; here, the number may have included pass-along circulation in addition to paid readership.
95. For example, see the *National Police Gazette*, February 3, 1883.
96. "Richard K. Fox and His Sporting Representatives," *National Police Gazette*, August 25, 1883, 13.
97. Ibid.
98. "A Word About Ourselves," *National Police Gazette*, October 17, 1885, 2.
99. See David W. Shaw, *Daring the Sea: The True Story of the First Men to Row Across the Atlantic Ocean* (Seacaucus, NJ: Birch Lane, 1998) for a rather fanciful account of Fox's supposed conversation with the immigrants when they approached him in his office with the idea. The men did ultimately complete the journey, in an eighteen-foot boat, which they rowed from New York to England in fifty-five days. Their time, set in 1896, still stands.
100. See "A Word to Strong Men," *National Police Gazette*, May 5, 1884, 2, for a Fox editorial on the Cyr-Sandow match, which Fox said was necessary to settle once and for all the question of who was strongest.
101. "Police Gazette a Factor in Manly Sport," *National Police Gazette*, May 20, 1899, 7.
102. "Suppose and Suppose," *National Police Gazette*, May 30, 1885, 2.
103. "Richard K. Fox Vs. Snide Reformers," *National Police Gazette*, May 30, 1885, 2.
104. "They All Do It," *National Police Gazette*, April 4, 1885, 2.
105. Ibid.
106. Mott, *A History of American Magazines*, vol. 3, 123.
107. *National Police Gazette*, September 16, 1882, 11.
108. Van Every, *Sins of New York*, 271.
109. "Another Victory!" *National Police Gazette*, February 17, 1883, 10.
110. Ibid.
111. "Richard K. Fox Wins," *National Police Gazette*, February 24, 1883, 10.
112. For example, see *National Police Gazette*, July 27, 1889, 6.
113. *National Police Gazette*, April 7, 1883, 4.
114. *National Police Gazette*, April 14, 1883, 2.

115. "The Prize Ring," *National Police Gazette*, May 19, 1883, 10.

116. See Van Every, *Sins of New York*, and Isenberg, *John L. Sullivan and His America*, for differing views on the amounts earned by Fox.

117. Hazel Dicken-Garcia, *Journalistic Standards in Nineteenth-Century America* (Madison: University of Wisconsin Press, 1989), 224.

118. *National Police Gazette*, November 1, 1845. For a discussion of the *Gazette*'s role in the rise of journalism objectivity, see Dan Schiller, *Objectivity and the News: The Public and the Rise of Commercial Journalism* (Philadelphia: University of Pennsylvania Press, 1981).

119. "A Bad System," *National Police Gazette*, May 22, 1880, 2.

120. Isenberg, *John L. Sullivan and His America*, 130.

121. John Dinan, *Sports in the Pulp Magazines* (Jefferson, NC: McFarland & Co., 1998), 8.

122. *National Police Gazette*, June 30, 1883, 11. For a fictional account of the romance between John L. and Annie, see Mathias P. Harpin, *Trumpets in Jericho* (West Warwick, RI: Commercial Printing Publishing, 1961). Despite her claim in the *Gazette*, two years later Annie Bates Bailey would sue John L. Sullivan for divorce, accusing him of abuse on numerous occasions, including one instance in which the beating was so severe she had to use house paint to cover her wounds. Her petition was denied on the grounds that she had condoned Sullivan's actions. See Isenberg, *John L. Sullivan and His America*, for a complete recounting of the marriage.

123. Van Every, *Sins of New York*, 269.

124. Ibid.

125. Isenberg, *John L. Sullivan and His America*, 176. Gilbert Odd, in his *Encyclopedia of Boxing* (London: Hamlyn Publishing, 1983), tells of how the sportsmen of Boston awarded Sullivan his own belt because of Sullivan's disdain for Fox's. It contained 397 diamonds that spelled out his name. Sullivan, who was in deep debt at various times of his life, later sold the belt for a few hundred dollars, having pried out all the diamonds.

126. Van Every, *Sins of New York*, 271.

127. The *Gazette* would describe a portion of the jury selection this way: "After several rejections along came William McBride, who admitted he did not approve of boxing to excess. To illustrate, he said he had often played checkers all night and considered that excess. When he said 'checkers' the court room [*sic*] smiled right out loud and the checker fiend was excused."

128. Isenberg, *John L. Sullivan and His America*, 181. Isenberg noted that this claim by Sullivan was undoubtedly a "whopper."

129. Van Every, *Sins of New York*, 274.

130. Ibid.

131. Van Every, *Sins of New York*, 261.

132. *National Police Gazette*, January 7, 1888, 4.

133. Jeffrey T. Sammons, *Beyond the Ring: The Role of Boxing in American Society* (Chicago: University of Illinois Press, 1988), 9.
134. Van Every, *Sins of New York*, 276.
135. Isenberg, *John L. Sullivan and His America*, 275.
136. *National Police Gazette*, July 20, 1889, 2.
137. Ibid., 4.
138. Mott, *A History of American Magazines*, vol. 2, 334. Interestingly, Sullivan managed to eventually swear off drinking for good, and the date is considered reliable by most historians because Sullivan and others testified repeatedly as to what happened: On March 5, 1905, the day after Theodore Roosevelt's inauguration, Sullivan ordered a glass of champagne in a hotel bar in Terre Haute, Indiana. As he was waiting to be served, he began thinking about how much he'd spent on alcohol over the years. After coming up with an outlandish figure of $500,000, he poured the champagne in a spittoon and vowed never to drink again. He apparently kept his word.
139. *National Police Gazette*, November 10, 1888, 7.
140. Gail Bederman, *Manliness & Civilization: A Cultural History of Gender and Race in the United States, 1880–1917* (Chicago: University of Chicago Press, 1995), 1.
141. "John L. Sullivan," *National Police Gazette*, April 26, 1884, 7.
142. *National Police Gazette*, January 17, 1885, 2.
143. Isenberg, *John L. Sullivan and His America*, 59.
144. Elliott J. Gorn, *The Manly Art: Bare-Knuckle Prize Fighting in America* (Ithaca, NY: Cornell University Press, 1986), 247.

6   THE GIRL ON THE *POLICE GAZETTE*

Epigraph. Irving Berlin, "The Girl on the Police Gazette," from the 1937 film *On the Avenue*. A soundtrack was released in 1999 by Disconforme, available at www.disconforme.com

1. *National Police Gazette*, September 27, 1879, 1; July 17, 1880, 5, 9; January 26, 1884, 1; January 26, 1889, 1; June 2, 1894, 1; February 16, 1895, 1; July 27, 1895, 1; January 25, 1902, 1.
2. Sexually suggestive illustrations in the *Gazette* took different forms, but often included activities of acrtresses or showgirls in provocative poses. They also included women in scanty or ruffled clothing. In the coding instructions (see Appendix A), coders were instructed that sexually suggestive "pictures are sexually tantalizing in nature and generally include provocative poses of actresses or showgirls, plus women in skimpy attire or who are flirting, playing with each other, carousing, or engaged in prostitution or temptation."
3. "Masks and Faces," *National Police Gazette*, March 10, 1894, 2.
4. "Chorus Girls Are Anxious to Display Their Figures," *National Police Gazette*, February 2, 1895, 2.

5. "All Five Were Lynched," *National Police Gazette*, May 11, 1895, 6.
6. Stanley Cohen and Jock Young, eds., *The Manufacture of News: Social problems, Deviance and the Mass Media* (London: Constable, 1973), 15–16.
7. Mary P. Ryan, *Womanhood in America: From Colonial Times to the Present* (New York: New Viewpoints, 1975), 256–57.
8. Carolyn Kitch, *The Girl on the Magazine Cover: The Origins of Visual Stereotypes in American Mass Media* (Chapel Hill: University of North Carolina Press, 2001), 20.
9. Ibid., 37, 39.
10. Mark Gabor, *The Illustrated History of Girlie Magazines: From National Police Gazette to the Present* (New York: Harmony Books, 1984), 31.
11. Ibid., 15.
12. Ibid., 25–26.
13. "Gems from the Gay Dog's Companion," *American Heritage* 11 (October 1960): 105–111.
14. Donald J. Mrozek, "Sport in American Life: From National Health to Personal Fulfillment, 1890–1940," in *Fitness in American Culture: Images of Health, Sport, and the Body, 1830–1940*, ed. Kathryn Grover (Amherst: University of Massachusetts Press, 1989), 27; T.J. Jackson Lears, *Fables of Abundance: A Cultural History of Advertising in America* (New York: Basic Books, 1993).
15. Dorothy Dix, "The Girl of Today," *Good Housekeeping*, March 1916, 289.
16. Gabor, *The Illustrated History of Girlie Magazines*, 21.
17. Kitch, *The Girl on the Magazine Cover*, 58.
18. Ibid., 60.
19. Ibid., 59.
20. Ibid., 67–68.
21. Kenneth A. Yellis, "Prosperity's Child: Some Thoughts on the Flapper," *American Quarterly* 21 (Spring 1969): 44–64.
22. Margaret A. Hawkins and Thomas K. Nakayama, "Discourse on Women's Bodies: Advertising in the 1920s," in *Constructing and Reconstructing Gender: The Links Among Communication, Language, and Gender*, ed. Linda A.M. Perry, Lynn H. Turner, and Helen Sterk (Albany: State University of New York Press, 1992), 62.
23. Kitch, *The Girl on the Magazine Cover*, 182.
24. Ibid., 191–92.
25. Michael Capuzzo, *Close to Shore: A True Story of Terror in an Age of Innocence* (New York: Broadway Books, 2001), 49.
26. David Loth, *The Erotic in Literature: A Historical Survey of Pornography as Delightful as it is Indiscreet* (New York: Julian Messner, 1961), 117.
27. Joseph W. Slade, *Pornography in America: A Reference Handbook* (Santa Barbara, CA: ABC-CLIO, 2000), 5.
28. Ibid., 57.
29. Loth, *The Erotic in Literature*, 119.

30. Ibid., 124.
31. Ibid., 143.
32. Ibid., 144.
33. Helen Lefkowitz Horowitz, *Rereading Sex: Battles over Sexual Knowledge and Suppression in Nineteenth-Century America* (New York: Alfred A Knopf, 2002), 369.
34. Loth, *The Erotic in Literature*, 144.
35. Elliot J. Gorn, "The Wicked World: The *National Police Gazette* and Gilded-Age America," *Media Studies Journal* 6, no. 1 (Winter 1992): 2.
36. Walter Kendrick, *The Secret Museum: Pornography in Modern Culture* (New York: Viking, 1987), 130.
37. Ibid., 138.
38. *Sunday Flash*, September 12, 1841, 1.
39. Horowitz, *Rereading Sex*, 160.
40. Ibid., 179.
41. Joseph W. Slade, *Pornography and Sexual Representation: A Reference Guide*, vol. 1 (Westport, CT: Greenwood Press, 2001), 47.
42. Horowitz, *Rereading Sex*, 187.
43. *The Herald*, September 15, 1842.
44. George Wilkes, *The Mysteries of the Tombs; A Journal of Thirty Days Imprisonment in the New York City Prison; for Libel* (New York: 1844), 63.
45. Zenger was defended by Andrew Hamilton after he published materials critical of the British New York governor. Hamilton said Zenger admitted publishing the articles, but successfully argued that to prevail, a libel action first had to prove that the account it challenged was false. Zenger had been accused of seditious libel, which protected the government against criticism. Other types of libel laws protect individuals against false accounts of their activities that reflect on their reputations. See Richard E. Labunksi, *Libel and the First Amendment: Legal History and Practice in Print and Broadcasting* (New Brunswick, NJ: Transaction Publishers, 1987).
46. Horowitz, *Rereading Sex*, 191, 202.
47. Marjorie Heinz, *Sex, Sin, and Blasphemy: A Guide to America's Censorship Wars* (New York: The New Press, 1993), 19.
48. Frederick F. Schauer, *The Law of Obscenity* (Washington: Bureau of National Affairs, 1976), 10.
49. Horowitz, *Rereading Sex*, 224–27.
50. Ibid., 230.
51. Ibid., 323.
52. Ibid., 369.
53. Ibid., 203.
54. Ibid., 203–4.
55. Kendrick, *The Secret Museum*, 145.
56. Gabor, *The Illustrated History of Girlie Magazines*, 17–18.
57. Stanley Cohen, "Mods and Rockers: the inventory as manufactured news," in *The Manufacture of News: Social problems, deviance and the*

mass media, ed. Stanley Cohen and Jock Young (London: Constable, 1973), 228. The essay is an abbreviated form of material that appeared in Chapter 2 of Cohen's book *Folk Devils and Moral Panics: The Creation of the Mods and Rockers* (London: MacGibbon & Kee, 1972).

58. Cohen, "Mods and Rockers," 238.
59. *National Police Gazette*, July 27, 1895, 1, 2.
60. Ibid., "Masks and Faces," 2.
61. Kenneth Thompson, *Moral Panics* (London: Routledge, 1998), 60.
62. Erich Goode and Nachman Ben-Yehuda, *Moral Panics: The Social Construction of Deviance* (Oxford, England: Blackwell, 1994), 42.
63. As noted previously, Pamela Shoemaker and Stephen D. Reese discuss the affect of ideology on news content in their models described in *Mediating the Message: Theories of Influences on Mass Media Content*, 2nd ed. (New York: Longman, 1996).
64. Howard P. Chudacoff, *The Age of the Bachelor: Creating an American Subculture* (Princeton: Princeton University Press, 1999), 19.
65. Ibid., 35.
66. Timothy J. Gilfoyle, *City of Eros: New York City, Prostitution, and the Commercialization of Sex* (New York: W.W. Norton Co., 1992), 112–14.
67. Chudacoff, *Age of the Bachelor*, 36.
68. Ibid., 48.
69. Ibid., 55–67; quotation from Chudacoff, *Age of the Bachelor*, 67.
70. Jack Black, *You Can't Win* (New York: Macmillan, 1926), 12.
71. Ibid., 12.
72. Chudacoff, *Age of the Bachelor*, 124–25.
73. Ibid., 186.
74. See Lee Coyle, *George Ade* (New York: Twayne Publishers, 1964).
75. George Ade, *Single Blessedness and Other Observations* (Garden City, NY: Doubleday, Page and Co., 1922), 15–16.
76. Chudacoff, *Age of the Bachelor*, 187.
77. Ibid., 192.
78. Ibid., 193.
79. Ibid., 194.
80. Ibid., 195.
81. Ibid., 197.
82. See, e.g., "1,000,000 Readers Every Week!" *National Police Gazette*, November 3, 1883, 2.
83. Chudacoff, *Age of the Bachelor*, 198.
84. Ibid., 206.
85. Ibid.
86. Alan Trachentenberg, foreword to *Horrible Prettiness: Burlesque and American Culture*, by Robert C. Allen (Chapel Hill: University of North Carolina Press, 1991), xii.
87. Ibid.
88. Allen, *Horrible Prettiness*, 200.

89. *National Police Gazette*, March 18, 1899, 3.
90. New York *Clipper*, March 4, 1871, cited in Allen, *Horrible Prettiness*, 378.
91. *National Police Gazette*, October 31, 1896, 2; Allen, *Horrible Prettiness*, 244.
92. Chudacoff, *Age of the Bachelor*, 209, 210.
93. Kevin White, *The First Sexual Revolution: The Emergence of Male Heterosexuality in Modern America* (New York: New York University Press, 1993), 7.
94. Ibid., 188.
95. "Gems from the Gay Dog's Companion," *American Heritage* 11 (October 1960): 106.
96. Berlin, "The Girl on the Police Gazette."
97. Edward Van Every, *Sins of New York as "Exposed" by the Police Gazette* (New York: Frederick A. Stokes Co., 1930), xv.
98. Ibid., vi.
99. Gabor, *The Illustrated History of Girlie Magazines*, 25.

7 PATRON OF SPORT

Epigraph. "An Open Letter," *National Police Gazette*, July 2, 1887, 2.
1. "The Cranes Again," *National Police Gazette*, October 8, 1887, 2.
2. Mark Gabor, *The Illustrated History of Girlie Magazines: From* National Police Gazette *to the Present* (New York: Harmony Books, 1984), 21.
3. Richard K. Fox, *Rube Burrows' Raids. Historic Highwaymen. Night Riders of Ozark; Or, the Bald Knobbers of Missouri* (New York: Richard K. Fox, 1891). Rube Burrows was described as a "noted outlaw, train robber and murderer" who was a "bold and adventurous desperado."
4. See Fox's books of the 1890s for advertisements highlighting his order department, run by a "thoroughly competent man." The sporting goods department also sold "Base Balls, Base Ball Bats, Base Ball Masks, Catchers' Gloves, Breast Protectors, Lawn Tennis, Croquet, Hammocks, Fencing Foils, Fencing Masks, Ice Skates, Roller Skates, the American Hoyle . . ." and so on.
5. Stewart Pearson, *Building Brands Directly: Creating Business Value from Customer Relationships* (New York: New York University Press, 1996), 6.
6. M.M. Manring, *Slave in a Box: The Strange Career of Aunt Jemima* (Charlottesville: University Press of Virginia, 1998), 72–76. Davis even found a real woman to play Aunt Jemima: Nancy Green of Chicago, a fifty-seven-year-old former slave, who appeared at the 1893 World's Fair in Chicago as the legendary cook.
7. Fox's books, published through the Richard K. Fox publishing house in New York City, included an instructional manual on the art of poker as well as books chronicling tales of the Old West. His boxing books included *The Life and Battles of Jake Kilrain* (1888), *The Great Battle*

Between John L. Sullivan and Jake Kilrain (New York: Richard K. Fox, 1889), *The Black Champions of the Prize Ring from Molineaux to Jackson* (New York: Richard K. Fox, 1890), *Life and Battles of James J. Corbett, the Champion of the World* (New York: Richard K. Fox, 1894), and *The Life and Battles of Jack Johnson, Champion Pugilist of the World* (New York: Richard K. Fox, 1909).

8. Margaret Mark and Carol S. Pearson, *The Hero and the Outlaw: Building Extraordinary Brands Through the Power of Archetypes* (New York: McGraw-Hill, 2001), 5–7.

9. "Dangers of Fiction," *National Police Gazette*, June 21, 1884, 2.

10. "A Young Murderer," *National Police Gazette*, February 2, 1884, 11.

11. Walter Davenport, "The Dirt Disher," *Collier's*, March 24, 1928, 52–53.

12. Douglas Sutherland, *The Yellow Earl: The Life of Hugh Lowther, 5th Earl of Lonsdale, 1857–1944* (New York: Coward-McCann, 1965), 99–105. Before the race with Shrewsbury, one of Lonsdale's biggest claims to fame was his supposed defeat of John L. Sullivan in an illegal boxing match in the early 1880s. The two met at Central Park Academy in New York, after Lonsdale made the voyage specifically to fight Sullivan. They fought with illegal six-ounce gloves, and Lonsdale survived a heavy beating before breaking his hand when he punched Sullivan in the torso. Sullivan collapsed and did not rise again. There were not many witnesses to the fight, and Sullivan never spoke of it. Fox, however, characteristically, called Lonsdale the winner. See Sutherland, *The Yellow Earl*, 56–60.

13. In 1872 Pulitzer bought the *St. Louis Post* for $3,000. He later purchased the *St. Louis Dispatch*, then combined the two publications and used them for crusades against government corruption, lotteries, gambling, and tax fraud. By 1883 Pulitzer was a wealthy man and was able to purchase the *New York World* for $346,000. The newspaper, which had been losing $40,000 a year, concentrated on human-interest stories, scandal, and sensationalism. He also used it to advocate reforms that included tax policy. In 1887, at age twenty-three Hearst became proprietor of the *San Francisco Examiner*. Inspired by Pulitzer, Hearst turned the newspaper into a combination of reformist investigative reporting and lurid sensationalism. At his peak he owned twenty-eight major newspapers and eighteen magazines, along with several radio stations and movie companies. See W.A. Swanberg, *Pulitzer* (New York: Charles Scribner's Sons, 1967); David Nasaw, *The Chief: The Life of William Randolph Hearst* (Boston: Houghton Mifflin, 2000).

14. Gabor, *The Illustrated History of Girlie Magazines*, 21.

15. Franklin P. Adams, introduction to *Sins of New York as "Exposed" by the Police Gazette*, by Edward Van Every (New York: Frederick A. Stokes Co., 1930), vii.

16. Ibid., v–vi. Adams commented in the introduction that he felt "old, writing about the *Police Gazette*," and joked that he wanted to answer an old *Gazette* ad "to assure me that I could regain my Vanished Virility for a

dime, ten cents, the tenth of a dollar." In an attempt at prophecy, he figured that his two-year-old son would someday be "getting his 10,000,000 circulation newspaper over the television radio" while writing an introduction to Van Every's grandson's "history of the 1931 tabloids, and how we Old Gentlemen used to get a kick out of those outworn one-hoss shays of journalism. But he'll need this book for reference, the little upstart!"

17. Tom Wolfe, foreword to *The Police Gazette*, Gene Smith and Jayne Barry Smith, eds. (New York: Simon and Schuster, 1972), 10.
18. Smith and Smith, *The Police Gazette*, 18.
19. Ibid.
20. Ibid.
21. Ibid., 19.
22. Howard P. Chudacoff, *The Age of the Bachelor: Creating an American Subculture* (Princeton, NJ: Princeton University Press, 1999), 192.
23. Ibid., 193.
24. Frank Luther Mott, *A History of American Magazines*, vol. 2 (1938; reprint, Cambridge, MA: Harvard University Press, 1957), 336.
25. Chudacoff, *Age of the Bachelor*, 193.
26. Mott, *A History of American Magazines*, vol. 2, 336.
27. Alan Nourie and Barbara Nourie, *American Mass-Market Magazines* (New York: Greenwood Press, 1990), 289.
28. "Richard K. Fox's Death," Red Bank *Register*, November 15, 1922, 9.
29. "Richard K. Fox Dies; Patron of Sports," New York *Times*, November 15, 1922, 19.
30. "Funeral of Richard K. Fox," New York *Times*, November 21, 1922, 19.
31. "R.K. Fox Left $3,000,000," New York *Times*, December 22, 1922, 15.
32. "Richard K. Fox Left Estate of $1,796,169," New York *Times*, June 19, 1923, 21.
33. Ibid.
34. Ibid.
35. "Richard K. Fox's Death," Red Bank *Register*, November 15, 1922, 9.
36. Lincoln died in 1865 but Fox did not arrive in America until 1874.
37. George Jean Nathan and H.L. Mencken, "Repetition Generale," *Smart Set*, February 1923, 33–35; Nathan and Mencken, 35.
38. "The Richard K. Fox Era," New York *Herald*, November 16, 1922, 11.
39. Ibid.
40. "Richard Kyle Fox," *National Police Gazette*, December 2, 1922, 2.
41. Simon Michael Bessie, *Jazz Journalism: The Story of the Tabloid Newspapers* (1938; reprint, New York: Russell & Russell, 1969), 230–31 (page citations are to the reprint edition).
42. See Bessie, *Jazz Journalism*, for a discussion of this point.
43. Theodore Dreiser, *Sister Carrie* (1900; reprint, New York: Bantam Books, 1982), 82 (page citations are to the reprint edition).

44. Michael Parenti, *Inventing Reality: The Politics of the Mass Media* (New York: St. Martin's Press, 1986), 220.

45. Wendy Lesser, *Pictures at an Execution* (Cambridge: Harvard University Press, 1993), 22.

46. Ibid., 51.

47. Michael Kimmel, *Manhood in America: A Cultural History* (New York: Free Press, 1996), 335.

48. Bessie, *Jazz Journalism*, 65.

49. Elliott J. Gorn, "The Wicked World: The *National Police Gazette* and Gilded-Age America," *Media Studies Journal* 6, no. 1 (Winter 1992), 15.

50. Frank Luther Mott, *American Journalism: A History: 1690–1960*, 3rd ed. (New York: Macmillan, 1962), 673.

51. Colin Sparks, introduction to *Tabloid Tales: Global Debates Over Media Standards*, ed. Sparks and John Tulloch (Oxford, England: Rowman and Littlefield, 2000), 10.

52. See Marvin Kalb, *One Scandalous Story: Clinton, Lewinsky, and Thirteen Days that Tarnished American Journalism* (New York: The Free Press, 2001).

53. Erika J. Pribanic-Smith, "Sensationalism and Tabloidism," in *American Journalism: History, Principles, Practices*, ed. W. David Sloan and Lisa Mullikin Parcell (Jefferson, NC: McFarland & Co., 2002) 267, 272.

54. Jostein Gripsrud, "The Aesthetics and Politics of Melodrama," in *Journalism and Popular Culture*, ed. Peter Dahlgren and Colin Sparks (London: Sage, 1992), 91.

55. David J. Kracjicek, *Scooped: Media Miss Real Story on Crime While Chasing Sex, Sleaze, and Celebrities* (New York: Columbia University Press, 1998), ix.

56. Sparks, *Tabloid Tales*, 33.

57. There is a paradox here: Fox always claimed he illustrated immoralities and misdeeds so that the foul acts could be exposed and their perpetrators rooted out. If that is true, in that sense he and Comstock were actually on the same side. Fox claimed he wanted right action to prevail, so he exposed wrong action. Comstock wanted right action to prevail, partly through stamping out the depiction of wrong action. The converging goals, and Fox's genuine belief that the *Gazette* was not a scandalous publication, may have part of the reason Comstock was treated gently in the *Gazette*'s pages. Of course, ulterior motives no doubt saw their way into the actions of both sides.

58. Sparks, *Tabloid Tales*, 184.

59. Barry Glassner, *The Culture of Fear: Why Americans are Afraid of the Wrong Things* (New York: Basic Books, 1999), 23.

60. *National Police Gazette*, January 20, 1894, 1.

61. Sparks, *Tabloid Tales*, 27.

62. Ibid., 28.

63. Gripsrud, "The Aesthetics and Politics of Melodrama," 84–95.

64. Mott, *A History of American Magazines*, vol. 5, 346.

65 Ibid., 346–47.

66. Oliver Wendell Holmes, *The Professor at the Breakfast-Table* (Boston: James R. Osgood and Co., 1871), 148. The quotation first appeared in a series of Holmes essays published in the *Atlantic Monthly*, 1859–1860.

Epilogue

1. Arthur Meier Schlesinger, *The Rise of Modern America: 1865–1951* (New York: Macmillan, 1951).

2. Michael Kimmel, *Manhood in America: A Cultural History* (New York: The Free Press, 1996), 89, 90–91.

3. E. Anthony Rotundo, *American Manhood: Transformations in Masculinity from the Revolution to the Modern Era* (New York: Basic Books, 1993), 3.

4. Ibid., 5–6.

5. Ibid., 6–7, 8. See Rotundo, *American Manhood*, 271, for a discussion of use of gender-charged terms in nineteenth-century politics. Male abolitionists and reformers were often branded as woman-like or allied with females.

6. Ibid.

7. Kimmel, *Manhood in America*, 104.

8. Rotundo, *American Manhood*, 239.

9. The notion of "separate spheres" of public and private, as well as of men and women, is familiar to any student of women's history. Carroll Smith-Rosenberg, Nancy F. Cott, and Linda K. Kerber, among many others, have explained the way in which women have driven strength and influence from a "sphere" of friendship, work, and utility outside the immediate domain of men. For some historians, the notion of separate spheres is essential for a complete understanding of the forces of history. Kerber took the notion a step further, arguing that men often affected the supposed "separate sphere" of women; in turn, the women's sphere affected and influenced the activities of men in many ways. To be sure, the idea that the spheres may not have been so separate—as women began challenging men in their own spheres—was one of the themes of the *Gazette* illustrations. For a discussion of separate spheres theory, see Linda K. Kerber, *Toward an Intellectual History of Women* (Chapel Hill: University of North Carolina Press, 1997).

10. Ibid., 287.

11. Kimmel, *Manhood in America*, 320.

12. Marc Fasteau, "Vietnam and the Cult of Toughness in Foreign Policy," in *The American Man*, Elizabeth H. Pleck, Joseph H. Pleck, eds., 384, 386, 393.

13. Kimmel, *Manhood in America*, 149.

14. Ibid., 291.

15. Kimmel, *Manhood in America*, 292.
16. Ibid., 298.
17. Ibid., 326.
18. Ibid., 327.
19. See the *National Police Gazette*, April 21, 1888, and February 23, 1889.

Bibliography

Adams, Franklin P. Introduction to *Sins of New York as "Exposed" by the Police Gazette*, by Edward Van Every. New York: Frederick A. Stokes Co., 1930.

Ade, George. *Single Blessedness and Other Observations*. Garden City, NY: Doubleday, Page and Co., 1922.

Allen, Robert C. *Horrible Prettiness: Burlesque and American Culture*. Chapel Hill: University of North Carolina Press, 1991.

"All Five Were Lynched." *National Police Gazette*, May 11, 1895, 6.

"Almost a Mob." *National Police Gazette*, February 28, 1846, 2.

"Another Bridge Jumper." *National Police Gazette*, August 10, 1885, 6.

"Another Victory!" *National Police Gazette*, February 17, 1883, 10.

"The Assassin's Story." *National Police Gazette*, December 17, 1881, 11.

"Atrocious Murder." *New York Herald*, April 11, 1836, 1.

"A Bad System." *National Police Gazette*, May 22, 1880, 2.

"The Bandit's Boast." *National Police Gazette*, April 1, 1882, 10.

"A Barbarous Lynching." *National Police Gazette*, February 18, 1893, 2.

"The Bartender's Medal." *National Police Gazette*, November 16, 1901, 6.

Basso, Matthew, Laura McCall, and Dee Garceau. *Across the Great Divide: Cultures of Manhood in the American West*. New York: Routledge, 2001.

Betts, John Rickards. "The Technological Revolution and the Rise of Sport, 1850–1900." In *The American Sporting Experience: A Historical Anthology of Sport in America*, edited by Steven A. Riess. New York: Leisure Press, 1984.

———. "Sporting Journalism in Nineteenth-Century America." *American Quarterly* 5 (spring 1953): 39–56.

Bederman, Gail. *Manliness and Civilization: A Cultural History of Gender and Race in the United States, 1880–1917*. Chicago: University of Chicago Press, 1995.

Bellamy, Edward. *Looking Backward: 2000–1887*. 1888. Reprint, Boston: Magnum Books, 1968.

Bessie, Simon Michael. *Jazz Journalism*. New York: E.P. Dutton, 1938.

Beynon, John. *Masculinities and Culture*. Philadelphia: Open University Press, 2002.

"Billy the Kid's Dash for Liberty." *National Police Gazette*, October 26, 1901, 6.

Black, Jack. *You Can't Win*. New York: Macmillan, 1926.

Boyd, Andrew. "The Orange Order, 1795–1995." *History Today*, September 1, 1995, 17.

Browning, Reed. *The Duke of Newcastle*. New Haven: Yale University Press, 1975.

Burrows, Edwin G. and Mike Wallace. *Gotham: A History of New York City to 1898*. New York: Oxford University Press, 1999.

Campbell, W. Joseph. *Yellow Journalism: Puncturing the Myths, Defining the Legacies*. Westport, CT: Praeger, 2001.

Capuzzo, Michael. *Close to Shore: A True Story of Terror in an Age of Innocence*. New York: Broadway Books, 2001.

Carlson, Oliver. *The Man Who Made News: James Gordon Bennett*. New York: Duell, Sloan and Pearce, 1942.

"Chorus Girls Are Anxious to Display Their Figures." *National Police Gazette*, February 2, 1895, 2.

Chudacoff, Howard P. *The Age of the Bachelor: Creating an American Subculture*. Princeton: Princeton University Press, 1999.

Cohen, Stanley. *Folk Devils and Moral Panics: The Creation of the Mods and Rockers*. London: MacGibbon & Kee, 1972.

Cohen, Stanley and Jock Young, eds. *The Manufacture of News: Social problems, Deviance and the Mass Media*. London: Constable, 1973.

Connell, R.W. *Masculinities*. Berkeley: University of California Press, 1995.

Coyle, Lee. *George Ade*. New York: Twayne Publishers, 1964.

"The Cranes Again." *National Police Gazette*, October 8, 1887, 2.

Cutlip, Scott M. *Public Relations History from the Seventeenth to the Twentieth Century*. Hillsdale, NJ: Lawrence Erlbaum Associates, 1995.

"The Dalton Gang Killed." *National Police Gazette*, October 22, 1892, 6.

"Dangers of Fiction." *National Police Gazette*, June 21, 1884, 2.

Davenport, Walter. "The Nickel Shocker." *Collier's*, March 10, 1928, 26–40.

———. "The Dirt Disher." *Collier's*, March 24, 1928, 26–52.

Desmond, Robert W. *The Information Process: World News Reporting to the Twentieth Century*. Iowa City: University of Iowa Press, 1978.

"A Desperate Woman Killed." *New York Times*, February 6, 1889, 1.

Dicken-Garcia, Hazel. *Journalistic Standards in Nineteenth-Century America*. Madison: University of Wisconsin Press, 1989.

Dinan, John. *Sports in the Pulp Magazines*. London: McFarland & Co., 1998.

Dix, Dorothy. "The Girl of Today." *Good Housekeeping*, March 1916, 289.

Douglas, Susan. *Inventing American Broadcasting, 1899–1922*. Baltimore: Johns Hopkins University Press, 1987.

"Do We?" *National Police Gazette*, June 20, 1885, 2.

Dreiser, Theodore. *Sister Carrie*. 1900. Reprint, New York: Bantam Books, 1982.

Dribble, R.F. *John L. Sullivan: An Intimate Narrative*. Boston: Little Brown, 1925.

Durkheim, Emile. *The Rules of the Sociological Method*. Edited by Steven Lukes, translated by W.D. Halls. New York: Free Press, 1982.

"Editorial notes." *National Police Gazette*, March 23, 1889, 2.

Ellman, Richard. *Oscar Wilde*. New York: Alfred A. Knopf, 1987.

Emery, Edwin and Michael Emery. *The Press and America: An Interpretive History of the Mass Media*. Englewood Cliffs, NJ: Prentice Hall.

Ewen, Stuart. *PR! A Social History of Spin*. New York: Harper Collins, 1996.

"The Fall of Oscar Wilde." *National Police Gazette*, May 4, 1895, 6.

Ferrell, Jeff and Neil Websdale, eds. *Making Trouble: Cultural Constructions of Crime, Deviance, and Control*. New York: Walter de Gruyter, Inc.

Ferrero, Gina Lombroso. "The Criminal Man." In *Criminological Theory: Past to Present*, edited by Francis T. Cullen and Robert Agnew. Los Angeles: Roxbury Publishing, 1999.

"For Heaven's Sake, Stop." *National Police Gazette*, July 17, 1880, 2.

Fox, Richard K. *Bella Starr, The Bandit Queen, or The Female Jesse James. A Full and Authentic History of the Dashing Female Highwayman, with Copious Extracts from Her Journal. Handsomely and Profusely Illustrated*. New York: Richard K. Fox, 1889.

———. *The Black Champions of the Prize Ring from Molineaux to Jackson*. New York: Richard K. Fox, 1890.

———. *The Great Battle Between John L. Sullivan and Jake Kilrain*. New York: Richard K. Fox, 1889.

———. *The Life and Battles of Jack Johnson, Champion Pugilist of the World*. New York: Richard K. Fox, 1909.

———. *The Life and Battles of Jake Kilrain*. New York: Richard K. Fox, 1888.

———. *Life and Battles of James J. Corbett, the Champion of the World*. New York: Richard K. Fox, 1894.

———. *Rube Burrows' Raids. Historic Highwaymen. Night Riders of Ozark; Or, the Bald Knobbers of Missouri*. New York: Richard K. Fox, 1891.

———. "Friend John." *National Police Gazette*, May 2, 1885, 2.

Fox, Richard Wightman. *Trials of Intimacy: Love and Loss in the Beecher-Tilton Scandal*. Chicago: University of Chicago Press, 1999.

"Funeral of Richard K. Fox." *New York Times*, November 21, 1922, 19.

Gabor, Mark. *The Illustrated History of Girlie Magazines: From National Police Gazette to the Present*. New York: Harmony Books, 1984.

Garraty, John A. and Mark C. Carnes, eds. *American National Biography*. Vol. 8. Oxford: Oxford University Press, 1999.

"Gems from the Gay Dog's Companion." *American Heritage* 11 (October 1960): 105–111.

Gilfoyle, Timothy J. *City of Eros: New York City, Prostitution, and the Commercialization of Sex*. New York: W.W. Norton Co., 1992.

Glassner, Barry. *The Culture of Fear: Why Americans are Afraid of the Wrong Things*. New York: Basic Books, 1999.

Goode, Erich and Nachman Ben-Yehuda. *Moral Panics: The Social Construction of Deviance*. Oxford, England: Blackwell, 1994.

Gordon, Richard. *Jack the Ripper*. New York: Athenaeum, 1980.

Gordon, Welche. *Jesse James and His Band of Notorious Outlaws*. Chicago: Laird and Lee, 1891.

Gorn, Elliott J. "The Wicked World: *The National Police Gazette* and Gilded-Age America." *Media Studies Journal* 6 (Winter 1992): 1–15.

———. *The Manly Art: Bare-Knuckle Prize Fighting in America*. Ithaca, NY: Cornell University Press, 1986.

Gripsrud, Jostein. "The Aesthetics and Politics of Melodrama." In *Journalism and Popular Culture*, edited by Peter Dahlgren and Colin Sparks (London: Sage, 1992).

Gross, Gerald. *Masterpieces of Murder*. New York: Bonanza Books, 1961.

Hantover, Jeffrey P. "The Boy Scouts and the Validation of Masculinity." In *The American Man*, edited by Elizabeth H. Pleck and Joseph H. Pleck. Englewood Cliffs, NJ: Prentice Hall, 1980.

Harpin, Mathias P. *Trumpets in Jericho*. West Warwick, RI: Commercial Printing Publishing, 1961.

"The Harry Hill Benefit." *National Police Gazette*, April 28, 1884, 10.

Hartshorne, Thomas L. *The Distorted Image: Changing Conceptions of the American Character Since Turner*. Cleveland: Case Western Reserve University Press, 1968.

Hawkins, Margaret A. and Thomas K. Nakayama. "Discourse on Women's Bodies: Advertising in the 1920s." In *Constructing and Reconstructing Gender: The Links Among Communication, Language, and Gender*, edited by Linda A.M. Perry, Lynn H. Turner, and Helen Sterk. Albany: State University of New York Press, 1992.

Heinz, Marjorie. *Sex, Sin, and Blasphemy: A Guide to America's Censorship Wars*. New York: New Press, 1993.

Higham, John. "The Reorientation of American Culture in the 1890s." In *Writing American History: Essays in Modern Scholarship*, edited by John Higham. Bloomington: Indiana University Press, 1970.

Hoffer, Richard. "John L. Sullivan & Jake Kilrain in the Outlaw Brawl that Started it All." *Sports Illustrated*, May 6, 2002, 64–73.

Holmes, Oliver Wendell. *The Professor at the Breakfast-Table*. Boston: James R. Osgood and Co., 1871.

Horowitz, Helen Lefkowitz. *Rereading Sex: Battles over Sexual Knowledge and Suppression in Nineteenth-Century America*. New York: Alfred A. Knopf, 2002.

James L. Huston. *Panic of 1857 and the Coming of the Civil War*. Baton Rouge: Louisiana State University Press, 1987.

Isenberg, Michael T. *John L. Sullivan and His America*. Chicago: University of Illinois Press, 1988.

E.M. Jellinek. "Recent Trends in Alcoholism and Alcohol Consumption." *Quarterly Journal of Studies on Alcohol* 8 (June 1947): 2–11.

"John L. Sullivan." *National Police Gazette*, April 26, 1884, 7.

Johnson, Allen and Dumas Malone, eds. *Dictionary of American Biography*. Vol. 6. New York: Charles Scribner's Sons, 1931.

Jones, Robert W. *Journalism in the United States*. New York: E.P. Dutton, 1947.

Joyce, James. *Ulysses*. New York: Random House, 1934.

Juergens, George. *Joseph Pulitzer and the New York World.* Princeton, NJ: Princeton University Press, 1966.

Kalb, Marvin. *One Scandalous Story: Clinton, Lewinsky, and Thirteen Days that Tarnished American Journalism.* New York: Free Press, 2001.

Kamphoefner, Walter D., Wolfgang Helbich, and Ulrike Sommer, eds. *News from the Land of Freedom: German Emigrants Write Home.* Ithaca: Cornell University Press, 1991.

Kasson, John F. *Houdini, Tarzan, and the Perfect Man: The White Male Body and the Challenge of Modernity in America.* New York: Hill and Wang, 2001.

Kendrick, Walter. *The Secret Museum: Pornography in Modern Culture.* New York: Viking, 1987.

Kimmel, Michael. *Manhood in America: A Cultural History.* New York: Free Press, 1996.

Kingsdale, Jon M. "The 'Poor Man's Club': Social Functions of the Urban Working-Class Saloon." In *The American Man,* edited by Elizabeth H. Pleck and Joseph H. Pleck. Englewood Cliffs, NJ: Prentice Hall, 1980.

Kitch, Carolyn. *The Girl on the Magazine Cover: The Origins of Visual Stereotypes in American Mass Media.* Chapel Hill: University of North Carolina Press, 2001.

"Known the World Over." *National Police Gazette,* January 28, 1893, 2.

Kobre, Sidney. *The Yellow Press and Gilded Age Journalism.* Tallahassee: Florida State University Press, 1964.

Kooistra, Paul. *Criminals As Heroes: Structure, Power & Identity.* Bowling Green, OH: Bowling Green State University Press, 1989.

Kracjicek, David J. *Scooped: Media Miss Real Story on Crime While Chasing Sex, Sleaze, and Celebrities.* New York: Columbia University Press, 1998.

Kroeger, Brooke. *Nellie Bly: Daredevil, Reporter, Feminist.* New York: Random House, 1994.

Labunksi, Richard E. *Libel and the First Amendment: Legal History and Practice in Print and Broadcasting.* New Brunswick, NJ: Transaction Books, 1987.

LaMay, Craig and E. Dennis, eds. *The Culture of Crime.* New Brunswick, NJ: Transaction Books, 1995.

Lardner, Rex. *The Legendary Champions.* New York: American Heritage Press, 1972.

Lears, T.J. Jackson. *Fables of Abundance: A Cultural History of Advertising in America.* New York: Basic Books, 1993.

Leonard, Thomas C. *The Power of the Press: The Birth of American Political Reporting.* New York: Oxford University Press, 1986.

———. *News for All: America's Coming-of-Age with the Press.* New York: Oxford University Press, 1995.

Lesser, Wendy. *Pictures at an Execution.* Cambridge: Harvard University Press, 1993.

Levi-Strauss, Claude. *Structural Anthropology.* Vol. 1. New York: Basic Books, 1963.

Lofficier, Jean-Marc. *French Science Fiction, Fantasy, Horror and Pulp Fiction: A Guide to Cinema, Television, Radio, Animation, Comic Books and Literature from the Middle Ages to the Present*. Jefferson, NC: McFarland, 2000.

Lombroso, Caesar and William Ferrero. *The Female Offender*. New York: Philosophical Library, 1958.

Loth, David. *The Erotic in Literature: A Historical Survey of Pornography as Delightful as it is Indiscreet*. New York: Julian Messner, 1961.

Lyon, Peter. *The Wild, Wild West*. New York: Funk and Wagnalls, 1969.

Mandelbaum, Seymour J. *Boss Tweed's New York*. New York: J. Wiley, 1965.

Manring, M.M. *Slave in a Box: The Strange Career of Aunt Jemima*. Charlottesville: University Press of Virginia, 1998.

"Maria, This is a Wicked World." *National Police Gazette*, July 17, 1880, 6.

Mark, Margaret and Carol S. Pearson. *The Hero and the Outlaw: Building Extraordinary Brands Through the Power of Archetypes*. New York: McGraw-Hill, 2001.

"Masks and Faces." *National Police Gazette*, March 10, 1894, 2.

"Masks and Faces." *National Police Gazette*, July 27, 1895, 2.

McCullough, David. *The Great Bridge: The Epic Story of the Building of the Brooklyn Bridge*. New York: Touchstone Books, 1982.

Messaris, Paul and Linus Abraham. "The Role of Images in Framing News Stories." In *Framing Public Life: Perspectives on Media and Our Understanding of the Social World*, edited by Stephen D. Reese, Oscar H. Gandy Jr., and August E. Grant. Mahwah, NJ: Lawrence Erlbaum, 2001.

Messerschmidt, James W. *Nine lives: Adolescent Masculinities, the Body, and Violence*. Boulder, CO: Westview Press, 2000.

Meyers, Marian. *News Coverage of Violence Against Women: Engendering Blame*. London: Sage, 1997.

"Midnight Pictures." *National Police Gazette*, November 22, 1879, 15–16.

Miller, Robert Keith. *Oscar Wilde*. New York: Frederick Ungar Publishing Co., 1982.

Montgomery, David. *Citizen Worker: The Experience of Workers in the United States with Democracy and the Free Market During the Nineteenth Century*. New York: Cambridge University Press, 1994.

Morison, Samuel Eliot. *The Oxford History of the American People*. New York: Oxford University Press, 1965.

Morris, Lloyd. *Incredible New York: High Life and Low Life of the Last Hundred Years*. New York: Random House, 1951.

Mosse, George L. *The Image of Man: The Creation of Modern Masculinity*. New York: Oxford University Press, 1996.

Mott, Frank Luther. *American Journalism: A History: 1690–1960*. 3rd ed. New York: Macmillan, 1962.

———. *A History of American Magazines*. 5 vols. 1938. Reprint, Cambridge: Harvard University Press, 1957.

Mrozek, Donald J. "Sport in American Life: From National Health to Personal Fulfillment, 1890–1940." In *Fitness in American Culture: Images of Health, Sport, and the Body, 1830–1940*, edited by Kathryn Grover. Amherst: University of Massachusetts Press, 1989.

Nasaw, David. *The Chief: The Life of William Randolph Hearst*. Boston: Houghton Mifflin, 2000.

Nathan, George Jean and H.L. Mencken. "Repetition Generale." *Smart Set*, February 1923, 33–35.

"A Naughty, Naughty Parson!" *National Police Gazette*, January 14, 1882, 6.

"A New Departure." *National Police Gazette*, March 20, 1880, 2.

"The New York Herald as Science Prophet." *Manufacturer and Builder*, July 1874, 158.

"Nigger Sam's Brain." *National Police Gazette*, May 4, 1878, 4.

Nourie, Alan and Barbara Nourie. *American Mass-Market Magazines*. New York: Greenwood Press, 1990.

Nye, David E. *American Technological Sublime*. Cambridge: MIT Press, 1994.

Odd, Gilbert. *Encyclopedia of Boxing*. London: Hamlyn Publishing, 1983.

"An Open Letter." *The National Police Gazette*, July 2, 1887, 2.

Oriard, Michael. *Reading Football: How the Popular Press Created an American Spectacle*. Chapel Hill: University of North Carolina Press, 1993.

"Our Celebration." *National Police Gazette*, June 16, 1883, 7.

"Our Fallacious Excise Laws." *National Police Gazette*, March 5, 1881, 2.

"Outraged by a Farm Hand." *National Police Gazette*, December 17, 1881, 11.

"Paddy Ryan." *National Police Gazette*, July 2, 1881, 4.

Parenti, Michael. *Inventing Reality: The Politics of the Mass Media*. New York: St. Martin's Press, 1986.

Pearson, Stewart. *Building Brands Directly: Creating Business Value from Customer Relationships*. New York: New York University Press, 1996.

Pleck, Joseph H. *The Myth of Masculinity*. Cambridge: MIT Press, 1981.

"The 'Police Gazette'." *National Police Gazette*, March 10, 1883, 7.

"Police Gazette a Factor in Manly Sport." *National Police Gazette*, May 20, 1899, 7.

Prassel, Frank Richard. *The Great American Outlaw: A Legacy of Faction and Fiction*. Norman: University of Oklahoma Press, 1993.

Pribanic-Smith, Erika J. "Sensationalism and Tabloidism." In *American Journalism: History, Principles, Practices*, edited by W. David Sloan and Lisan Mullinkin Parcell. Jefferson, NC: McFarland & Co., 2002.

Pritchard, David and Karen D. Hughes. "Patterns of Deviance in Crime News." *Journal of Communication* 47, no. 3 (September 1997): 49–67.

"The Prize Ring." *National Police Gazette*, May 19, 1883, 10.

"The Reason Why." *National Police Gazette*, November 27, 1880, 2.

"A Reign of Terror." *National Police Gazette*, January 12, 1895, 6.

"The Religious Editor." *National Police Gazette*, June 16, 1883, 7.

"Restell, the Female Abortionist." *National Police Gazette*, February 21, 1846, 6.

"R.K. Fox Left $3,000,000." *New York Times*, December 22, 1922, 15.

"Richard K. Fox." *National Police Gazette*, May 23, 1885, 2.

"Richard K. Fox's Death." Red Bank *Register*, November 15, 1922, 9.

"Richard K. Fox Dies; Patron of Sports." *New York Times*, November 15, 1922, 19.

"The Richard K. Fox Era." *New York Herald*, November 16, 1922, 11.

"Richard K. Fox Left Estate of $1,796,169." New York *Times*, June 19, 1923, 21.

"Richard K. Fox and His Sporting Representatives." *National Police Gazette*, August 25, 1883, 13.

"Richard K. Fox Vs. Snide Reformers." *National Police Gazette*, May 30, 1885, 2.

"Richard K. Fox Wins." *National Police Gazette*, February 24, 1883, 10.

"Richard Kyle Fox." *National Police Gazette*, December 2, 1922, 2.

Riess, Steven A. *City Games: The Evolution of American Urban Society and the Rise of Sports*. Urbanna, IL: University of Illinois Press, 1989.

Riffe, Daniel, Stephen Lacy, and Frederick G. Fico. *Analyzing Media Messages: Using Quantitative Content Analysis in Research*. Mahwah, NJ: Laurence Erlbaum Associates, 1998.

Riley, Sam G., "Richard Kyle Fox." In *Dictionary of Literary Biography*. Vol. 79, *American Magazine Journalists, 1850–1900*, edited by Riley. Detroit: Bruccoli Clark Layman, 1989.

Roosevelt, Theodore. *Ranch Life and the Hunting-Trail*. New York: Century Co., 1888.

Rosenberg, Charles E. *The Trial of the Assassin Guiteau: Psychiatry and Law in the Gilded Age*. Chicago: University of Chicago Press, 1968.

Ryan, Mary P. *Womanhood in America: From Colonial Times to the Present*. New York: New Viewpoints, 1975.

Sammons, Jeffrey T. *Beyond the Ring: The Role of Boxing in American Society*. Chicago: University of Illinois Press, 1988.

"Samuel Mackeever." *National Police Gazette*, April 3, 1880, 2.

Saxton, Alexander. "George Wilkes: The Disintegration of a Radical Ideology." Paper presented at the Conference on Labor History, Wayne State University, Detroit, October 1979.

"The Scandal Duet." *National Police Gazette*, April 27, 1878, 2.

Schauer, Frederick F. *The Law of Obscenity*. Washington, DC: Bureau of National Affairs, 1976.

Schiller, Dan. *Objectivity and the News: The Public and the Rise of Commercial Journalism*. Philadelphia: University of Pennsylvania Press, 1981.

Schmidgall, Gary. *The Stranger Wilde: Interpreting Oscar*. New York: Dutton, 1994.

Shaw, George Bernard. "My Memories of Oscar Wilde." In *Oscar Wilde, including My Memories of Oscar Wilde, by George Bernard Shaw*, edited by Frank Harris. East Lansing: Michigan State University Press, 1959.

Shaw, David W. *Daring the Sea: The True Story of the First Men to Row Across the Atlantic Ocean*. Seacaucus, NJ: Birch Lane, 1998.

Shirley, Glenn. *Belle Starr and Her Times: The Literature, the Facts, and the Legends.* Norman: University of Oklahoma Press, 1982.

Shoemaker, Pamela J. and Stephen D. Reese. *Mediating the Message: Theories of Influences on Mass Media Content.* 2nd ed. New York: Longman, 1996.

Slade, Joseph W. *Pornography in America: A Reference Handbook.* Santa Barbara, CA: ABC-CLIO, 2000.

———. *Pornography and Sexual Representation: A Reference Guide.* Vol. 1. Westport, CT: Greenwood Press, 2001.

Smith, Gene and Jayne Barry Smith, eds. *The Police Gazette.* New York: Simon & Schuster, 1972.

Sparks, Colin. Introduction to *Tabloid Tales: Global Debates Over Media Standards,* edited by Sparks and John Tulloch. Oxford, England: Rowman and Littlefield, 2000.

Stearns, Peter N. *Be a Man! Males in Modern Society.* New York: Holmes & Meier, 1979.

Stephens, Mitchell. *A History of News: From the Drum to the Satellite.* New York: Viking, 1988.

Stevens, John D. *Sensationalism and the New York Press.* New York: Columbia University Press, 1991.

Stiles, T.J. *Jesse James: Last Rebel of the Civil War.* New York: Alfred A. Knopf, 2002.

"Sullivan wins!" *National Police Gazette,* February 18, 1882, 2.

"Suppose and Suppose." *National Police Gazette,* May 30, 1885, 2.

Sutherland, Douglas. *The Yellow Earl: The Life of Hugh Lowther, 5th Earl of Lonsdale, 1857–1944.* New York: Coward-McCann, 1965.

Swanberg, W.A. *Pulitzer.* New York: Charles Scribner's Sons, 1967.

"They All Do It." *National Police Gazette,* April 4, 1885, 2.

"This Wicked World." *National Police Gazette,* July 9, 1887, 3.

Thompson, Kenneth. *Moral Panics.* London: Routledge, 1998.

"To Our Readers—Something New." *National Police Gazette,* December 5, 1874, 2.

Trachentenberg, Alan. Foreword to *Horrible Prettiness: Burlesque and American Culture,* by Robert C. Allen. Chapel Hill: University of North Carolina Press, 1991.

Tucher, Andie. *Froth and Scum: Truth, Beauty, Goodness, and the Ax Murder in America's First Mass Medium.* Chapel Hill: University of North Carolina Press, 1994.

———. "In Search of Jenkins: Taste, Style, and Credibility in Gilded-Age Journalism." *Journalism History* 27, no. 2 (Summer 2001): 50–55.

Turner, Hy B. *When Giants Ruled: The Story of Park Row, New York's Great Newspaper Street.* New York: Fordham University Press, 1999.

Valente, Joseph. "The novel and the Police (Gazette)," *Novel* 29, no. 1 (Fall 1995): 8–25.

"A Valuable Gift." *National Police Gazette,* November 27, 1880, 2.

Van Every, Edward. *Sins of New York as "Exposed" by the Police Gazette.* New York: Frederick A. Stokes, 1930.

Vivian, John. *The Media of Mass Communication*. 6th ed. Boston: Allyn & Bacon, 1991.

Welky, David B. "Culture, Media and Sport: The *National Police Gazette* and the Creation of an American Working-Class World." *Culture, Sport, Society* 1., no. 1 (May 1998): 78–100.

White, G. Edward. *The Eastern Establishment and the Western Experience: The West of Frederic Remington, Theodore Roosevelt, and Owen Wister*. New Haven: Yale University Press, 1968.

White, Kevin. *The First Sexual Revolution: The Emergence of Male Heterosexuality in Modern America*. New York: New York University Press, 1993.

"Whitechapel's Fiend." *National Police Gazette*, August 17, 1889, 3.

"Wilde on the Treadmill." *National Police Gazette*, June 15, 1895, 6.

Wilkes, George. *The Mysteries of the Tombs; A Journal of Thirty Days Imprisonment in the New York City Prison; for Libel*. New York: n.p., 1844.

Williams, Raymond. *Marxism and Literature*. New York: Oxford University Press, 1977.

Wilson, Colin, and Donald Seaman. *Scandal! An Encyclopedia*. London: Weidenfeld and Nicolson, 1986.

Wolfe, Tom. Foreword to *The Police Gazette*, edited by Gene Smith and Jayne Barry Smith. New York: Simon and Schuster, 1972.

"A Word About Ourselves." *National Police Gazette*, October 17, 1885, 2.

"A Word to Strong Men." *National Police Gazette*, May 5, 1884, 2.

Yellis, Kenneth A. "Prosperity's Child: Some Thoughts on the Flapper." *American Quarterly* 21 (spring 1969): 44–64.

"A. Young Murderer" *National Police Gazette*, February 2, 1884, 11.

INDEX